HISTORY FROM THE HIGH

WYOMING

HISTORY FROM THE HIGHWAYS

WYOMING

Thomas Schmidt and Winfred Blevins

PRUETT PUBLISHING COMPANY
BOULDER, COLORADO

Printed in the United States
10 9 8 7 6 5 4 3 2 1

Library of Congress Cataloging-in-Publication Data

Schmidt, Thomas, 1959–
    History from the highways : Wyoming / Thomas Schmidt, Winfred
Blevins.
        p.   cm.
    Includes indexes.
    ISBN 0-87108-833-9 (pbk. : acid-free paper)
    1. Wyoming—History, Local. 2. Wyoming—Guidebooks.
3. Automobile travel—Wyoming—Guidebooks. I. Blevins, Winfred.
II. Title.
F761.S32   1993
917.87′0433—dc20   92-43029
                                                                CIP

Cover design by Melanie Smith and Jody Chapel
Book design by Jody Chapel, Cover to Cover Design,
Denver, Colorado

This book is dedicated to Wyoming's people, all of them, from the distant past to the infinite future.

CONTENTS

ACKNOWLEDGMENTS

Thanks to Adam Blevins, who drove highways, took notes, and found pictures; to George Hufsmith, who lent us his research about Cattle Kate even before he published it; to the staff of the Teton County Library, tireless helpers; to the Western Heritage Center at the University of Wyoming and the Teton County Historical Society for help with photos; and to all the people who wrote down and remembered the stories of life in Wyoming so we could condense it in this form.

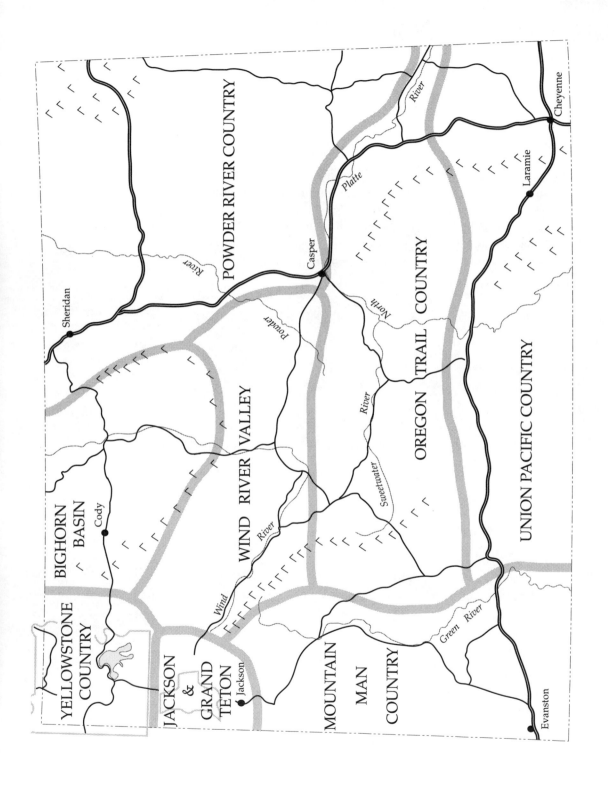

INTRODUCTION

Wyoming is a state of relentless, inexorable change.

Imagine that you are in Wyoming two hundred years ago, a visitor, perhaps from the civilized New York City of that day, come to observe and set down what you see in writing.

You see a state sparsely settled, or more accurately not settled at all, for the inhabitants move about, hunting, gathering, sometimes warring, often dancing and performing rituals. They stay nowhere long. They live in tipis that are raised and dismantled in only minutes.

When you query them in sign language, they sign back that their way of life has not changed since before the memories of the grandfathers of the oldest men. In the spring, after a long winter, they hunt the buffalo. In the summer they gather together and have a dance called Gazing-at-the-Sun Dance, or Dry-Standing Dance, or simply Sun Dance, on behalf of the common good. In the autumn they have big buffalo hunts and make meat against the cold season. In the winter they stay close to their lodge fires and tell the ancient stories of their people, the stories that constitute their central mythos.

At all times of year they hunt when they can, gather what they can, make clothing and lodges and utensils, seek spiritual power, and live in the way spirit reveals to them. Like the stars, the sun, the earth, life itself, they travel the same circle over and over.

Perhaps you, an outsider, at first see their lifeway as barbarous. If you stay long enough, you may begin to see its timeless beauty.

Perhaps they see it as more timeless than it truly is. They have not walked this part of the earth since time immemorial—they came from elsewhere, the Shoshones from the Great Basin, the Crows from the Missouri River, the Arapaho, Cheyenne, and Lakota from the woodlands on the western edge of the Great Lakes. In these places they lived in permanent villages of earth huts, or in bark wigwams, or in temporary shelters of brush. They hunted not the immense buffalo but smaller game, and gathered roots, berries, and other vegetables. They did not roam on horseback, but walked.

The pace of change, like a river's current, has begun to quicken for these people. Pressure from the Ojibwa, who got some guns from the white man, forced the Lakotas westward. Pressure from the Lakotas forced the Cheyennes and Arapahos westward. The Shoshones have been attracted eastward by the buffalo.

Many of these people now have steel points for their arrows. Glass beads. Blankets, knives, or metal hatchets. Though the vast majority of them have not yet seen the white man, through trade they have a few artifacts of white culture. The current is picking up the tempo, but so far very gradually.

Now suppose you return to these people fifty years later, in 1840. They are at the height of their material wealth and their temporal power. They have gotten rich, by their standards, trading common items like the skins of beaver and buffalo for rarities like cloth, kettles, powder, and guns. They shoot buffalo from wonderfully trained horses and make meat more quickly than ever before. Though white men come among them, they are few, and powerless. The poor creatures don't even have any women—they have to trade for them.

Nevertheless, these people's lives have changed more in this half-century than in the previous couple of centuries. The next half-century, for them, will be a cataclysm.

1890: Wyoming has become first a territory and then, just this year, a state. The buffalo are nearly exterminated. Where they once grazed, millions of cattle crop the grass. Over the Black Hills, sacred to the Lakotas and the Cheyennes, gold miners bustle like ants. A railroad crosses the bottom half of Wyoming, a sequence of towns dropped along the line. A series of great battles has been fought between the horse Indians and the U.S. cavalry—all through the Powder River country, on the Rosebud, on the Little Big Horn north of the state line. Though many of these fights were won, the battle is lost.

The people are now confined to reservations. The Shoshones and Arapahos are along the Wind River. The Crows are on the Big Horn, just north of the state's northern border. The Cheyennes are on the Tongue River, across the line in Montana. The Lakotas are in North and South Dakota. There, just before the new year, Big Foot's band will be slaughtered on the banks of Wounded Knee Creek, the last major bloodletting of the Indian Wars.

Everything is new, different, out of sync. Tipis are now canvas—there are no buffalo hides to sew them from. Food amounts to handouts from the government, irregular and insufficient. Men hunt, but the game is gone. Many of the old ways are forbidden. According to the new ways, a man can't take a second wife even if he can afford it, and even if she's his wife's sister. Counting coup, stealing horses, taking scalps—all are forbidden. Many ceremonies that keep the people right with the powers are forbidden. The sacred hoop is broken, and the people wither.

Thus a century of violent change for Indian peoples. The river of time did not flow gently for them but erupted in terrible rapids.

Of course things changed for the Indians, you say. They went from "barbarism" to "civilization."

No, things changed for whites as well—changed fast, perplexingly, messily. Of all the human survival tools, perhaps the most important in Wyoming the last two centuries has been the ability to adapt quickly and as comfortably as possible to change.

White explorers first touched Wyoming in the early 1740s. Trappers wandered through in the first two decades of the nineteenth century. Then, in 1823, the fur men stumbled on South Pass and the great beaver grounds of the Green River. They were here to stay.

Though some disliked the life and quickly headed back to the blandishments of civilization, others loved it. You traveled about with other trappers and with Indians, trapped the cold streams, hunted the mighty buffalo, adventured over worlds of new country, met up with the other fellows and the mule train from St. Louis once a year to trade your furs for some deep drafts of whiskey, powder, lead, and some other essentials. Later you got skilled at trading with the Indians and learned to speak their languages. Then you could endure the cold winters in one of their villages. You even took an Indian woman. Before long you realized you had a wife and kids, a family.

These men were the first white citizens of Wyoming. Their lifestyle lasted, at the outside, about twenty years. Then the price of beaver bottomed out and the great migration across the Oregon Trail came full flood. Most of the mountain men found their lives violently dislocated. The emigrants called them "squaw men," and thought them "worse than Indians." The fellows went back to Missouri, where their wives and kids were often treated as inferior, or to Oregon or California to get the same treatment. At forty years old or less, the mountain men found that the life they wanted was gone and that they were faced with lousy choices. A few found work at the trading posts. A few stayed in the mountains to work as guides for the emigrants who despised them or for the soldiers. And a few lived with the Indians, utter outcasts from white civilization.

For the next generation, white life in Wyoming was mostly people going across the state at a high rate of speed, headed for one of several imagined paradises: Oregon, where crops grew so fast you had to beat them back; the Great Salt Lake and the Mormon paradise Deseret; California, where gold nuggets the size of fists lay on the ground waiting to be picked up; or Montana, where drinking the water meant peeing gold. This period, 1843 to 1868, was a time of emigration for white people. For the Indians and the remaining mountain men, it was a holding period.

But that latter year was a great divide. From 1865 through 1868, Wyoming tribes accepted reservations, lands that were to be their own, for their traditional way of life, forever. The Lakotas, thinking they'd won their war against the whites under the chief Red Cloud, thought they were preserving hunting grounds from central Wyoming to central Dakota Territory. But in 1868 came the iron horse.

Tie by tie, rail by rail, the railroad clanged across the lower part of the state in a rush to meet the rails coming from California. In its wake it left the first towns in Wyoming—hell-raising end-of-line towns at first, full of gamblers, prostitutes, and quick-buck artists. Then they became burgeoning commercial centers, points for supplying outlying ranches and for shipping cows back East, outfitting miners looking for fortunes hither and yon. The principal yon was the Black Hills. When whites discovered gold there in 1874, gold seekers paid no attention to the treaty that promised those sacred lands to the Indians forever. And the kickoff point for the Black Hills was Cheyenne. A state that had a handful of permanent white residents in 1840 had over twenty thousand by 1880.

With the railroad came a new lifestyle entirely, that of the cattle ranch. Grass was free, a way of saying cattlemen could make their profits on public lands without charge. And grass grew as high and wide as the plains themselves, with not a fence anywhere. Shipping was cheap enough. British and eastern U.S. money men saw cattle ranches as bonanzas. And so a new kind of Wyoming white man came into being, the successor of the mountain man, the emigrant, the scout, the soldier, and the miner. He was the cowboy.

The cataclysmic changes do not stop here. In the late 1860s, when the first big cattle herds arrived from Texas, the cowboy had open range in every direction, space for more cows than he could imagine. Two decades later, after the devastating winter of 1886–87, he had a country filling up with barbed wire fences and the carcasses of frozen cows. Though the cowboy is an important part of the Wyoming economy even today, his heyday was as brief as that of the mountain man.

An economist would describe all this change as a classic boom-and-bust economy. Until the nineteenth century, Wyoming had a subsistence and barter economy that changed little even by the introduction of manufactured goods toward the end. Starting in 1822, investors made fortunes in beaver and the Indian trade closely associated with it. About 1840, beaver went to hell. Though the Indian trade survived (in buffalo hides), the real money was in supplying emigrants, who were coming through the territory in hordes. After the Civil War, two major events caused another big economic dislocation: Huge herds of cows arrived from Texas, and the railroad came. For two decades fortunes were made (and lost) in cattle ranching.

Think of an Indian, born on the high plains of Wyoming in, say, 1823, the date when trappers came to Wyoming to stay. His grandfather would have lived a simple life in a sacred and timeless way. Advance our Indian now to the age of eighty. He has seen white people throwing their energies furiously into a series of different activities — beaver-trapping, emigrating, prospecting, soldiering, mining, ranching. He has seen the gun, the railroad, the camera, the electric light. If he hasn't seen the automobile, he soon will. They make little sense to him, most of these miracles of technology, because he does not see the whites as able to live in a sacred way. And he sees himself as having lost his own people's sacred way. Their gods apparently have failed (or the people have failed their gods) and the sacred hoop is broken, so the people can prosper no more. He huddles in his blanket by a stove in a shack, wishing he had a tipi, and wonders what has happened to his world.

The changes detailed above all occurred in the nineteenth century. But rapid, unsettling change didn't stop there. Nor did the boom-and-bust economy. In this century oil in Wyoming has gone boom and bust repeatedly. Uranium has peaked and bottomed out. Coal the same. Natural gas the same. Steel the same.

The pattern continues today. The Overthrust Belt of western Wyoming, a region of rich but deep deposits of oil and gas, was discovered in the late 1970s, leading to a fury of exploration and some drilling. The exploring crews and drilling rigs are now gone elsewhere.

People who think of ghost towns as old, quaint phenomena may be stimulated by Wyoming to rethink this assumption. Jeffrey City, Hanna, and Atlantic City became virtual ghost towns in the 1980s (that's 1980s) when uranium, coal, and steel-mining went bust. Other towns suddenly found themselves half-empty.

When jobs are lost and new ones are invented and then lost again, people change and lifestyles change. The drilling boom of the 1970s brought lots of workers to Wyoming, many of them from the industrial East. While they were here, land prices rose, rents soared, and building boomed. When the jobs and the people left, you could buy a house dirt cheap in a lot of towns. You still can.

Lots of those workers stayed and became Wyoming people. They found work in the endeavors that have lasted longer here. The cattle industry is muddling through, though with difficulty. (The descendants of the proud Wyoming cattlemen who once fought wars to keep sheep off their ranges will now often admit they raise cows for respectability and sheep for profit.) The government is a strong employer in Wyoming. We are full of national parks — including two of the most visited, Yellowstone and Grand Teton — and national forests and other public lands. The government is an enduring employer.

Those public lands create the industry that creates most of the jobs: tourism. People want to see our mountains and our cold creeks and swift rivers and the elk, buffalo, antelope, and other wonderful animals that live here. Which means we have jobs building roads, serving meals, pumping gas, putting up motels, guiding hunters and fishermen, selling ski-lift tickets, and doing the bookkeeping for all these businesses.

Some of the people who visit and look with open eyes and hearts fall in love and want to stay. That creates more change—more ranchland converted to condominiums, more trees cut to build houses, more septic systems, more wood stoves pumping out smoke, more boats on the rivers, more feet on the trails and mountaintops.

Wyoming probably needs it to be that way. No society can go static and stay healthy.

Change. Many newcomers to Wyoming dread it. The old-timers mostly welcome it.

A local rancher who's now around eighty will tell you the change is for the better. He rocks along on his horse—he's too vigorous for a rocking chair—and remembers the old times. His family used to come to town on Saturdays in wagons, an all-day excursion. Now they drive to town in fifteen minutes to pick up the mail. He hunted these hills, and the family ate what he shot. Now that they can afford it, he and his wife stick to store-bought beef. They chuckle at newcomers to the country eating that stringy antelope. Though they don't necessarily like the new-comers—"ain't got enough sense to close a gate behind 'em"—they like the modern world.

Maybe the best way to look forward when you're trying to grasp change with heart and mind is to look back. We asked a lifelong resident, for decades the town's piano teacher, to remember what our home country, Jackson Hole, was like fifty years ago, in 1942. Her memories, prompted by her journal, are a time capsule:

> Jackson Hole was then called Jackson's Hole.
> We knew everybody. Jackson's Hole was quiet—fewer cars, motor-cycles, airplanes, snowmobiles, trucks, buses, helicopters. Fewer people.
> Wallace Beery was in town for Independence Day. "Wally shelled peanuts all during our piano recital and was very noisy and crude."
> My husband and I bought the last available Chevrolet. General Motors had stopped making them because of the war.
> Motels cost three dollars a room.
> There was no television, and wouldn't be until 1960.
> I registered for sugar, which was rationed.
> The roads were rougher, so you couldn't speed, so there were fewer accidents.
> On January 3, 1942, it was thirty-eight degrees below zero.

A soap shortage was on (the war again).

I went to Salt Lake City and saw *Rigoletto* and *Cavalleria Rusticana*.

Jackson had illegal gambling. Since my husband was in law enforcement, I sometimes felt I was sitting on a powder keg.

Certain people were still poaching beaver.

Jackson was more primitive and pristine.

"I was fifty years younger, so had more fun."

Not that our friend would go back in all ways. In those times she couldn't have her favorite recreation of modern life — watching every professional basketball game that's on television, rooting for a few teams here in the West, but eager to watch *any* game.

Everyone wonders, though, what change will do to the lifestyle we came here for, to our sense of what is a good way to live on this land and be of this land. How long will we be able to breathe the best air there is? Drink our own good water? Get firewood from our own forests? Make meat from our animals? Live truly as a part of this big, complicated earth system we love.

We read that just fifty years ago some Indians regularly made the pilgrimage to the medicine wheel in the Big Horn Mountains by wagon. There's a parking lot there now, and tourists look on as modern Indians offer their prayers. We remember that just twenty years ago you could ride for weeks in the Thorofare country without seeing anyone. Now you'll see plenty of backpackers. We remember that just ten years ago certain mountain slopes were trackless all winter. Now the tracks of telemarkers litter them. We wonder whether this grandeur must all be compromised.

When we look back, we see that in the two centuries of white presence here, no one has been able to see the future clearly. So we look toward the undiscovered country ahead of us, and wonder.

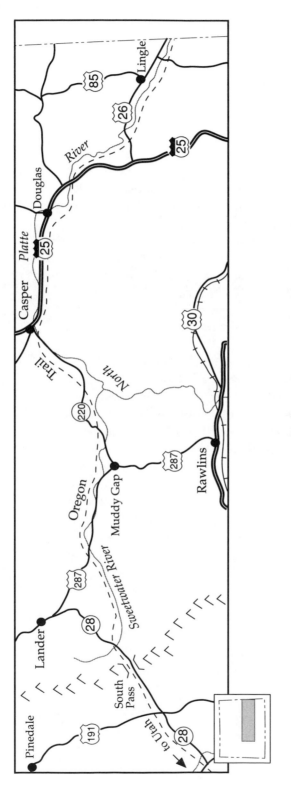

THE OREGON TRAIL

THE OREGON TRAIL: INTRODUCTION

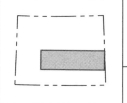

The Oregon Trail — backdrop for countless Westerns and springboard to a multitude of social hypotheses — was the single most important route for westbound settlers of the mid–nineteenth century. Stretching across the Great Plains and over the Rocky Mountains to the Pacific Coast, the trail followed a network of major western waterways that guided the emigrants and provided water and forage for the animals that pulled their wagons. Most jumped off at Independence, Missouri, and followed the Little Blue River through modern-day Kansas to Fort Kearny, Nebraska. Then they picked up the Platte River and trundled along its banks into Wyoming. Eventually, they hooked up with the Snake River in Idaho and followed it on to the Columbia River in Oregon.

The portion of the trip across Wyoming covered a bit more than four hundred miles and normally took three to five weeks to traverse. The route followed the North Platte until the river made its long southwestward curve around the Medicine Bow Mountains. Then it headed up the Sweetwater River, over South Pass, and across the Green River into Idaho or Utah.

Although isolated parties of settlers traveled through Wyoming as early as the mid-1830s, the first true wave of Oregon-bound settlers did not pass this way until 1843. Four years later the ranks swelled when Brigham Young led the first expedition of Mormons along the North Platte toward the Salt Lake basin in Utah. The following year gold was discovered in California, luring a vast stream of emigrants to the West. The covered-wagon era continued until after the Civil War, when the Union Pacific built the nation's first transcontinental railroad.

During the years 1841–68, somewhere between 350,000 and 400,000 emigrants rolled through Wyoming. The movement reached its peak during 1850 and 1852, when fifty thousand to sixty thousand settlers plodded up the trail each summer. In those years, the route clogged with wagons. People sometimes had to wait days for their turn at the river crossings, and it wasn't unusual for several thousand people to pass Fort Laramie in a single day. One emigrant watched two hundred wagons pass by while he stopped for lunch.

No wonder the Indians got nervous. Some even talked about moving East because surely few whites remained there.

Many people died along the trail, but contrary to the impression created by movies and novels, Indian violence accounted for a tiny proportion of the deaths.

"The actual dangers of the overland venture have been considerably misrepresented by the myth-makers' overemphasis on Indian treachery," writes historian John Unruh in *The Plains Across*. "The less than 400 emigrants killed by Indians during the antebellum era represents a mere 4% of the estimated 10,000 or more emigrant deaths."

Nine out of ten deaths were caused by diseases such as cholera, mountain fever, scurvy, and tuberculosis. About three hundred people drowned and many others were shot accidentally while handling firearms, which is not surprising when one considers the amazing arsenals the emigrants packed for the journey.

William Kelly, an 1851 traveler, wrote that his "well-equipped" group hit the trail with "each man carrying in his belt a revolver, a sword, and bowie knife; the mounted men having besides a pair of holster-pistols and a rifle slung from the horn of their saddles, over and above which there were several double and single shotguns and rifles suspended in the wagons, in loops, near the forepart, where they would be easily accessible in case of attack."

Unfortunately, these weapons were sometimes a little too accessible. Some people died while rearranging the loads in their wagons and tugging on shotguns barrel-first.

Others fell under moving wheels, got tangled in ropes, were kicked by horses, and got hit by lightning. One person died from overdrinking after a long desert crossing.

The trip was difficult, but emigrants from different parties tended to look after one another. They shared food, drink, and information. They helped one another fix broken-down wagons and replace lost or stolen equipment, supplies, and livestock. They banded together for mutual protection and extended aid to those in the most dire of straits. In 1849, for example, emigrant Bernard Reid and his party came across a seventeen-year-old girl caring for her cholera-stricken brother in the back of a wagon. Their parents had died, their oxen had vanished, and the group they had been traveling with had abandoned them. Reid took up a collection, bought the girl some livestock, and found a doctor to prescribe medicine for her brother. A group of Missourians took in the orphans and cared for them during the rest of the trip.

Reid's story and others like it are the stuff of myth and legend in the West. They lend credence to the benevolent image of one who, as the saying goes, rides tall in the saddle, or in Reid's case high on the buckboard. Fortunately, in many parts of the West, Reid's spirit has not yet deteriorated into the realm of myth and legend. People still tend to look after one another, even if the other happens to be a stranger.

As it parallels the banks of the North Platte River to Interstate 25, Highway 26 follows an incredibly rich vein of history. It is thick with the experiences of emigrants on the Oregon Trail, of course, but it also turns up an incredible survival story from the fur-trapping era, an encounter with a French trader in his cups, and some incidents from the turbulent and tragic history of relations between whites and Indians. The road passes Fort Laramie Historic Site, where beautifully restored buildings preserve the look and feel of what was the most important way station in Wyoming for settlers who passed that way in covered wagons. Farther along, it passes a site near Guernsey where the wheels of passing emigrant wagons carved ruts four to six feet deep in solid rock.

NORTH PLATTE RIVER

Long before the first emigrant wagon creaked across the prairie toward the West Coast, a highway of sorts existed here in the North Platte River Valley. Used by Indians traveling between the Great Plains and the high valleys of present-day Wyoming, the route must have seemed like a rich and effortless thoroughfare. The river attracted vast herds of buffalo for their meals, provided water and forage for their ponies, and guided them toward the important valleys of the Powder, Sweetwater, Big Horn, Wind, and Green rivers.

The first whites to traverse the route, in 1812, had a rougher time of it. Known as the "Astorians," they were a ragged band of fur traders who had passed easily enough through northeastern Wyoming the year before and had built a post at the mouth of Oregon's Columbia River for the New York entrepreneur John Jacob Astor. Problems on the Columbia, though, prompted the post's commander to send a small detachment of men back to New York to tell

John Jacob Astor, founder of the American Fur Company. *(University of Wyoming American Heritage Center)*

Astor that all was not well on the West Coast. The men lost their horses to Crow Indians in western Wyoming, soon got lost themselves, and then went without food for so long that they nearly drew lots to see which of the men should be killed to provide meat for the others.

Finally, a friendly Shoshone happened upon the group. He traded them a horse and gave them directions to the gentle South Pass and the North Platte River highway. They spent the winter of 1812–13 on the banks of the North Platte, near Torrington, and then followed the river down to the Missouri.

These men, stumbling backward from the interior West to Missouri, had in fact discovered an easy wagon route across the plains and the Rocky Mountains. The route later would be called The Oregon Trail, and it would draw hundreds of thousands of people to the banks of the North Platte here in southeastern Wyoming. But it would take more than thirty years for that wave of migration to begin.

In the meantime, fur trappers frequented the banks of the river, using it as the Indians did. They traveled upriver, pausing to shoot buffalo, bear, and elk for meat, and dispersed into the mountains with their traps. Pack trains followed every summer, bearing more traps, ammunition, coffee, and lots of whiskey for the annual mountain man rendezvous (see page 186). Downriver went the fruits of their labor: bundles of beaver pelts bound for St. Louis and the East, where they would be made into felt hats. Downriver also came the occasional hard-luck trapper, headed for the nearest outpost of white civilization, bereft of horse, rifle, and maybe even his clothes, probably starving, perhaps shot up by Indians or ripped up by a grizzly.

NORTH PLATTE: EMIGRANTS

By the mid-1830s, people unconnected to the fur trade — missionaries and pleasure travelers — started to accompany the annual pack trains to the mountain man rendezvous. Among the latter was William Marshall Anderson, a lawyer from Louisville, Kentucky, who accompanied the pack train to the 1834 rendezvous. Happily for us, Anderson kept a journal during the trip. Here he records some of his excitement:

> This evening, about 5 o'clock, I felled a mighty bison to the earth . . . I placed my foot upon his neck of strength and looked around, but in vain, for some witness of my first great "coup." I felt proud; I felt glorious; I thought myself larger than a dozen men. I tied little blackhawk [Anderson's horse] to his horns, danced upon his body, and made a fool of myself to my heart's content, then cut out his tongue and sat down to rest and moralize.

In the years following Anderson's trip, wagonloads of settlers bound for Oregon, California, and Utah rumbled along the North Platte in an ever-widening stream. By 1860, some 250,000 had rolled through Wyoming, leaving in some places a deeply rutted track that remains as a vivid monument to their passage. Later, an efficient stagecoach system transported mail along the North Platte and brought some famous people west. The journalist Horace Greeley, who is said to have coined the phrase "Go west,

young man," followed his own advice in 1859. Two years later, a young Mark Twain rolled along this stretch of the North Platte and passed a group of Mormon emigrants slogging their way toward Utah. Twain, reclining on a stack of mail sacks, later wrote:

> Tramping wearily along and driving their herd of loose cows, were dozens of coarse-clad and sad-looking men, women and children, who had walked as they were walking now, day after day for eight lingering weeks, and in that time had compassed the distance our stage had compassed in eight days and three hours — seven hundred and ninety-eight miles! They were dusty and uncombed, hatless, bonnetless and ragged, and they did look so tired!

TORRINGTON

By the time the Chicago, Burlington & Quincy railroad set tracks along the North Platte in 1900 and established the town of Torrington, the area's most interesting history had already faded from the scene. The trappers and emigrants had passed through long before, and ranchers had fattened cattle on the surrounding plains for nearly fifty years. One rancher, William G. Curtis, had even bothered to establish a post office on his ranch — and "bother" is the right word, because he had to pack in the mail from Fort Laramie at his own expense. Curtis named the post office after his hometown of Torrington, Connecticut. The name stuck when the railroad platted the town. Today, Torrington is an agricultural center serving an irrigated district where farmers raise sugar beets and, of all things, corn, an anomalous crop in Wyoming.

LINGLE

Across the North Platte from Lingle and a couple of miles west stood the trading post of

James Bordeaux, a Frenchman who occasionally grew quite lonely for his native land. At Bordeaux Station from 1849 to 1868 he provisioned emigrants, bartered with Indians, and shared meals, conversation, and champagne with the officers of nearby Fort Laramie.

One of the officers to enjoy Bordeaux's hospitality, Lt. Eugene Ware, met the trader in 1864 and commiserated with him late into the night:

> Mr. Bordeaux again got off onto the subject of his visit to "La Belle France," and he seemed to be very much pleased with the bitters he had and the attention with which I listened to his story . . . All at once he disappeared through the floor, by turning up a plank or puncheon, and the first thing I knew he came back from down below somewhere with two large, musty quart bottles of champagne, and sticking one down in front of me said, "We will drink to La Belle France." I was as much surprised as if the man had dug up a statue of Daniel Webster. The idea of a quart bottle of champagne in that dry, arid, heathen country almost paralyzed me.

After the Civil War, large herds of Texas longhorn cattle were driven north through the Lingle area to ranches in Wyoming and Montana, where they fattened up before being shipped to market. As the buffalo neared extinction, much of the demand for beef grew from the need to feed Indian tribes that had been forced onto reservations where they could no longer hunt for food. The drives continued until the mid-1880s. By then, rail lines had supplanted the trails, and the grazing lands of Wyoming and Montana had become crowded with herds of cattle capable of sustaining their numbers through reproduction.

JUNCTION 26 AND 85

Highway 85 heads north along the route of the old Cheyenne to Deadwood stage line. (See page 91.)

GRATTAN BATTLE

In 1854, thirty-one soldiers from Fort Laramie were killed about two and a half miles west of Lingle when they tried, ineptly, to arrest a Lakota warrior who had killed an emigrant's cow that was lame and perhaps dying.

Two days after the incident, the trader James Bordeaux said the cow had run into "the camp of the Indians, who were waiting for payment [under an 1851 treaty] and were out of provisions." The cow was butchered and eaten.

The 1851 treaty specified that Indian chiefs would make restitution for any offense that members of their tribes committed against whites. When Brave Bear, chief of the Brulé village, heard that the cow had been killed, he rode to Fort Laramie and offered to pay for it out of the treaty payments the tribe had been promised under the treaty.

The fort's commander, Lt. Hugh B. Fleming, refused the offer for compensation and ordered the arrest of those responsible for the death of the cow. Lt. John L. Grattan set out for the village with twenty-nine men and the fort's drunken interpreter, who loathed the Lakota. On the way, Brave Bear intercepted them and offered to pay for the cow with ponies. Grattan refused, insisting instead on arresting the offending warrior, a condition Brave Bear would not accept.

Grattan and his men formed a battle line across a creek from the village, wheeled up a cannon, and fired. Even though one Lakota was wounded, the Lakota chiefs managed to keep their braves from returning fire. However, when the next volley killed Brave Bear, the Lakota counterattacked and wiped out the soldiers.

After the battle, the warriors raided trading posts around the fort and attacked mail carriers, killing at least three.

Upper Platte Indian Agent Whitfield later said the incident probably could have been avoided had it not been for "Lt. Grattan's want of knowledge of the Indian character and the rash language used by a drunken interpreter."

Nonetheless, a year later, six hundred soldiers led by Gen. W. S. Harney sought revenge for the Grattan battle by attacking a village of entirely different Lakota near Ash Hollow in Nebraska. His troops killed eighty-six, wounded five, and captured seventy.

WYOMING'S OLDEST BRIDGE

After taking the turnoff to Fort Laramie, the road crosses the Laramie River beside the state's oldest standing bridge. Built in 1876, it arrived just in time to provide a reliable crossing of the North Platte for prospectors and others bound for the goldfields of the Black Hills.

FORT LARAMIE

Built in 1834 at the confluence of the North Platte and Laramie rivers, Fort Laramie casts a long shadow over Wyoming's early history. Even before the fort was built, Indians and trappers camped here to hunt, trap beaver, rest, trade with one another, and sometimes fight. During the emigrant years, the fort served as an important stopover and, at the height of the migration, became a vast dumping ground where over-burdened settlers disposed of surplus provisions and equipment. Stagecoach lines and the Pony Express used the fort as a relay point, and some of the earliest experiments in raising beef cattle occurred nearby.

The site also figured prominently in relations between whites and Indians. Soon after the trading post opened, bands of Lakota set up a semi-permanent village nearby. Troops were stationed

Fort Laramie as it appeared in 1870. The fort was the single most important way station in Wyoming for travelers on the Oregon Trail. But the fort in one form or another had existed since the 1830s, when it was built by fur trappers. *(University of Wyoming American Heritage Center)*

at the fort in 1849 to protect the trails, and two important treaties were signed here: one in 1851 and the other in 1868. Neither kept the peace for long. Whites completely shattered the latter in the mid-seventies when prospectors trespassed on Indian land and discovered gold in the Black Hills of South Dakota. During the subsequent rush, Fort Laramie was an important stop on the Cheyenne to Deadwood stagecoach line.

The Early Fort

The fort was built by William Sublette and Robert Campbell, trappers-turned-capitalists who wanted to control trade with the Indians frequenting the upper North Platte. They built the original fort across the river from the present town, on the north bank of the Laramie River and about a mile upstream from the confluence.

Like many of the West's military outposts, Fort Laramie takes its name from a white man killed by Indians. In this case, the man was Jacque LaRamee, a fur trapper believed to have been killed by Arapahos during the early 1820s on what became known as the Laramie River. But the fort wasn't always called Laramie. It picked up that name through local use. The trappers who built the place called it Fort William, presumably after their leader, William Sublette. But they also named it after William Anderson, a Louisville lawyer who rode west with them that summer and shared in the fort's ground-breaking ceremony.

Anderson wrote in his journal on May 31, 1834:

> This day we laid the foundation log of a fort, on Laramee's fork. A friendly dispute rose between our leader and myself, as to the name. He proposed to call it Fort Anderson. I insisted upon baptising it Fort Sublette and, holding the trump card in my hand [a bottle of champagne], was about to claim the trick. Sublette stood by, cup reversed, still object-

ing, when Patton offered a compromise which was accepted, and the foam flew, in honor of Fort William.

The original Fort William was probably just a simple enclosure made of cottonwood logs. The American Fur Company, which acquired the fort in 1836, built adobe walls in 1841 to improve on the cottonwood fortifications. The army occupied the fort from 1849 to 1890 and added officers' quarters, barracks, and many other buildings. It also called the place Fort John, a name that never stuck.

FORT LARAMIE TREATY OF 1851

When Sublette and Campbell built the fort, they invited the Oglalla and Brulé Lakota to move near the outpost in order to facilitate trade. The Indians obliged, and so, from almost the very start, travelers encountered a semipermanent encampment of Lakota when they arrived at the fort. Relations between early emigrants and Indians were for the most part quite good. However, concern grew among government officials as the volume of settlers swelled and then surged with the discovery of California gold in 1848. In order to head off potential trouble, the government bought Fort Laramie in 1849 and stationed troops there to protect the trail. Two years later, it proposed a treaty council that prompted the largest gathering of tribes in history.

During September 1851, about ten thousand representatives of the Lakota, Cheyenne, Arapaho, and Crow tribes converged on Fort Laramie for the proceedings and soon moved about thirty-five miles downriver to find better grazing land. The resulting treaty stipulated that the government promised to protect the tribes against white depredations and to pay them fifty thousand dollars in goods annually for the following fifty years as compensation for the

Father Jean Pierre DeSmet, the Jesuit who became influential among many of the western tribes. *(University of Wyoming American Heritage Center)*

depletion of buffalo, grass, and timber caused by white passage through the West. In exchange, the tribes agreed to allow the government to build roads and outposts, and promised to maintain peace between the tribes and to refrain from attacking whites. They also agreed to set and respect tribal boundaries.

Some whites had misgivings. They included Superintendent of Indian Affairs D. D. Mitchell, who worried that the treaty might not keep the Indians content for long. After all, he pointed out, fifty thousand dollars would not go far among the estimated fifty thousand members of the tribes. The money went even less far than Mitchell expected. When the treaty got to Washington, the Senate cut eighty percent of the promised sum by unilaterally reducing the term of the payments from fifty years to ten.

The Jesuit priest Father Pierre DeSmet, who spent a large portion of his life among the Indians in the West, gloomily wondered if the treaty marked the beginning of the end for the western tribes: "If they are again repelled and banished further inland, they will perish infallibly," he wrote shortly after the treaty was negotiated. "The Indians who refuse to submit or accept the definite arrangement . . . [will] close their sad existence as the bison and other animals on which they live vanish."

INDIAN WARS

By the mid-1860s, the concerns that had led the government to negotiate the 1851 treaty were realized. The immense westward movement of whites had disturbed important hunting grounds, killing off small game and changing the migration patterns of the buffalo. The mere presence of whites had infected the tribes with unfamiliar and deadly diseases, and the number of Indians killed by emigrants along the trail was higher than the number of whites killed by Indians. Some emigrants had even adopted the policy of shooting whatever Indians happened across their paths, friendly or not. Fifty thousand bucks a year wasn't about to make up for that.

Problems between whites and Indians in other parts of the country spilled over to Wyoming, and violence soon erupted (see page 79).

Protection was thin for emigrants along the trails because most of the army was busy fighting the Civil War. During 1862 the Lakota made the Oregon Trail so dangerous that the stagecoach operator, Ben Holladay, moved his operation south to the portion of Wyoming now crossed by Interstate 80. Though slowed, emigrant traffic continued along the Oregon Trail, with small wagon trains banding together for mutual protection. Emigrants were attacked, and so were army troopers, freight wagons, and telegraph and stage stations.

Troops of the 7th Infantry muster at Fort Laramie in 1885. *(University of Wyoming American Heritage Center)*

Serious violence continued through the Civil War years. Then, in 1866, after a U.S. Army campaign of retribution through the Powder River country had largely failed (see page 80), the federal government tried to end the dispute through negotiation. Talks began at Fort Laramie, and a treaty was quickly signed by the peaceful Lakota who were camped around the fort. But the warring Lakota, led by chiefs like Red Cloud, fought it out for another two years before they made peace, mostly on their own terms (see page 81).

GOLD RUSH

The 1868 Laramie treaty kept the peace until the mid-seventies, when Lt. Col. George Armstrong Custer's prospecting expedition discovered gold in the Black Hills of modern South Dakota. Although the 1868 treaty recognized the Black Hills as Indian land, the U.S. government seized the region, touching off the last of the great Indian Wars. During the conflict the Indians wiped out Custer and his men, but in the end they were defeated and forced onto reservations (see pages 81–83).

Meanwhile, thousands of white people hoping to strike it rich poured north through Fort Laramie, which had become an important stop on the trail leading from the Union Pacific tracks in Cheyenne to the mining town of Deadwood, South Dakota. There were prospectors, of course, and land developers, swindlers, gamblers, saloon-keepers, prostitutes, and bankers. Among these predictable opportunists traveled some truly ingenious entrepreneurs. A man named Phatty Thompson, for instance, paid kids in Cheyenne twenty-five cents apiece for cats. When he'd collected enough to fill an enormous crate, he set off for Deadwood and sold the animals for fifteen to twenty-five dollars each to the hard-working staffs of the bordellos.

As the gold rush faded and emigrants relied more on trains than trails to take them west, Fort Laramie diminished in importance. Government troops abandoned it in 1890. Today, it is a national historic site that is open to the public all year. Many of its structures have been restored and furnished in period style, including the post trader's store, the cavalry barracks, and the officers' quarters building, which is believed to be the oldest man-made structure standing in Wyoming.

HUGH GLASS

In early 1824, as Wyoming's fur trade got underway, mountain man Hugh Glass and several companions bobbed merrily down the North Platte in a bullboat—a makeshift vessel resembling a broad canoe, often constructed by stretching the hides of buffalo bulls over willow boughs. They were on their way from Fort Henry at the mouth of the Big Horn to Fort Atkinson at Council Bluffs in order to deliver a message to William Ashley, who commanded their operation. The journey was interrupted somewhere near the present site of Fort Laramie when a group of Indians hailed the boat and invited the men up to the village for a smoke and something to eat. The Indians looked to be Pawnee, which delighted Glass. He had spent considerable time on the Kansas prairie as the adopted son of a Pawnee chief, so he expected quite a reception from his long-lost brothers. He got it.

As they paddled to shore, Glass reassured his less-experienced companions and advised them to leave their rifles in the boat. It would be rude to carry them into a peaceful camp. And so, unarmed, they all went up to the village and settled in for a good time. For Glass, who was arguably the most resilient mountain man of all time, what followed was his fourth nearly fatal encounter with Indians in the space of a year.

He sensed that something wasn't quite right as soon as they cozied up in Elk Tongue's lodge at the village, but what he didn't understand until very late in the game was that the village was not Pawnee. The Indians were hostile Arickara posing as Pawnee. As soon as Glass understood his mistake, he and the others sprinted from camp with a bunch of Arickara warriors pounding after them. Their rifles were gone by now, of course, but the boat was still there, and the mountain men managed to cross the river and scatter. Glass found a place to hide and watched as two of his companions were cut down and butchered within a few feet of him. After dark he stole away and set out on foot for Fort Kiowa. He was undaunted by the trek.

"Although I had lost my rifle and all my plunder, I felt quite rich when I found my knife, flint and steel, in my shot pouch," he said later. "These little fixens make a man feel right peart when he is three or four hundred miles from any body or any place—all alone among the painters and wild varmints."

Glass was in fact traveling in high style. The last time he had set out for Fort Kiowa, just six months before, he had no knife, no flint, no steel. He couldn't even walk. A grizzly had mauled him on the Grand River in Nebraska before the rest of his party could kill her. Figuring he was a goner, most of his colleagues moved on, leaving John Fitzgerald and a very young man who may have been Jim Bridger behind to bury him when the time came. However, Glass lingered too long for Fitzgerald and Bridger. They took his gear and left him to die. Hugh held on.

After he was abandoned, he managed to drag himself to a spring. There he stayed, drinking water and eating berries until he found the strength to stand and begin hobbling toward Fort Kiowa, more than a hundred miles distant. Along the way, he came upon a pack of wolves who had killed a buffalo calf. He waited for them to eat their fill, then claimed the carcass as his own and lived by it for a few days, eating as much as he could. Then he set off again across the prairie, living off berries and carrion. Some say he made it all the way to Fort Kiowa on his own, others that he was picked up by a small party of men headed upriver.

In any case, by New Year's Eve 1824, Glass rejoined the party that had abandoned him and, for some unexplained reason, forgave Jim Bridger—perhaps on account of his youth. Fitzgerald had left the party of trappers by then. Glass caught up with him at Fort Kiowa after his scrape with the Arickaras near what would become Fort Laramie. Since Fitzgerald was under protection of the army, Glass could not kill him. Resupplied by the post's commander, Glass headed out and kept trapping for a few years until his luck ran out and his old enemies, the Arickaras, finally lifted his hair.

HARTVILLE AND SUNRISE

Long before whites arrived there in the nineteenth century, Hartville was the site of a large Indian settlement. A few white settlers arrived in the 1870s to raise cattle, but the town didn't boom until copper was discovered nearby in the 1880s. Then miners swarmed to the area, and saloons, dance halls, and gambling houses were built for them to blow off steam and whatever money they might carry in their pockets. Feelings occasionally ran high, and disputes were not always settled in the most chivalrous manner. Whoever killed Ed "Badman" Taylor in January 1883 didn't bother with the preliminaries one generally associates with western duels. Instead of calling Taylor out, the assailant simply poked a rifle through a saloon window when Taylor's back was turned and pulled the trigger.

At the turn of the century, the area's prosperity got a second, more lasting, shot in the arm when a massive deposit of iron ore was discovered near the present Sunrise. The deposit proved to be one of the largest in the nation.

Sightseers in the 1930s stand in trail ruts that were cut into the sandstone by wagons passing on the Oregon Trail near present-day Guernsey. *(University of Wyoming American Heritage Center)*

GUERNSEY: OREGON TRAIL RUTS

Some of the most impressive physical evidence of the covered-wagon era lies a little more than a mile south of Guernsey. There the Oregon Trail crossed a ridge of soft sandstone where the thousands of passing wagons eventually wore a rut two to six feet deep. Just downriver, many stopped to carve their names on a sandstone bluff called Register Cliff. Others died and were buried nearby.

CASTOFFS

As the wheel ruts cut into the sandstone near Guernsey, piles of debris grew along the trail. During the heaviest years of emigration, the road from Fort Laramie to modern Glenrock became cluttered with top-quality junk. Emigrants could obtain virtually anything they needed—food, clothes, tools, even furniture—by simply picking it up. This amazing collection of stuff accumulated because many emigrants overloaded their wagons. As they creaked across the plains, they saw that their livestock would not endure unless their burdens were lightened. Many delayed the inevitable until they reached Fort Laramie in hopes of selling their surplus goods at a small profit, or at least at not much of a loss. Of course, with so many emigrants thinking the same way, supply completely outran demand, and the would-be wheeler-dealers couldn't sell at any price. So they just dumped their goods. By June 1, 1849, emigrants had abandoned twenty thousand pounds of bacon next to Fort Laramie, which was dubbed "Camp Sacrifice." Howard Stansbury, one of many who headed west in 1849, catalogued the trash he came across beyond Fort Laramie:

> The road has been literally strewn with articles that have been thrown away. Bar-iron and steel, large blacksmith's anvils and bellows, crow-bars, drills, augers, gold-washers, chisels, axes, lead, trunks, spades, ploughs, large grindstones, baking-ovens, cooking stoves without number, kegs, barrels, harnesses, clothing, bacon, and beans.

Others reported that they never lacked for good reading material because many ahead of them had jettisoned their family libraries. One emigrant wrote that when he finished one book he filed it in the "prairie library" by tossing it off the bench of his wagon, confident that he'd come across an equally interesting volume before he'd gone much farther.

While many dumped goods, others scavenged. The Mormons sent out parties from Salt Lake to garner provisions and raw materials, such as cast iron, for their settlements. And emigrants often traded in their own second-rate food and clothing for better stuff they found along the road. One man stopped to trim the fat from all his bacon and replace the weight with bacon he trimmed from a large heap by the trail. Aban-

doned wagons provided spare parts. Abandoned cookstoves were used as overnight kitchens by those who camped beside them. One lucky party even found four kegs of whiskey buried next to the trail.

WARM SPRINGS

Warm Springs, about two and a half miles west of Guernsey, was a popular camping area for travelers on the Oregon Trail. Two free-flowing springs provided plenty of water: one poured from a rock ledge, the other bubbled up in a large pool.

Modern travelers can camp beside a much larger pool of water—the Guernsey Reservoir, created in the late 1920s when the government dammed the North Platte at Hartville. Local lore

A cowpoke bellies up for a drink at Warm Springs, a favorite emigrant campsite near modern Guernsey. *(University of Wyoming American Heritage Center)*

has it that the town's namesake, rancher Charles A. Guernsey, rerouted a trainload of U.S. senators to Hartville in 1909 to convince them of the project's merit. The reservoir helps irrigate surrounding farmland, and the dam creates hydroelectric power.

JUNCTION WITH INTERSTATE 25

From this point to Casper, Highway 26 joins northbound I-25 and continues to follow the route of the Oregon Trail.

OREGON TRAIL

During the years 1841–68, more than 350,000 emigrants drove their wagons along the North Platte and across Wyoming toward Oregon, Utah, and California. Like motorists on I-25 today, the emigrants followed the great bend of the river as it skirts the foothills of the Medicine Bow range. And like the mountain men and Indians who traveled this route before them, the emigrants relied on the North Platte for guidance, water, and forage for their livestock.

But the state's history here pushes well beyond the emigrant era. Cattle ranchers and railroads helped settle the land and established many of the towns along this route. The discovery of rich coal and oil deposits also spurred development.

HORSESHOE STATION

During the early 1860s, one of the West's well-known gunslingers, Jack Slade, frequented Horseshoe Station, which stood about two miles south of present Glendo. Slade, the son of an Illinois congressman, earned his gunfighting reputation by hunting and ruthlessly disposing of stagecoach robbers along a six-hundred-mile stretch of the Oregon Trail.

First, the Russell, Majors & Waddell stagecoach line put him in charge of the road from Julesburg, Colorado, to South Pass. While cleaning up this stretch, Slade often made his headquarters at the Horseshoe Station, a relay point for both stagecoach drivers and Pony Express riders. When Slade wasn't running off crooked ranchers or presiding at the executions of stage robbers and horse thieves, he entertained travelers at the Horseshoe Station. The Englishman Sir Richard Burton met him here in 1860.

He had the reputation of having killed his three men and a few days afterwards the grave that concealed one of his murders was pointed out to me. This pleasant individual for an evening party wore the revolver and bowie-knife here, there, and everywhere. He had lately indeed had a strong hint not to forget his weapon. One M. Jules, a French trader, after a quarrel which took place at dinner, walked up to him and fired a pistol, wounding him in the breast. As he [Slade] rose to run away, Jules discharged a second, which took effect upon his back, and then without giving him time to arm, [Jules] fetched a gun and favoured him with a dose of slugs.

Burton was referring to Jules Reni, who some say had lost his position as district manager of the stage line to Slade. Slade eventually caught up with Jules and killed him. Accounts of Jules's death say that Slade dropped him from his horse with one shot and tied him, still living, to a fence post. Then Slade spent the better part of an afternoon drinking and firing away at Jules, announcing before each shot where the bullet would strike. Some say Slade cut away the man's ears after he finished him off and carried them around for years afterward.

ELKHORN CREEK

About three miles north of Glendo, a dirt road heads west toward Laramie Peak, a major landmark for emigrants and other travelers. The road leads to Esterbrook, a tiny community that was once a copper-mining town. An old log-cabin church stands there with Laramie Peak framed by one of its windows.

ORIN: BRIDGER'S FERRY

Jim Bridger, the fabled mountain man, trader, and guide, built a ferry in 1864 near the present site of Orin. Located about fifteen hundred feet upstream of where I-25 now crosses the North Platte, Bridger's Ferry was an important jumping-off point for the short-lived Bozeman Trail.

DOUGLAS

An abundance of water and plenty of native grassland lured ranchers to the Douglas area in the late 1860s, but the town did not form until 1886, in anticipation of the coming railroad. It started as a tent town, with three streets and many businesses, including a newspaper. But the early residents of Douglas guessed wrong about where the railroad intended to lay track. Instead of hammering spikes right up to the canvas roofs, officials announced that the Fremont, Elkhorn & Missouri River Valley Railroad would pass ten miles to the east. Well, Douglas people were nothing if not flexible. They packed up their busy little town and moved it across the river.

In the early years, drinking and playing cards were the chief forms of relaxation for the cowboys. A guy could get pretty relaxed on a Saturday night in Douglas, considering that the early town had twenty-five saloons. George Pike, Douglas's most famous cowboy, frequented them and played a lot of cards. After losing big in a rigged game, Pike returned to the saloon in disguise, drew his gun, and held up the cheater for $2,500. Pike was a good wrangler—so good, rumor had it, that he often supplemented his wages by selling any unbranded cattle (called "mavericks") he could find. In those days, the herds of different ranches roamed together, and often it was anybody's guess who the mavericks belonged to. Individual employers, recognizing that Pike's talent for petty rustling could redound to their benefit, paid him high wages to continue his pursuits as long as they got a cut of the

proceeds. Pike was such a valued hand that when he died his final employer bought an expensive tombstone and had the following verse inscribed:

> Underneath this stone in eternal rest
> Sleeps the wildest one of the wayward west.
> He was gambler and sport and cowboy, too,
> And he led the pace in an outlaw crew.
> He was sure on the trigger and staid to
>   the end
> But was never known to quit on a friend.
> In the relations of death all mankind's alike
> But in life there was only one George W. Pike.

The gravestone still stands in the Douglas Park Cemetery.

During World War II, the federal government built a prisoner of war camp a mile south of Douglas. The camp, 180 buildings in a wire perimeter, housed Italian and German POWs from 1943 to the autumn of 1945. The prisoners worked in lumber camps and helped out on nearby farms.

Wyoming residents enthusiastically greeted news of the government's plans to build the camp. Douglas merchants liked the money it would bring in, and farmers and ranchers needed laborers. Citizens took pride in the camp, with its well-appointed 150-bed hospital and canteen where the men could buy cigarettes, candy, and soft drinks.

Wyoming's attitude toward captured enemy soldiers stood in sharp contrast to the greeting it accorded American citizens of Japanese descent, who had been forced from their West Coast homes and interned at a large camp near Powell (see page 161).

JUNCTION WITH STATE ROUTE 59

State Route 59 leads north through Bill and Gillette to the Montana border (see page 103).

JUNCTION WITH
STATE ROUTE 93

A short trip from the interstate on State 93 leads to the site of restored Fort Fetterman, which was the start of the Bozeman Trail and a staging area for army troops during the Indian Wars of the 1860s and 1870s (see page 29).

BOXELDER CREEK

On July 12, 1864, a band of Oglalla Lakota attacked a small wagon train on Boxelder Creek. The wagons crossed the creek at more or less the same point that I-25 does today and traveled about a half-mile upstream. The sun was setting, and one of the men was singing a favorite song about Idaho.

"Without a sound of preparation or a word of warning, the bluffs before us were covered with a party of about 250 Indians, painted and equipped for war," wrote Fanny Kelly in her book, *My Captivity Among the Sioux.*

The emigrants corraled their wagons and watched a detachment of Indians circle round and round. After a while, the Indians came forward to parley. They said they wanted peace. The emigrants did not believe them but decided to give them anything they asked for without a fight in the hope that another, larger wagon train would arrive and help them out of the mess. The Indians' demands for goods grew bolder and bolder, Kelly wrote. Finally, at dusk, the Indians opened fire. One man died at Kelly's feet.

"I never can forget his face as I saw him shot through the forehead with a rifle ball," she wrote. "He looked at me as he fell backward to the ground a corpse."

Three men were killed immediately, two were wounded, and two managed to escape, including Kelly's husband, who had been off collecting firewood. The Indians plundered the train

and rode off with Fanny Kelly and her young niece, Mary, as well as Sarah Larimer and her son.

Kelly managed to slip Mary into the brush the following night with instructions to get back to the road and hail the next emigrant train to come along. Mary got to the road. Soldiers approached her but stopped some distance off, thinking she might be a decoy. Just then, they caught sight of some Indians who had gone back to find Mary. The soldiers galloped off and the Indians killed the little girl. Fanny Kelly did not learn of the child's fate until much later, when one of her captors rode up beside her: "At his saddle hung a bright and well-known little shawl, and from the other side was suspended a child's scalp of long fair hair," Kelly wrote. "I dropped from the saddle as if dead, and rolled upon the ground at the horse's feet."

Mary's grave and those of the three men killed in the initial attack lie on a private ranch a couple of miles south of where the interstate crosses Boxelder Creek.

The Larimers soon managed to escape. Kelly, though, lived with the Lakota for five months before a white trader bought her freedom. Both women wrote about their experiences, fanning white hatred for the Indians.

GLENROCK

Here, where Deer Creek meets the North Platte, the main branch of the Oregon Trail continued along the south bank of the river to Casper. Most emigrants went that way, but many chose to cross here. During low water, wagons could ford just south of the present bridge. In the summer of 1849, though, four crude ferries plied the river. One was owned by Joseph Bissonette, who opened a trading post that summer and operated his ferry about a quarter-mile upstream of the present bridge.

Old Muddy, a stage and Pony Express station in southwest Wyoming, as it appeared in the 1860s. Many such primitive stations dotted the Wyoming plains before the coming of the Union Pacific Railroad, and they were the subjects of many travelers' complaints and adventures. *(University of Wyoming American Heritage Center)*

Two years later John Richard built a log bridge across the river. It was the first over the North Platte, but it didn't last long. It washed out the following spring.

Bissonette remained on the scene much longer, and prospered. Richard Burton, the English adventurer, stopped at Bissonette's post in 1860: "[He] was the usual creole, speaking a French not unlike that of the Channel Islands and wide awake to the advantages derivable from travelers," Burton wrote. "I wish my enemy no more terrible fate than to drink excessively with M. Bissonette."

During the early 1850s, the Mormons built a substantial way station at Deer Creek for their long trains of Zion-bound brethren. There Mormon travelers could rest, repair their wagons, and eat vegetables grown nearby in irrigated gardens. The vegetables were more than a treat for emigrants, because scurvy was a major cause of death along the trail. The Mormons abandoned their buildings in 1857 when the U.S. Army threatened to invade their settlements in the Salt Lake valley.

Known as Deer Creek early on, the settlement picked up several other names, including Mercedes and Nuttell, before taking its present one from a prominent rock in a glen near the railroad station. Located near a lucrative oil field named Big Muddy, Glenrock was home to an oil refinery in the 1930s. One visitor during that period remarked that the smell of crude oil permeated the town. Today, a large coal-fired plant produces electricity for Wyoming and other states.

A BRITON COMPLAINS

Although the English traveler and explorer Richard Burton had it better than most, he still found plenty to complain about during his overland stage journey in 1860. Very few of his stops were pleasant ones, and the station at Muddy Creek (between Glenrock and Casper) was no exception: "A wretched place, built of 'dry stones,' viz, slabs without mortar," he wrote.

"The furniture was composed of a box and a trunk, and the negative catalogue of its supplies was extensive, — whiskey forming the only positive item."

Meals also failed to come up to Burton's standards. He wrote this about the food at another station:

> Our breakfast was prepared in the usual prairie style. First the coffee — three parts burnt beans — which had been duly ground to a fine powder and exposed to the air, lest the aroma should prove too strong for us, was placed on the stove to simmer till every noxious principle was duly extracted from it. Then the rusty bacon, cut into thick slices, was thrown into the fry-pan; here the gridiron is unknown, and if known would be little appreciated, because it wastes the "drippings", which form with the staff of life a luxurious sop. Thirdly, antelope steak, cut off a corpse suspended for the benefit of flies outside, was placed to stew within influence of the bacon's aroma. Lastly came the bread, which of course should have been cooked first.

Still, Burton hadn't forgotten to provision himself against the hardships of the trail, and he recommended others do the same: "Captain Marcy outfits his prairie traveler with a little blue mass, quinine, opium, and some cathartic medicine put up in doses for adults," he wrote. "I limited myself to the opium, which is invaluable when one expects five consecutive days and nights in a prairie wagon."

Cigars, he said, "must be bought in extraordinary quantities, as the driver either receives or takes the lion's share."

To cure snakebite, Burton recommended plenty of whiskey: "It has the advantage of being a palatable medicine; it must also be taken in large quantities, a couple of bottles sometimes producing little effect."

And there was this last bit of advice for his British readers: "Above all things, as you value your nationality let no false shame cause you to forget your hat-box and your umbrella."

CHILD'S GRAVE

Just west of Glenrock lie the remains of Ada Magill, a six-year-old who came down with dysentery at Fort Laramie and died near Glenrock. She fell the same way most people did on the Oregon Trail: from a disease rather than an Indian attack.

CASPER

The city of Casper takes its misspelled name from a young cavalry officer, Caspar Collins, who died nearby while fighting Indians in 1865 (see page 63). Long before Collins was born (he died at twenty), people traveling through Wyoming had crossed the North Platte in the vicinity of the present city.

In the early days of the fur trade, trappers usually forded the river near the Red Buttes, about twelve miles southwest of town on State 220. Taking their lead from the mountain men, early emigrants also used that ford. But at the height of the westward movement, most emigrants crossed near the present U.S. 26 bridge.

In 1847, Brigham Young and the first wagon train of Mormons built a skiff there to ferry their wagons. Before they crossed, though, a train of Missourians overtook them and asked if they could rent the ferry. Young charged them $1.50 a wagon and accepted payment in flour, bacon, and meal — provisions dearly needed by the Mormons. Seeing the commercial opportunity, Young asked nine of his flock to stay behind at the crossing to ferry other Gentiles. The proceeds resupplied the Mormon trains that followed.

Business was brisk at as much as five dollars per wagon. James A. Pritchard, who lined up behind 175 wagons in June 1849, had to wait three days to cross. Total proceeds for seven weeks of ferrying gold-rush emigrants came to somewhere between $6,465 and $10,000.

Competitors soon moved in. John Richard built another of his log bridges across the Platte three miles northeast of Casper in 1852–53. This one lasted longer than his Glenrock bridge, earning him tens of thousands of dollars in tolls as the emigrants streamed by. In 1858, Louis Guinard built a better bridge upstream, thirteen feet wide and one thousand feet long. The site of Guinard's bridge became known as the Platte Bridge Station, and it is where the army built its fort, later named Fort Caspar.

Some emigrants cleverly avoided tolls on both ferries and bridges. They bought scows and makeshift boats from those ahead of them, ferried their goods across, and then sold the vessel to the next party for an identical price.

In 1938, Fort Caspar was reconstructed at its original location and now serves as a historic site and excellent pioneer museum. To get to the museum, take the State 220 exit and follow the signs.

While looking at this stretch of the North Platte and imagining how the emigrants crossed, keep in mind that today's river is a much diminished waterway due to upstream dams and heavy irrigation.

For more about Casper's history, see pages 63–65.

JUNCTION WITH 220

From Casper, State Route 220 heads southwest, loosely following the Oregon Trail (see page 31).

JUNCTION WITH 26

Highway 26 crosses the North Platte and continues northwest over a classic high-plains landscape through the Wind River Indian Reservation and up the Wind River Valley to Grand Teton National Park (see page 56).

State 93 breaks away from I-25 at Douglas and passes the sites of Fort Fetterman, an important military outpost during the 1860s and 1870s, and the Hog Ranch, a frontier saloon and whorehouse.

FORT FETTERMAN

Built in 1867 on a bench of land overlooking the North Platte, Fort Fetterman was supposed to protect emigrants traveling on the Oregon Trail and the Bozeman Road. It was named for Capt. William J. Fetterman, who led eighty-one men to their deaths in an ambush sprung by the Lakota (often called Sioux*) near Fort Phil Kearny the previous year (see page 86).

Remnants of the fort survive today as a state historical park. Still visible are the former officers' quarters, the armory, and the cemetery. Occupied by the army from 1867 to 1882, Fetterman was not a popular billet. Troopers serving here considered it a disciplinary assignment, and many of them deserted. Even some of the civilians who frequented Fort Fetterman found social conditions less than ideal. Bill Hooker said that the civilian wagon drivers, or "bullwhackers," who freighted supplies to Fort Fetterman looked so disreputable that the officers didn't care to rub elbows with them. Sim Waln, for instance, wore a pair of elkskin breeches, a greasy sombrero, a buckskin shirt, and a belt with two revolvers, forty rounds of ammunition, and a butcher knife with a ten-inch blade.

Bullwhackers had need of such abundant weaponry because Fort Fetterman was built during a peak of hostilities between whites and Indians. During the Civil War, when troops for the West were scarce, the tribes did their best to shut down emigration on the Oregon and Bozeman trails, both of which led north to the goldfields of Montana. They were especially intent on closing the Bozeman Trail because it led through the Lakota's last great source of food (see page 79). Fort Fetterman lay at the southern edge of this territory.

The war kicked off by the Bozeman Trail ended in 1868 with yet another treaty at Fort Laramie (see page 18). This treaty recognized the entire northeast quarter of Wyoming as Indian land, over which no white was allowed to pass. The treaty closed down the Bozeman Trail, and the army abandoned most of the forts that had been built to protect it. A form of peace (an awful lot of killing went on during the 1860s) held from the date of that treaty to the mid-1870s, when a federal mineral survey found gold on Indian land in the Black Hills. Then the rush was on, and war resumed between Indians trying to defend their land and whites determined to seize it.

Here at Fort Fetterman in the fall of 1875, a band of Lakota killed several soldiers on the parade ground in front of the command's officers and men. Earlier in the summer, Indians had attacked a wagon train loaded with supplies for the fort and killed one of the bullwhackers, George Throstle, who was buried in the fort's cemetery.

On March 1, Gen. George Crook and a command of one thousand men headed north from Fort Fetterman as part of a campaign to break the power of the Lakota. His winter expedition was the first in a long series of army disappointments that continued throughout the

---

*The word "Sioux" is a term that has been used traditionally by white historians. The members of this tribe refer to themselves as *Lakota* or *Dakota,* and we use these terms preferentially, adding the word "Sioux" wherever a recorded historical incident warrants this additional identification.

summer and that included Custer's death on the Little Big Horn (see page 83).

From the gazebo beyond the fort you can look across a farm field to the site of the Hog Ranch, a notorious gambling hall, saloon, dance hall, and whorehouse. It attracted some interesting characters, such as Alferd Packer, who was arrested there in 1883 and later convicted of having killed and eaten five prospectors while they were snowbound in the Colorado Rockies.

A BUM STEER

While moseying along the banks of the North Platte with a group of mountain men in 1834, lawyer William Anderson came across an anatomical curiosity that shows how tough life on the plains could be for animals.

"Emmanuel killed a very large and exceedingly fat steer buffalo," Anderson wrote. "This is no very remarkable circumstance. The Crow Indians alter a great many calves, and some suppose that accidents arising from the attacks of the wolves reduce others to this condition."

The Oregon Trail included many branches and shortcuts, and emigrants crossed the North Platte at many different points. However, most crossed to the north bank of the river before leaving the vicinity of Casper and then headed southwest until they picked up the Sweetwater River. State Route 220 follows the same general course, but it crosses the river farther upstream and parallels the trail closely for only about twenty miles. While thick with stories about the emigrants, the road also passes sites where Indians, mountain men, explorers, lynching parties, cattle barons, and cowboys left their marks on Wyoming's history.

RED BUTTES

About a half-dozen miles southwest of Casper's outskirts, a set of high red cliffs rises above the waters of the North Platte. Called the Red Buttes, these cliffs of rusty sandstone mark the point where early western travelers finally bid adieu to the valley of the Platte River, which they had followed for hundreds of miles. Although travelers could cross to the north bank at many points along the river, this was considered the uppermost ford. It was heavily used by fur trappers and early emigrants, but traffic slacked off after various ferry services and bridges began operating downstream in the late 1840s. From here the emigrants veered off a bit more to the west to pick up the Sweetwater River, which guided and sustained them until they reached South Pass.

Indians had plotted their travels in relation to the Red Buttes long before the first wagons rolled west, and it most probably was an Indian who told the first whites about the landmark. These were the returning Astorians, a small band of men making a painful overland journey in 1812 from the mouth of the Columbia River to New York (see page 12). The Astorians reached

A small party of emigrants arrives on the banks of the North Platte River at Red Buttes in 1870. The site is about a dozen miles west of modern Casper on State Route 220. It was a traditional fording point for Indians, mountain men, and emigrants. In 1856 a Mormon handcart company met with disaster here when an early winter storm struck as they forded the river on foot. *(University of Wyoming American Heritage Center)*

Red Buttes in late autumn, built a small cabin, stocked it with meat, and intended to settle in for the winter. But Indians chased them off, and they had to spend the winter east of the Medicine Bow Mountains.

By the time William Anderson came west with a caravan of trappers in 1834, the Red Buttes crossing was heavily traveled by the mountain men. Anderson, a lawyer taking a break from his Louisville, Kentucky, practice, seems to have had a more peaceful sojourn at Red Buttes than did the Astorians. He wrote in June:

> Here I am, at a beautiful spring, my skewer in the ground at a hot fire of buffalo dung, a set of good, sweet hump-ribs roasting before me, legs crossed, knife drawn, and mouth watering, waiting for the attack

. . . These clear mountain springs are charming places. They do so sweetly wash down a savory meal of buffalo meat. And is such meat really good? What a question to a hungry man. Ask a Catholic if he loves or believes in the Virgin Mary.

Anderson probably carried warm memories of Red Buttes with him for the rest of his days, but the crossing was an agony to a company of roughly 550 Mormons who arrived here on a frigid October day in 1856 starving and nearly exhausted from pulling their handcarts through Iowa, Nebraska, and a third of Wyoming.

ORDEAL OF THE MORMON HANDCARTS

The experience of this handcart company, along with that of another that preceded it by two weeks, ranks as one of the most tragic stories of the emigrant era.

It began smoothly enough, with four boatloads of European Mormon converts arriving in America and swiftly traveling by rail and steamboat to eastern Iowa under the efficient guidance of their church. From there the emigrants would have to walk, because neither they nor the church could afford to buy the necessary wagons and livestock to carry them west. Instead, the emigrants would travel light, pulling a few belongings behind them in handcarts. A small train of wagons drawn by livestock would follow with provisions, and a herd of cattle would be driven along for meat. At a pace of twenty miles a day they would arrive in Salt Lake before winter and in better physical shape than when they started.

As farfetched as it may seem today, when people depend on cars to reach the corner grocery, in the nineteenth century the idea of Mormon handcart companies crossing the continent proved generally to be a sound one. Three

companies, with a total of some eight hundred persons, made the trip with comparative ease in 1856. And in later years, other Mormon handcart companies reached Salt Lake with few problems. But the last of the 1856 groups—the Martin and Willie companies—jumped off far too late to cross the mountains in safety.

They left eastern Iowa in late July and began crossing Nebraska in late August. Some had doubts. They thought the companies ought to hole up for the winter while they still could, and finish the trip in the spring. Brigham Young later said that this was exactly what the church leadership had expected them to do. But they were driven forward by zeal on the part of nearly everyone, including those who should have known better, and ignorance on the part of those who might have been more cautious had they known about the early winter storms that could strike the Rocky Mountains.

The trek was difficult even through Iowa. Some company members died. A large portion of the beef herd ran off with stampeding buffalo. Rations grew scarce and the nights got cold. But the true ordeal did not begin until October at Red Buttes.

In the Mormons' day, the North Platte was a much wider, much wilder river than it is today. And because they were too poor to pay the ferry and bridge tolls farther downstream, the handcart company had no choice but to plunge in and drag their carts across.

"The crossing of the North Platte was fraught with more fatalities than any other incident of the entire journey," wrote Josiah Rogerson, of Martin's handcart company. "More than a score or two of the young female members waded the stream that in places was waist deep. Blocks of mushy snow and ice had to be dodged."

Men carried some of the women across on their backs, but a few were so weak they could not cross the river even without a burden. One was Aaron Jackson, whose wife, Elizabeth, had taken over the task of pulling the handcart. From shore, she watched him struggle:

He had only gone a short distance when he reached a sandbar in the river, on which he sank down through weakness and exhaustion. My sister . . . waded through the water to his assistance. She raised him up to his feet. Shortly afterward, a man came along on horseback and conveyed him to the other side. My sister then helped me to pull my cart with my three children and other matters on it. We had scarcely crossed the river when we were visited with a tremendous storm of snow, hail, sand, and fierce winds.

Aaron Jackson died that night in camp, not far beyond the icy waters of the Platte. Rogerson, who shared his tent, stumbled across Jackson's stiff legs at midnight: "Reaching my hand to his face, I found that he was dead with his exhausted wife and little ones by his side all sound asleep." Jackson's wife soon made the same discovery:

I called for help to the other inmates of the tent. They could render me no aid, and there was no alternative but to remain alone by the side of the corpse till morning . . . When daylight came, some of the male part of the company prepared the body for burial . . . They wrapped him in a blanket and placed him in a pile with thirteen others who had died, and then covered him up with snow. The ground was frozen so hard that they could not dig a grave.

The ordeal continued for another dreadful month as the two companies made their way along the length of the Sweetwater River toward South Pass. Deep snow, subzero temperatures, lack of food and proper clothing all combined to reap a grim harvest of the faithful.

"Life went out as smoothly as a lamp ceases to burn when the oil is gone," wrote John Chislett, with Willie's company. "At first the deaths occurred slowly and irregularly, but in a few days at more frequent intervals, until we soon thought it unusual to leave a campground without burying one or more persons . . . Many a father pulled his cart, with his little children on it, until the day preceding his death."

A blizzard stalled both companies. Willie's group, which had started two weeks earlier, bogged down close to South Pass. Martin's company got just twelve miles past Red Buttes. Help was on the way from Salt Lake City, but many people died before it arrived.

"Captain Martin stood over the grave of the departed ones with shotgun in hand, firing at intervals to keep the crows and buzzards away," wrote John Bond, who was twelve years old at the time.

Nine desperate days after Martin's company crossed the Platte, hope arrived in the form of three riders from a Salt Lake City relief train. Unfortunately, they had little but hope to offer. The wagons with food, clothing, and blankets were still about forty grueling miles to the west at Devil's Gate. Cold, wet, hungry, some dying, others maimed by frostbite, the Mormons had no choice but to break camp and walk for it.

"The train was strung out for three or four miles," wrote one of the riders, Dan Jones. "There were old men pulling and tugging their carts, sometimes loaded with a sick wife or children—women pulling along sick husbands—little children six to eight years old struggling through the mud and snow. As night came on the mud would freeze on their clothes and feet. There were two of us, and hundreds needing help. What could we do?"

By the time relief wagons finally reached the spent emigrants sixteen miles east of Independence Rock, not more than a third of them could walk. In the nine days between crossing the Platte and greeting the express riders of the relief train, Martin's company had lost fifty-six people. More died before the wagons got through, and still more died on the way to Devil's Gate and Salt Lake. No one knows precisely how many died, but probably between 135 and 150. In Willie's company of five hundred, between sixty-two and sixty-seven perished. Many others were maimed for life because their frozen feet, hands, or legs had to be amputated.

For more about the handcart ordeal, see page 39.

BILL CODY'S FAMOUS RIDE

In the years after disaster struck the Mormon handcart companies, a stage and Pony Express station was built on the north bank of the Platte at Red Buttes. From that station, young Bill Cody (later Buffalo Bill) made the third-longest Pony Express ride ever. His usual circuit ran seventy-six miles up the Sweetwater River to Three Crossings, near modern Jeffrey City. But one day he trotted into Three Crossings and learned that the next rider had been killed. So he rode another eighty-five miles along the Sweetwater to Rocky Ridge Station, then back again with the mail, on time. The total round-trip distance was 322 miles, which he is said to have covered in twenty-one hours, forty minutes.

ALCOVA

In 1891, eastern developers planned to build a health spa here based at a nearby hot springs that pours out of the rock walls of a canyon. The promoters gave up their idea, but the town took root. The Alcova Dam, across the reservoir to the southwest, was built in 1935–38. In 1955 a hydroelectric plant was added.

THE POOREST USE OF CATTLE KATE

By the 1880s, large herds of cattle grazed the hills and bottomland of the Sweetwater Valley. In those days, vast tracts of valuable grassland belonged to no one — or, rather, the land belonged to the government, which allowed ranchers to graze their cattle on it without charge. Grazing rights were not leased and were not assigned. The open range was just that, open. At least that was the official version. In practice, much of the public land was controlled by handfuls of powerful ranchers who had come to regard it as their own. They did not take kindly to those who challenged their claim — people such as Cattle Kate.

Cattle Kate, whose real name was Ella Watson, came to the Sweetwater Valley in early 1888. The big cattlemen later painted her as a worn-out Rawlins whore who, at the ripe old age of twenty-seven, came to the Sweetwater to trade her services for rustled cattle. But recent research by Jackson Hole composer George Hufsmith shows her to have been an innocent homesteader persecuted by the landed interests of the local ranchers. In any event, Watson staked out a homestead a couple of miles east of Independence Rock. Her claim lay close to that of another homesteader, Jim Averell, who had been living in the valley for about five years and ran a small store and saloon popular with local cowboys. Though labeled as Watson's lover and pimp and a rustler to boot, he was Ella's husband.

Crucial is the fact that both of their homesteads lay on public land where a rancher named Albert Bothwell grazed his cattle. To Bothwell, their mere presence was a challenge to his interests. Averell had written bitter letters to the Casper newspaper about how Bothwell and two other ranchers controlled one hundred miles of open range along the Sweetwater. He complained about how large ranching interests wielded absolute control over the registration of new brands, a fact that made it impossible for homesteaders like himself to get a legitimate start. He had tried for five years running to get his brand approved so he could legally run cattle, but each year the Carbon County brand committee turned him down. Watson's application for a brand was also turned down in 1888.

On July 20, 1889, Watson and a cowboy who worked for her returned to her cabin and found six local ranchers, including Bothwell, waiting. The ranchers ordered Watson into a wagon and rode over to Averell's place, where they told him they had a warrant for his arrest. Averell asked to see the warrant, then climbed into the wagon when a couple of the ranchers patted their rifles and said the guns were warrant enough. The cowboy who had worked for Watson, along with a fourteen-year-old neighbor, watched all this happen and tried to follow the wagon as the ranchers drove toward Independence Rock. They were turned back at gunpoint, but Frank Buchanan, a cowboy who had been at Averell's store, tracked the wagon around the western end of Independence Rock and up Spring Creek Canyon.

Buchanan later testified that when he caught up with the ranchers, they had tossed ropes over a branch of a scrub pine. Bothwell had a rope around Averell's neck. A rancher named McLain was trying to put the other noose around Watson's neck, but she was moving her head around too much for him to do it. Buchanan said he opened fire but was driven off. He rode back to Averell's store and told a group of cowboys about the hangings. While they started making coffins, Buchanan rode on to Casper to tell the sheriff.

By the time the posse reached Spring Creek gulch, almost three days had passed. Averell and

James Averell, the husband of Ella Watson, also known as Cattle Kate. Both drew the wrath of large cattle ranchers by homesteading on public land the ranchers regarded as their own. They were lynched together near Independence Rock in August 1889. *(University of Wyoming American Heritage Center)*

Watson hung lifeless from the ropes. Apparently they had strangled slowly to death, because the ledge they were forced to jump from was only a two-foot drop.

The coroner's inquest, held at Averell's place, determined that Watson and Averell had been killed by ranchers Albert J. Bothwell, Tom Sun, John Durbin, R. M. Gailbraith, Bob Conners, E. McLain and one other, unknown, man. When a grand jury was convened, all of the key witnesses had died or disappeared. The ranchers were never indicted.

"The men of Wyoming will not be proud of the fact that a woman . . . has been hanged within their territory," wrote an editor of the *Salt Lake Tribune*. "That is about the poorest use that a woman can be put to."

Cattle Kate was the only woman in Wyoming ever put to such a poor use—legally or otherwise.

SWEETWATER STATION

Located about a mile east of Independence Rock, Sweetwater Station was built in the early 1860s to protect emigrants and the transcontinental telegraph line.

Caspar Collins, the infantry lieutenant killed on the North Platte near modern Casper in 1865, commanded a small military post at Sweetwater

Station in 1862. He wrote to tell his mother that the winds in this area were the worst he had ever experienced.

SALERATUS LAKE

Not far from Sweetwater Station lay Saleratus Lake, part of a chain of alkaline springs emigrants came across on the approach to Independence Rock. It looked like a frozen lake in the middle of a desert. Mormon emigrants scooped up the alkali dust by the pailful and baked with it. Gentiles said it made their bread look suspiciously green.

Emigrants had to be careful of alkaline water along this stretch of the trail. Guidebooks, veterans of the passage, and the hard-luck stories of those who had gone on ahead warned that the brackish water could kill their livestock. Many failed to get the word or could not manage to prevent thirsty livestock from lapping it up. "During the afternoon we passed the carcasses of many animals, mostly cattle," wrote Albert Dickson in 1864. "The stench became more nauseating as we advanced. Why they had perished here in such numbers we could only conjecture."

They soon found out. Before they could herd their oxen down to the river that evening, the animals drank from standing water. Dickson woke the next morning to find that one of his oxen had died in the night.

There lay Jerry, my off wheel ox, stark. He would never carry a yoke again. Red Tom, one of Dad Ridgley's leaders, was just able to rise. The others, including the two cows, were in a bad way . . . Like most tenderfeet we knew nothing of alkali or its effects upon stock . . . As we watched the poor creatures writhing in their misery, we were confronted with the possibility that all of them might lay their bones among the skeletons by the wayside, leaving us stranded out in these wilds.

Dickson and his party had heard of a cure. They stuffed about two pounds of fat bacon down the mouths of each animal. It worked.

INDEPENDENCE ROCK

This oblong dome of grayish brown stone just south of the road was the most noted Wyoming landmark west of Fort Laramie during the emigrant era. In the years 1841–68, thousands stopped here to clamber over the rock and add their own autographs to the names of those who had come before. Even in the earliest days of emigrant travel it was clear to those who stopped that they were by no means among the first. In the spring of 1842, Rufus B. Sage described an Independence Rock liberally marked up with the scribblings of passersby:

The surface is covered with names of travelers, traders, trappers and emigrants engraved upon it in almost every practicable part, for the distance of many feet above its base . . . But most prominent among them is the word, "Independence," inscribed by the patriotic band who first christened this lonely monument of nature in honor of Liberty's birthday.

That patriotic band was composed of fur trappers. Some say they were led by William Sublette and that the rock was named on July 4, 1830. Others say an earlier group of trappers named it while camped here in 1823. Whenever it happened, the mountain men threw themselves a big party at the base of the rock and sanctified the rowdy proceedings by naming the landmark Independence Rock.

During the great wave of emigration, the rock was one of the most popular campsites on

Independence Rock, in Wyoming's Sweetwater Valley.This famous landmark of the Oregon Trail is inscribed with hundreds of names of people who came this way in covered wagons. *(University of Wyoming American Heritage Center)*

the trail. A trader set up shop here in 1859 and chained a grizzly bear out front to draw in customers. A party of Mormon stonecutters also sought to turn a good buck at the rock by offering to inscribe names for one to five dollars, depending on length. Emigrants pored over the granite surfaces looking not only for the names of friends but also of famous frontier personalities.

"Many of the names were carved high above our heads," wrote Albert Dickson, who came West in 1864. "I still remember the signatures of Kit Carson and generals Harney, Fremont and Kearney."

Today the names from covered-wagon days are not so obvious along the base of the rock. However, plenty of old-time signatures survive on top.

PRAIRIE POST OFFICE

Although Independence Rock is the most prominent registry of emigrant graffiti on the Oregon Trail, it was only one of many such billboards. They served a more practical purpose than simply preserving marks for later generations to ponder. They were parts of what became known as the "prairie post office" or "roadside telegraph." Most of what might be called mailboxes in this system were not such lasting

monuments as Independence Rock. The emigrants left letters in hollow tree trunks, carved their names on trees, and painted messages on boulders, planks, abandoned wagons, even the bleached skulls of dead livestock. Usually the message was simple, just a name and a date. But such information proved useful. The name told relatives or friends in a subsequent wagon train that the person who left the message had passed the intervening miles in safety. The date indicated how far apart the two parties were.

Other messages passed on news, rumors, advice, changes in travel plans, and the like. They described where major shortcuts broke off from the main trail and bad-mouthed those that saved neither time nor effort. They warned of approaching stretches of desert, pointed out which watering holes had sickened people or livestock, and gave directions to freshwater springs and good campsites. Occasionally the roadside telegraph flashed bulletins of national importance. In 1850, an eastbound traveler tacked up a notice that President Zachary Taylor had died.

Sometimes even love letters were left along the way. Such was the case, in 1851, with John Lawrence Johnson and Jane Jones, the sixteen-year-old daughter of a Presbyterian minister. The couple fell for each other after meeting and traveling together in the same emigrant train. But when the Reverend Jones uncovered the mutual attraction, he found an excuse to move his family to another wagon train. Before the couple separated, they vowed that the one traveling ahead would leave letters on buffalo skins for the other code-named "Laurie." The system worked, but no one knows whether the two ever saw each other again.

Many of the roadside notices dealt with rumors of Indian attacks, but Indian attacks on emigrant trains were rare and greatly exaggerated. Overlanders discounted many of the rumors that reached them, but they could never be sure, so such rumors tended to keep them on guard. Even so, the comments of John Benson, who crossed in 1849, held true for most of the emigrants: "I have traveled about four and a half months and probably over 2,000 miles, most of the way in what was supposed to be a hostile Indian country," Benson wrote. "Rumors of depredation were afloat much of the time, but I have not seen a single hostile Indian. All I have met are extremely friendly."

Even at the height of real Indian trouble during the 1860s, most of the alarms were unwarranted. Albert Dickson stayed up most of one night in 1864 waiting behind corraled wagons for an attack that never came: "Morning was well along before I opened my sleep-clogged eyes and crawled out of my wagon. The others were up before me and breakfast was cooking. Lon had been relieved and was snoring in his wagon. I felt a little disappointed."

DEVIL'S GATE OVERLOOK

Driving west from Independence Rock, you'll see a large tongue of stone slanting down toward the road from the right. Near the end of the tongue there is a cleft. That's Devil's Gate, another important landmark on the Oregon Trail.

Although it doesn't look like much from the highway, the gorge is 1,500 feet long, 370 feet deep, and as tight as 50 feet across in some places. The Sweetwater River plunges through the gate, but you can't see that part of the river from the road or from the marked overlook.

The first Anglos to take note of Devil's Gate were probably the returning Astorians (see page 12). They stumbled past in miserable condition in 1812 but did not get quite so intimate with the feature as mountain man Tom Fitzpatrick did a dozen years later.

After a very good winter of trapping and skinning beaver in the Green River valley, Fitzpatrick and the large group of mountain men he worked with needed to get the fur back to St. Louis. From where they had camped much farther upstream, floating down the Sweetwater River seemed like just the way to do it. Fewer men would be needed to make the trip, so more trappers stayed in the mountains for the start of the fall hunt.

Fitzpatrick and two others loaded the fur into a bullboat, made of skins stretched over a light wooden frame, then set off. The bullboat rafted the men happily down the tame waters of the upper Sweetwater until they reached Devil's Gate, where the character of the river suddenly changed. Rapids capsized the boat and swallowed the rich load of furs.

Fitzpatrick and the other two men spent a few days in the rough water diving for the packs of furs and recovered most of them. They dried them, cached them near Independence Rock, and then started walking for Fort Atkinson, a mere 750 miles away, near modern Omaha. They arrived, nearly starved, in late summer. After regaining his strength, Fitzpatrick headed back for the furs and packed them out—this time by horse.

Devil's Gate was famous among emigrants. The Oregon Trail skirts it a half-mile to the south. Many pulled off to camp here and explore the phenomenon after their evening chores were done.

"We walked down into the passage of the river," wrote J. M. Harrison in 1846. "It looked like we might jump from one wall to the other, it was so narrow at the top."

The tall cliffs overlooking the rushing water lured emigrants to the tops of the bluffs, too. The climb on the south bluffs was easy, but they had trouble getting close enough to the edge to get a glimpse of the drop. Some tried human chains with the last man leaning out over the void and shouting back what he could see.

MARTIN'S COVE

A woeful landmark, Martin's Cove stands on the north side of the Sweetwater River about two miles northwest of Devil's Gate. There, on November 3, 1856, the haggard remnants of Martin's company of Mormon handcart emigrants staggered to the edge of the Sweetwater River. This ill-equipped and starving train of European converts had been caught in a blizzard near Red Buttes while trying to walk to Salt Lake City far too late in the season (see page 31). Many had died by the time a rescue party reached them sixteen miles east of Independence Rock. Many more would die here in the Devil's Gate vicinity and on the way to Salt Lake City despite the food, blankets, and warm clothing brought to them by relief wagons. Their hardships were far from over, and they were about to face another one here.

The rounded granite wall on the north bank of the river offered shelter from the snowstorms and severely cold weather that had afflicted them for more than two weeks. But the river separating them from the cove was choked with ice, and most of them shrank from the prospect of wading. Fortunately, three young men from the relief party were willing to carry most across on their backs.

The emigrants camped in the cove for several days, trying to stay warm in temperatures that dropped to eleven degrees below zero. It was clear that many of them would not make it to Salt Lake unless they could be carried by wagon. Fortunately, wagons were available.

On the snowy trail east of Devil's Gate, the Salt Lake rescue parties saved not only Martin's company but also two Mormon wagon trains loaded with the belongings of 385 emigrants who were only slightly less forlorn than those who had trudged west by handcart. The leaders of the rescue operation decided to empty the

wagons so the weakest of the handcart company could ride. On November 9, they broke camp and headed west. The snow was deep, the cold severe, and they still had 325 miles to go to Salt Lake City. (For more about the travail of the handcart companies, see page 43.)

PACK-SADDLE STEW

When the members of Martin's handcart company trudged off into the wintry landscape of central Wyoming, twenty volunteers from the rescue party agreed to stay behind at Devil's Gate and guard the belongings that had been unloaded from the wagon train. They watched the pitiful column of emigrants leave, then settled in for the winter.

They nearly starved. The men had been left with some crackers and a herd of seventy-five broken-down beef cattle, which they were not supposed to eat if they could help it. Large packs of wolves helped themselves, however, downing twenty-five head in the first week. Because protecting the herd proved futile, the men butchered the rest of the skinny animals and lived well for a while. But even forty to fifty head of cattle disappear quickly when twenty hungry men have nothing to eat but meat. Soon the beef was gone, and the Mormons, who didn't live by the mountain-man motto of "meat's meat," would not consider eating the hundred or so wolf carcasses they had stacked near the cabins. In fact, to remove the temptation, they chopped a hole in the Sweetwater River and dropped the remains through the ice. They tried hunting but had little success.

Instead, they boiled up the hides of the cattle they had butchered. Their first attempt produced a gluey slop none of them could stomach, but they soon hit upon a recipe: Scorch and scrape the hair from the hide. Boil for an hour and pour off the glue. Wash carefully, rinsing with cold water. Boil again until pliable. Let cool. Serve with a pinch of sugar.

This hardy fare kept them going for six weeks, but winter lasts a long time in the Rockies, and they were soon hungry again. Fortunately, they had some windfalls. A hungry Shoshone showed up about the same time that a mail coach got stuck in the snow near the fort. After eating through the mail crew's provisions the men formed a hunting party, and the Shoshone killed them a buffalo. Later, other Indian hunting parties dropped in, and the men were able to barter goods from the emigrant wagons for meat. Some unlucky oxen strayed into camp and were butchered. The men's own hunting improved. But they still went for long stretches without meat. During one lean period they ate every scrap of rawhide in the place, including worn-out moccasins and the buffalo hide they had been using as a doormat. They even dropped a pack saddle in the pot, but before they carved, a group of Mormon mail

carriers arrived at the fort with meat on their mules. After the pack-saddle episode, the quality of the victuals steadily improved until the men were able to return to Salt Lake in early summer.

TOM SUN RANCH

The ranch owned by one of the men implicated in Cattle Kate's lynching, Tom Sun, is now a national historic landmark. Located at the foot of the Devil's Gate overlook, the ranch still includes the original log cabin Sun built when he set up his cattle operation.

JUNCTION WITH 287

Here at the base of Muddy Gap, Highway 287 runs south thirty-three miles to Rawlins through country where the history seems as sparse as the vegetation. By following Highway 287 the other way, travelers continue along the route of the Oregon Trail for roughly fifty miles.

The road parallels the Oregon Trail for about thirty-five miles before slanting up to the Lander area and the Wind River Indian Reservation. Along this stretch of highway, the state's history deals with the continuing saga of the Mormon handcart ordeal, glances at a company of drunk soldiers, and turns up more landmarks along the Oregon Trail.

WHISKEY GAP

In 1862, Ben Holladay bought out the stage line that ran along the Oregon Trail and decided to move operations to the Overland Trail, which stretched across the southern portion of modern Wyoming. Soldiers from the 11th Ohio Volunteer Cavalry were assigned to protect one of the wagon trains freighting the stage line's equipment south. About three miles east of Muddy Gap, the group of soldiers and bullwhackers stopped to camp for the night. But as Maj. O'Farrell moved among his men, he noticed something odd—a telltale lurch in the step of some, a slur in the speech of others. It didn't take a West Point education to see that some of the men were drunk.

O'Farrell ordered a search of the wagons and soon found the culprit—a large barrel of whiskey in a civilian wagon. The officers broke open the barrel, poured the liquor on the ground, and watched it run into a small pool of cold spring water. Instead of enforcing sobriety, the exercise accelerated the process of inebriation. Officers couldn't keep the delighted soldiers and civilians from grabbing the nearest cup, bucket, pot, or ladle and scooping up a ready-made highball of whiskey and water. O'Farrell later wrote about his deep sense of relief that Indians had not attacked that night.

SPLIT ROCK

Another big landmark for emigrants and others traveling through the Sweetwater Valley,

Split Rock was the site of a stage and Pony Express station in the early 1860s. Although there is no trace of the station now, fifty soldiers garrisoned the outpost to protect the road. On a July day in 1862 they counted two hundred passing wagons. If they had been stationed there at the very height of the westward migration, say ten years earlier, they could have counted many more.

SWEETWATER RIVER VALLEY

The Sweetwater Valley was the second major leg of the Oregon Trail as it led through Wyoming. After following the North Platte around its great curve to modern Casper, the emigrants—and before them the mountain men and Indians—looked for the Sweetwater, which led them to South Pass.

The river picked up its name during the fur-trapping era, 1820–40. "The trappers found the water superior for drinking purposes and claimed that it left a pleasant taste in their mouth," wrote the early Wyoming historian C. J. Coutant. "General Ashley consequently named it Sweetwater." Ashley was the man who kicked off the Rocky Mountain fur trade in 1822, when he advertised in a St. Louis newspaper for enterprising young men to trap beaver in the mountains. Some of those who answered the ad would become legends: Jim Bridger, William Sublette, Tom Fitzpatrick, and Jedediah Smith, just to name a few.

Some trappers connected the Sweetwater's name with accidents. "This river owes its name to the accidental drowning in it of a mule loaded with sugar," according to W. A. Ferris. Mountain man A. J. Allen's variation substituted drunk trappers for the drowned mule: "A company were once passing the stream and, during a drunken carousel, emptied into it a large bag of sugar, thereby, as they said, christening it, and

A nineteenth-century party of campers relaxes near Split Rock and the Sweetwater River. *(University of Wyoming American Heritage Center)*

declaring that it should hereafter be called Sweetwater Valley."

Although anyone could see that the river changed tremendously from its mountain headwaters to the plains below, it took years of watching the valley surrounding it to detect other transformations. By 1834, trappers were already noticing the start of one of the most fundamental shifts in the western landscape. William Anderson, a southern lawyer out West for a summer of adventure, heard them talk about it while camped by the Sweetwater.

> The old hunters in the camp conversed about the diminution of the buffalo . . . There is a contrariety of opinion. Some assert that the number is fearfully less. Others merely that they have changed their regions of pasturage. Though I have seen millions and tens of millions at a view, I believe they are fast diminishing. And why should they not? Mr. Fontenelle asserted this evening, to knowing ones, that the American Fur Company, at their posts on the Mississippi and Missouri rivers, traded with the Sioux alone, in one winter, for 50,000 robes. For this trade, it is to be remembered the cows only are killed.

THREE CROSSINGS

East of Jeffrey City, and among the islands of rock north of the road, emigrants on the Oregon Trail splashed through the Sweetwater

The stage station at Three Crossings in 1870. *(University of Wyoming American Heritage Center)*

three times in the space of a couple of miles. Hence the name Three Crossings. The crossings started in a large meadow about four miles east of the present town and led through a deep canyon strewn with the remnants of broken and burned wagons.

"This is a very narrow and rugged pass," wrote the 1849 emigrant J. Goldsborough Bruff, who estimated the perpendicular walls to be four hundred to six hundred feet high. "The rocks here, wherever accessible, are marked all over with inscription, as usual."

During the emigrant years, one of the best road ranches on the trail stood about a mile east of the first crossing. Even the English traveler Sir Richard Burton, who delighted in griping about primitive accommodations along the trail in 1860, heralded the virtues of the station at Three Crossings: "We found the 'miss' a stout, active, middle-aged matron, deserving of all the praises that had so liberally been bestowed upon her," Burton wrote. "Miss Moore's husband, a decent appendage, had transferred his belief from the Church of England to the Church of Utah, and

the good wife, as in duty bound, had followed in his wake."

But when Miss Moore learned that some Mormons took several wives, "then did our stout Englishwoman's power of endurance break down never to rise again. Not an inch would she budge."

Burton praised Moore's food, enjoyed an evening on the veranda as the sun set, and took a swim in the river.

THE MORMON HANDCART ORDEAL CONTINUES

By the time the gaunt survivors of the Martin handcart company of 1856 reached Three Crossings they had been rescued from starvation by a relief party from Salt Lake City, and many were riding in wagons provided for them at Devil's Gate. However, the group remained in desperate straits. Snowstorms, which had halted the company's transcontinental hike at Red Buttes in late October, now slowed their advance even in covered wagons. Cold weather, which had killed fifty-six of them in nine days by the North Platte, continued to take its toll. And food supplies once again sank to dangerous levels because the weather had also mired the next wave of relief wagons sent out from Salt Lake.

Fortunately, a tough Mormon scout named Ephraim Hanks was driving one of those relief wagons. Stalled by deep snow on the far side of South Pass, Hanks grew impatient waiting for the weather to clear. He abandoned his wagon and sought out the group on horseback. Along the way he shot a buffalo cow, butchered it, and packed the meat onto his horses. An hour before sunset, he saw the column of weary Saints trundling along in the distance. He wrote later:

> The sight that met my gaze as I entered the camp can never be erased from my memory. The starved forms and haggard countenances of the poor sufferers, as they moved about slowly, shivering with cold, to prepare their scanty evening meal was enough to touch the stoutest heart. When they saw me coming, they hailed me with joy inexpressible, and when they further beheld the supply of fresh meat I brought into camp, their gratitude knew no bounds.

Within five minutes the hungry camp had stripped his horses of their burden of buffalo meat. Then Hanks got busy with a more gruesome task. The cold weather—subzero on some days—had done its horrid work on poorly protected flesh. Many lost limbs, either whole or in part. Hanks recounted:

> Many such I washed with water and castile soap, until the frozen parts would fall off, after which I would sever the shreds of flesh from the remaining portions of the limbs with my scissors. Some of the emigrants lost toes, others fingers, and again others whole hands and feet.

It was now mid-November and the worst of the ordeal was over for the Martin company. The Saints would find many relief wagons and milder weather on the west side of South Pass, and they would roll into the Salt Lake valley November 30.

JEFFREY CITY

Nearly a ghost town now, Jeffrey City was once a boomtown living off the prosperity of uranium ore processed there by the Western Nuclear Company. Its mill, built in 1957, was the first in Wyoming. It processed more than $30 million worth of ore every year from mines in the Gas Hills Uranium Mining District to the north and in the Crook's Gap fields to the south.

Uranium wasn't the only extraordinary material found in the Jeffrey City area. It was also a rich district for jade. In 1943 Verla Rhoads found a chunk weighing 3,366 pounds. Two years later Rhoads gathered forty-two pieces weighing a total of seven thousand pounds. During the same period a Lander grocer found a hunk weighing 2,410 pounds. During the summer today, rockhounds still comb the hills looking for the stones.

ICE SLOUGH

About nine miles west of Jeffrey City, U.S. 287 passes a highway sign marking the approximate site of Ice Slough, a refreshing stop for emigrants on the Oregon Trail.

After plodding through the summer heat for hundreds of miles, emigrants were delighted to come across this deposit of crystal-clear ice in the middle of what they considered a desert. Here the valley sags a bit in a marshy area where water collected during the summer under a layer of turf. In the winter, of course, it froze solid. The layer of turf acted as insulation during the warm months and kept the ice from completely melting.

"The ice is found about 8 to 10 inches beneath the surface," wrote James A. Pritchard in his 1849 diary. "There is from four to six inches of water above the ice, and of turf or sod of grass apparently floating on the water . . . To get to the ice you take a spade or ax and cut away the sod and there strike down and cut it out in square blocks. The ice is clear and pure, entirely free from any alkali and other unpleasant taste. It is from 4 to 10 inches thick, and as good as any I ever cut from the streams in Kentucky."

Many stopped to refresh themselves with iced drinks. Some even made ice cream.

Today very little ice forms in the slough because most of the water has been drawn off for irrigation.

JUNCTION WITH STATE 135

From here, U.S. 287 slants northwest and pulls away from the route of the Oregon Trail, which begins its long southwestern slant over South Pass toward Fort Bridger.

JUNCTION WITH STATE 28

To continue following the Oregon Trail route, follow State 28 southwest to the Green River.

Just to the east of this junction, Wyoming's first oil well was drilled in 1884. Long before that particular steel bit whirled into the ground, mountain men knew there was oil in the area. In the early 1830s, the trapper Osborne Russell and his chums entertained themselves at a well-known oil spring in the area.

This spring produces about one gallon per hour of pure oil of coal, or rather coal tar, the scent of which is often carried on the wind five or six miles. The oil issues from the ground within 30 feet of the stream and runs off slowly into the water . . . We set fire to the spring when there was two or three barrels of oil on the ground about it. It burned very quick and clear, but produced a dense column of thick black smoke. The oil above ground being consumed, the fire soon went out.

Trappers held in high regard the medicinal qualities of the oily substance oozing from the ground. They used the stuff to salve their horses' saddle sores and to alleviate the rheumatism endemic to a trade that required men to spend much of their time wading ice-cold mountain streams.

Here State Route 28 follows the Oregon Trail over its most important landmark—South Pass. While heavily weighted toward the emigrant era, history along State 28 also deals with boom-towns and disappointing mining claims, women's rights and relations between whites and Indians.

ATLANTIC CITY

After the road climbs to the edge of spectacular Red Canyon, State 28 drops over into the South Pass area. Prospectors overran the place in 1867 when a deceptively rich-looking deposit of gold ore was discovered near South Pass City. A few miles north of that town miners uncovered another lode in 1868, and Atlantic City was born.

Upwards of two thousand people lived in the South Pass area during the height of the rush, but neither the lode near Atlantic City nor the Carissa lode near South Pass City nor any of a handful of lesser claims proved to be worth all the excitement. Most of the miners soon moved on. However, activity did continue at Atlantic City longer than at the other town. Five years after the streets of South Pass City had become deserted, stamp mills in Atlantic City continued to process ore. Renewed excitement swept the area in the 1890s and again in the 1930s, when hopes soared over the promise (ultimately broken) of more efficient mining techniques to revive the industry.

Memorabilia from the gold-rush days are on display in saloons, restaurants, and inns that still operate in the town.

SOUTH PASS CITY

Although prospectors scratching the dirt near South Pass found gold as early as 1842, no one uncovered enough of the stuff to kick off a

South Pass City as it appeared in the 1860s. (It doesn't look much different today.) Gold strikes near South Pass City and neighboring Atlantic City in the late 1860s fueled short-lived booms in both towns. *(University of Wyoming American Heritage Center)*

boom until June 1867. That's when a group of Mormon miners struck the Carissa lode, a rich hard-rock deposit. Exaggerated accounts of their discovery made the rounds in Salt Lake City, and soon Mormon and Gentile miners alike had flocked to the area. By winter, the town's population had swelled to seven hundred, and by the following summer it could brag two thousand residents. Every day, two stage lines ferried people and goods between South Pass City and Point of Rocks on the Union Pacific rail line. In South Pass City there were five hotels, thirteen saloons, three butcher shops, a couple of bakeries, four law firms, a newspaper, bowling alley, and beer garden.

Other gold strikes in the surrounding hills fanned the flames and led to the founding of Atlantic City and Hamilton City. At the height of the boom, twelve stamping mills operated in the South Pass vicinity. But the returns were limited, and every winter the population plummeted. In the autumn of 1868, for example, a *Chicago Tribune* reporter found scores of deserted cabins and only fifty to sixty people in each of the three towns. Interest remained high during the summers of 1868 and 1869, but by the early 1870s it was clear that the gold had all but played out. Many of the miners packed it in and moved south to find a more dependable source of income in the coal mines owned by the Union Pacific railroad. By 1873, South Pass City was nearly deserted.

Before it died, though, the town made history. In 1869, one of its residents, William H. Bright, introduced a woman suffrage bill that passed the territorial legislature, making Wyoming women the first in the world to receive the right to vote. A year later, another South Pass City resident, Esther Hobart Morris, became the first woman justice of the peace and served for a little over eight months. Sadly, she suffered under the cruel hand of her husband, a saloon-keeper who beat her regularly. She eventually divorced him and, lacking a means of support, she moved to Cheyenne and lived with a son.

In recent years, large-scale mining resumed in the South Pass area, but not for gold. The U.S. Steel corporation strip-mined for taconite, a low-grade iron ore that the company crushed, formed into pellets, and shipped to Provo, Utah, for further processing. The closing of this operation in 1983 hurt the economy of the area, especially in the town of Lander.

THE MORMON HANDCART ORDEAL CONTINUES

In October 1856, an early winter storm blasted through the Wyoming mountains and came close to annihilating two large groups of ill-equipped and starving Mormon emigrants. One of the groups, led by James Willie, reached the climax of its agony while camped about twenty miles east of what would become South Pass City.

Organized into companies of roughly five hundred people, these groups of European converts had set off on foot from eastern Iowa in August, pulling their belongings behind them on handcarts. They made good progress across Iowa and Nebraska but ran low on food in Wyo-

ming just as the trail got tougher and the nights colder. In Willie's company, about one hundred miles ahead of Martin's group, the strain began taking its toll along the Sweetwater River. Crude burials of one or more people became part of the grim morning routine.

"We travelled on in misery and sorrow day after day," wrote John Chislett. "Finally we were overtaken by a snowstorm which the shrill wind blew furiously about us. The snow fell several inches deep as we travelled along."

The snow kept falling and the ragged line of Saints kept pushing forward until it finally reached a good camp that became known as St. Mary's Station. Thickets of willows offered shelter from the howling winds, and there was plenty of firewood and water. But the food had almost run out. When the travelers turned in for the night, they knew they had eaten the last of the flour. All they had left for nearly five hundred hungry people were a couple of barrels of hardtack, some sugar, dried fruit, and a few scrawny beef cattle.

In the morning, five more people died. But by then the survivors knew help was on the way. A light wagon had pulled through the day before, driven by two Salt Lake City men who told the group that wagons full of food and warm clothing were close behind.

"Being surrounded by snow a foot deep, out of provisions, many of our people sick, and our cattle dying, it was decided that we should remain in our present camp until the supply train reached us," Chislett wrote. "The scanty allowance of hard bread and poor beef . . . was mostly eaten the first day by the hungry, ravenous, famished souls. We killed more cattle and issued the meat. But eating it without bread did not satisfy hunger, and to those who were suffering from dysentery it did more harm than good. This terrible disease increased rapidly . . . and several died."

Mormon settlers pose for a group shot at South Pass in 1866. From here it was downhill pretty much all the way to Salt Lake. *(University of Wyoming American Heritage Center)*

They waited for three days before the wagons finally reached them with flour, potatoes, onions, buffalo robes, and wool socks.

"The change seemed almost miraculous, so sudden was it from grave to gay, from sorrow to gladness, from mourning to rejoicing," Chislett wrote. "With the cravings of hunger satisfied, and with hearts filled with gratitude to God and our good brethren, we all united in prayer and then retired to rest."

And to die. Nine more were buried the next morning. Help had come too late for them, and for others. Several died each day as Willie's company, aided by half the rescue party, struggled on toward South Pass. They buried thirteen before breaking camp at Willow Creek, then interred two more that evening. Men who dug graves for their family and friends in the morning sometimes died themselves before night. In all, somewhere between sixty-two and sixty-

seven people would die before reaching Salt Lake.

Conditions improved at South Pass. The weather moderated and more wagons from Salt Lake met the company.

"We found more brethren from the valley, with several quarters of good fat beef hanging frozen on the limbs of the trees where they were encamped," Chislett wrote. "These quarters of beef were to us the handsomest pictures we ever saw. The statues of Michelangelo or the paintings of the ancient masters would have been to us nothing in comparison to these life-giving pictures."

Willie's company arrived in Salt Lake on November 9. It would take another three weeks to bring in the remnants of Martin's company, which would lose between 135 and 150 people.

For more about the experiences of the Willie and Martin handcart companies, see page 32.

South Pass Station, also known as Burnt Ranch, as W. H. Jackson imagined it appeared at the height of westward migration along the Oregon Trail. *(University of Wyoming American Heritage Center)*

LANDER ROAD EXHIBIT

A few miles southwest of South Pass City hangs a sign describing the Lander Road, which skirted the foothills of the Wind River Mountains and crossed the Green River valley far to the north of the Oregon Trail's main branch. Built in 1857–58, the road offered emigrants a more dependable source of wood, water, and forage for their animals. It also avoided Mormon country, an important consideration at the time because of grave tensions between Mormons and Gentiles. In 1857, the U.S. government had narrowly averted a war with the Mormons, and in the same year a wagon train of 120 emigrants was massacred by Mormon zealots and Indians at Mountain Meadows, Utah.

The road began roughly nine miles east of the exhibit at a place called Burnt Ranch. Not visible from the road, Burnt Ranch was originally a stage station built in 1859 by the Russell, Majors & Waddell line. The site went by various names, including Gilbert's Station, Upper Sweetwater Station, and South Pass Station. When Mark Twain passed through in a stagecoach in 1861, he called it South Pass City:

> As we sat with raised curtains enjoying our early-morning smoke and contemplating the first splendor of the rising sun . . . we hove in sight of South Pass City. The hotel keeper, the postmaster, the locksmith, the mayor, the constable, the city marshal and the principal citizen and property holder, all came out and greeted us cheerily, and we gave him good day . . . Bemis said he was a perfect Allen's revolver of dignities. And he said that if he were to die as postmaster, or as blacksmith, or as postmaster and blacksmith both, the people might stand it. But if he were to die all over, it would be a frightful loss to the community.

The heavy emigrant traffic made Burnt Ranch a natural target for Indians who were trying to prevent whites from settling the West and disrupting their way of life. They burned the station to the ground twice, thus the name.

Troops of the 11th Ohio Volunteer Cavalry were garrisoned here in 1862 to protect the road, but they weren't able to keep a lid on hostilities. In August of that year, emigrant Henry Herr noted that even with one hundred soldiers camped in the area, "50 head of mules were stolen and several men shot dead by Indians."

The graves of at least eight people can be found near the station, including that of Charles Miller, Lander's meteorologist, who was killed in 1858 by a Mormon.

SOUTH PASS EXHIBIT

A roadside exhibit about four miles down the road from the Continental Divide commemorates the importance of South Pass on the Oregon Trail. The exhibit faces the pass — a long gradual ramp of sagebrush and prairie grass across the valley. Reaching an elevation of roughly seventy-five hundred feet, South Pass still bears the double-track marks left by the wheels of emigrant wagons. The trail came down the slope to the foot of Pacific Butte, to the right, and passed within a mile of the exhibit.

From the early 1840s to the late 1860s hundreds of thousands of people rolled their wagons over this gentle sag in the spine of the Rocky Mountains. It marked the halfway point for those heading to Oregon or California and served as the principal gate to the Far West in much the same way that the Cumberland Gap opened up Kentucky and the first western frontier in the late eighteenth century. Twenty miles wide, the plain of South Pass inclines at such a slight angle that many emigrants did not know they had cleared the summit until they came across a stream flowing west.

"A pass it is not," wrote the English traveler Sir Richard Burton after creaking over South Pass in a stagecoach during the summer of 1860. "This majestic level-topped bluff, the highest steppe of the continent, upon whose iron surface there is space enough for the armies of the globe to march over, is the grandest and the most appropriate of avenues."

It was an avenue for travelers long before the first whites saw it. To the Indians, like the emigrants who followed, it was the principal pass on the east-west route through present Wyoming. Whites learned about it in 1812 when a Shoshone Indian pointed it out as a favor to a rundown band of traders he had found starving in the Green River valley. He also told the whites, the returning Astorians (see page 000), how to follow the Sweetwater River from the east side of the pass to the North Platte River and hence to the Missouri and civilization. This route, which would become the Oregon Trail, was then forgotten by whites until 1824, when it was rediscovered by a party of mountain men.

The missionary Samuel Parker, who rode over South Pass in 1835 with a caravan of mountain men, may have been the first to note that the pass would make a good route for a railroad. "There would be no difficulty in the way of constructing a railway from the Atlantic to the Pacific Ocean," he wrote. "Probably the time may not be very far distant when trips may be made across the continent as they have been made to Niagara Falls to see nature's wonders."

It would take more than thirty years before the first transcontinental railroad was built, and it would not run over South Pass. Instead, it was built across southern Wyoming, largely because of the rich coal deposits there that the Union Pacific would pick up through its land grant from the government.

In the early years, before western railway

travel, most of the wagon trains aimed southwest from the pass to Fort Bridger. From there, those bound for the West Coast steered northwest to modern Sage and up the Bear River valley into Idaho. The Mormons, who began their migration to Salt Lake in 1847, continued heading southwest from Fort Bridger to Utah.

In later years, several major shortcuts, or "cutoffs," emerged along the main trail. The Sublette or Greenwood Cutoff ran almost due west from the pass, crossing roughly forty-five miles of waterless terrain from the Big Sandy River to the Green. From the Green, it led over the mountains into the Bear River valley, where it picked up the old trail. The Sublette Cutoff was popular among those who charged west in 1849 to get a piece of the action in the California goldfields, but the route bypassed Fort Bridger. This development so alarmed mountain man Jim Bridger and his partner Louis Vasquez that Vasquez rode up to South Pass and spent the better part of June 1849 badmouthing the shortcut. He talked many into continuing on the old trail to Fort Bridger that year, but the cutoff proved too popular, and soon most of the West Coast traffic bypassed Fort Bridger to the north.

Another alternate to the old Oregon Trail, the Lander Road, broke away from the main branch on the other side of the pass (see page 49).

Although South Pass offered wagon and stagecoach travelers one of the mildest routes possible through the Rockies, it did climb high enough to make them feel as if they had reached the top of the world. Some dropped their jaws in wonder and scribbled down their thoughts. Near the summit, Mark Twain gazed across the land to the east and in his mind traced the watershed from a small stream he could see to the Mississippi River, which he had learned intimately as a riverboat pilot.

We knew that long after we should have forgotten the simple rivulet it would still be plodding its patient way down the mountain sides . . . and by and by would join the broad Missouri . . . and enter the Mississippi, touch the wharves of St. Louis and still drift on, traversing shoals and rocky channels, then endless chains of bottomless and ample bends, walled with unbroken forests, then mysterious byways and secret passages among woody islands . . . then by New Orleans and still other chains of bends—and finally, after two long months of daily and nightly harassment, excitement, enjoyment, adventure, and awful peril of parched throats, pumps and evaporation, pass the Gulf and enter into its rest upon the bosom of the tropic sea, never to look upon its snow-peaks again or regret them. I freighted a leaf with a mental message for the friends at home, and dropped it in the stream. But I put no stamp on it and it was held for postage somewhere.

PACIFIC SPRINGS

These springs, at the foot of Pacific Butte across the valley from the South Pass exhibit, were the first waters encountered by travelers on the Pacific side of the Continental Divide.

Sir Richard Burton, who paused here in 1860, seemed to regard it as a pleasant-enough spot. "The springs are a pond of pure, hard, and very cold water surrounded by a strip of shaking bog, which must be boarded over before it will bear a man," he wrote.

FALSE PARTING OF THE WAYS

About twenty-four miles northeast of Farson, a monument beside the road purports to mark the spot where the Sublette Cutoff veered west from the main branch of the Oregon Trail. Instead, it marks the spot where the trail crossed a wagon route that ran between the South Pass

City goldfields and the Union Pacific tracks at Green River. Even so, this is a fine spot to see the wagon ruts left 150 years ago by emigrants on the Oregon Trail, which skirt the fence line here.

The true Parting of the Ways lies several miles off the highway, roughly fifteen miles northeast of Farson. It saved emigrants about forty-five miles, but the gain came at the risk of their livestock because they had to cross the Little Colorado Desert before reaching Green River. That meant nearly fifty miles without water. The cutoff picked up mountain man William Sublette's name due to an error in a guidebook many of the emigrants carried with them. Former mountain man Caleb Greenwood, at the startling age of eighty-one, actually pioneered the route in 1844 while guiding an emigrant train to Oregon.

The main branch of the Oregon Trail continued southwest at the Parting of the Ways, following Sandy Creek to the Green River.

LITTLE SANDY CROSSING

The remains of a stagecoach station still stand where emigrants on the main branch of the Oregon Trail crossed Little Sandy Creek. They crossed about seven miles northeast of Farson and about three miles north of State 28. The stage station, with thirteen graves nearby, is less than a quarter-mile from the crossing, on the west bank of the stream.

FARSON

In the summer of 1847, mountain man Jim Bridger spent an evening camped near here with the Mormon leader Brigham Young, who was leading the first large wagon train of Mormon emigrants to the Salt Lake valley. They passed a long, chatty evening together, and Bridger did

most of the talking while three of Young's assistants wrote down everything he said. The Mormons could not have found a mind better suited than Bridger's to fill them in on the land they intended to settle. After twenty-five years of trapping, fighting, and exploring throughout the country between the Rockies and the West Coast, Bridger had an encyclopedic knowledge of the land. During the course of the evening he told them he thought the Salt Lake valley would make a good place for a settlement, although the nights might get a little too cold for corn. He described the Bear River valley and the eastern rim of the Great Basin and then launched out on a lengthy, though disjointed, report about the country all the way to Oregon.

This amiable encounter stands in glaring contrast to the bitterness and violence that colored relations between the Mormons and the mountain men several years later, when Brigham Young sought control of Fort Bridger and the lucrative ferry crossings of the Green River. In 1853, large groups of armed Mormons attacked the fort and the crossings. They killed two men and stole much property, but failed to take the fort (see page 54).

At Farson, the main branch of the Oregon Trail crossed the Big Sandy River. State 28 roughly parallels the route to the Green River. Watch for concrete posts that mark the trail out on the flat sagebrush plain.

JUNCTION WITH 191

Highway 191 stretches north to Yellowstone National Park and south to the Utah border. See page 192.

UTAH WAR

In October 1857, a Mormon force under Lot

Smith intercepted and destroyed twenty-three wagons carrying supplies through Simpson's Hollow, about nine and a half miles southwest of Farson. A stone marker indicates the site.

The supplies had been intended for a column of twenty-five hundred U.S. Army troops poised to invade Utah. Federal appointees in the territory, angered by Brigham Young's reluctance to cooperate with them, had persuaded President James Buchanan that the Mormons were guilty of lawlessness and rebellion and that troops were needed to enforce the federal will. Some observers say talk of secession among southern states at the time may have prompted Buchanan to seize the opportunity to suppress secession in the West. In addition to ordering out troops, Buchanan fired Brigham Young as territorial governor and appointed in his place the former mayor of Augusta, Georgia.

The Mormons—who had been hounded, murdered, and driven from two states by Gentiles already—assumed the army had been sent to annihilate them. Rather than confront the troops, Young decided to avoid direct conflict. He ordered the Mormons to burn or abandon the supply outposts they had built along the Oregon Trail, and he made plans to evacuate Salt Lake City and burn it down. In the meantime, Mormon forces tried to stall the army's march. The strategy of interrupting the army's supply lines worked quite well. Without killing anyone, the Mormons attacked three major supply trains in southwestern Wyoming during the autumn of 1857. These attacks denied the army 368,000 pounds of rations and forced it to halt for the winter at Fort Bridger.

By spring, negotiations brought the affair to a peaceful conclusion.

GREEN RIVER: EMIGRANT CROSSINGS

Emigrants heading west on the Oregon Trail crossed Green River at many points. The Lander Road crossed it near Big Piney. The Sublette Cut-off crossed it near Names Hill, about ten miles south of LaBarge. Those who kept to the main branch of the Oregon Trail crossed it at several points in the vicinity of State Route 28, but probably the most important was the Lombard Ferry, located roughly five miles downstream of the present highway bridge.

During the years of heaviest emigration, the men who ferried wagons across the Green could make a tremendous amount of money during a short season of work. Thousands of wagons crossed the Green every summer during the late 1840s and early 1850s, each paying somewhere between three and fifteen dollars a wagon. The fee depended on weight, on whether the river was too deep to ford, and on whether the ferryman had any nearby competition.

Mormons running a ferry on Green River exacted tolls as high as sixteen dollars a wagon during the California gold rush summer of 1849, even though their charter from the Utah legislature limited them to charges of three to six dollars. John Riker, a forty-niner, wrote that the Mormon ferrymen refused to carry his party across for less than eleven dollars a wagon, or eighty-eight dollars for the train:

This our captain refused to pay, offering them $50, which we all considered a sufficient compensation. After a little delay, the teams were all crossed but one, which they refused to bring over until the full amount of ferriage was paid. At this the captain became angry, and immediately the company were ordered a short distance to camp, when nine of the men, well armed, returned to the ferry, determined to bring over the remaining team at all hazards. The captain then demanded their charter, which was reluctantly produced and, upon examination, it was found that they were allowed to charge but $3 a team. Then the captain drew

The Green River in southwestern Wyoming. This area is called the "Pallisades." *(University of Wyoming American Heritage Center)*

his revolver, and threatened them with instant death if the team was not immediately carried over. They seemed to think the latter preferable.

Of course, it wasn't just Mormon ferrymen who charged exorbitant rates. Several ferries operated on a thirty-mile stretch of the Green, and the former mountain men who ran other ferry outfits also charged as much as the traffic would bear. During the summer of 1852, two of these mountaineer ferrymen are said to have earned $65,000, which they promptly lost to gamblers. With that kind of money floating around the ferry landings, no wonder the mountain men and the Mormons clashed over who would control the trade.

In the early 1850s, the Mormons tried to monopolize it through legislative action. But the mountaineers drove off groups of Mormon ferrymen who arrived at their landings with charters from the Utah legislature. They also turned away a group of Mormon bridge-builders. In 1853, a posse of some 150 Mormons attacked the mountaineers at their ferries, killing two and riding off with the property of many others. But mountain men were tough to kill and even harder to dislodge. The Mormons did not gain control of the crossing trade until 1855, when a church representative bought out the interests of the mountaineer ferrymen as well as Fort Bridger.

Booking passage across the river wasn't the only sort of commerce to take place on the Green during the 1850s. Horace Greeley, publisher of the *New York Tribune,* rode across the West by stagecoach in 1859 and reported that Green River valley was the site of a lively trade in Indian women.

> White men with two or three squaws each are quite common throughout this region, and young and relatively comely Indian girls are bought from their fathers by white men as regularly and openly as Circassians at Constantinople . . . The usual range of prices is from $40 to $80—about that of Indian horses. I hear it stated that though all other trade may be dull, that in young squaws is always brisk on Green River.

Indians of the Green River valley, mostly Shoshone, gained a reputation for being quite helpful to emigrants. In 1859, Frederick Lander, who pioneered a branch of the Oregon Trail through southwestern Wyoming, reported that the life of an emigrant had been saved by an Indian at Green River Crossing and that great assistance had been rendered at the same dangerous ford for passing trains by other members of the Shoshone tribe.

During the heavy years of emigration, Indians of many tribes helped the pioneers roll across the trails to the West. Elsewhere in Wyoming, for instance, the Lakota (often called Sioux) helped emigrants swim their cattle across the Platte and Laramie rivers. They acted as guides. They trotted letters back to trading posts.

They hired out to cut and carry grass for emigrant cattle crossing arid stretches of the trail. They guarded cattle, gathered wood, acted as translators, and shared their knowledge of edible plants.

All was not sweetness and light, of course. Indians did attack wagon trains without reason that was apparent to the whites. But emigrants did the same thing, sometimes traveling under the policy of shooting every Indian they came across—regardless of whether the Indian was friendly or not or of how such a policy might affect subsequent emigrant trains.

Among the hundreds of thousands of people who crossed Green River before it was obliterated as an obstacle by the Union Pacific Railroad in 1868 was Sir Richard Burton, an English adventurer. Burton didn't think much of the landscaping around the stage station in 1860.

> A few trees, chiefly quaking asp, lingered near the station, but dead stumps were far more numerous than live trunks. In any other country their rare and precious shade would have endeared them to the whole settlement. Here they were never safe when a log was wanted. The Western man is bred and perhaps born . . . with an instinctive dislike to timber in general. He fells a tree naturally as a bull terrier worries a cat, and the admirable woodsman's axe which he has invented only serves to whet his desire to try conclusions with every more venerable patriarch of the forest.

JUNCTION WITH 372

State Route 372 connects I-80 on the south with Highway 189 on the north. The forty-nine-mile stretch of road runs across a high plains landscape rich in antelope.

From Casper, U.S. 26 passes over the North Platte along the same stretch of river crossed by hundreds of thousands of emigrants during the years 1841–68. It runs close to where two log toll bridges were built in the 1850s and cuts across the river near the site of a lucrative ferry established by Mormons in 1847. It also leads past reconstructed Fort Casper, site of an important battle between the army and the Indians (see page 63).

The road diverges from the Oregon Trail just west of Casper and stretches northwest across a classic high plains landscape that grows thick in early summer with antelope. It skirts the southern slopes of the Big Horn Mountains to the Wind River Indian Reservation.

WALTMAN: THE BRIDGER TRAIL

After gold was discovered in Montana in the early 1860s, the Oregon Trail was the safest route across Wyoming to the boomtowns, but it was also the longest. Prospectors followed it all the way through Wyoming, then headed north through Idaho. For years it remained the safest route, even though two attempts were made to find a shortcut. The first was blazed by John Bozeman in the early 1860s, but it ran north from modern Douglas through the sensitive Powder River country. The Lakota, Arapaho, and Cheyenne shut down the Bloody Bozeman in 1864 to protect what they regarded as their last good hunting ground.

The same year, former mountain man Jim Bridger traced an alternate route to Montana that ran fairly close to this stretch of highway. Bridger's route avoided the Powder River country by rounding the southern bend of the Big Horn mountains before breaking north through the Big Horn basin. U.S. 26 crosses the trail at Waltman. Bridger's route was shorter than Bozeman's and it avoided hostile Indians, but it never

caught on. It was a very difficult road for wagons and there was not enough water or forage for draft animals.

Although emigrants avoided the trail, trappers had followed the general route for many years. One mountain man who became more familiar with the terrain than he would have liked was Osborne Russell.

In the early winter of 1837, Russell and a few others stumbled down the south slopes of the Big Horn Mountains and out across the plains near the present highway. They had been trapping along the Big Horn River when a band of Crow Indians stole their horses and some of their gear. It was early November: cold, windy, and the first wet snows of the winter had begun to fall. Without horses they foresaw a difficult time surviving the season. So they burned their saddles and started walking for Fort Laramie, a distance of roughly 250 miles. Their trek offers a classic example of what mountain men down on their luck did.

Russell, writing about it later, took things philosophically: "Experience is the best teacher, hunger good sauce and I really think to be acquainted with misery contributes to the enjoyment of happiness."

If that's true, the trip must have cheered him up considerably. He wrote:

> Myself and Allen had one blanket between us. The others had a blanket each. The wind blew cold and the snow drifted along the brow of the mountain around us. When we arose in the morning our fire had gone out. The snow was three inches deep on our covering and it still kept snowing.

Every day they got up and trudged a bit farther through the blowing snow, sometimes losing their way. After they had walked out of the mountains and down to the plains, the snow turned from sleet to heavy rain. Drenched, they managed to build a small fire and pass the most uncomfortable night of the trip:

> We had plenty of water under, over and all around us, but could not find a stick for fuel bigger than a man's thumb. We sat down round the fire with each holding a piece of beef [the trappers sometimes called buffalo "prairie beef"] over it on a stick with one hand while the other was employed in keeping up the blaze by feeding it with wet sage and weeds until the meat was warmed through . . . After supper (if I may be allowed to disgrace the term by applying it to such a Wolfish feast) we spread the Bull skin down in the mud in the dryest place we could find and laid down upon it.

The rain immediately doused their fire.

> We lay tolerably comfortable whilst the skin retained its animal warmth and remained above the surface. But the mud being soft the weight of our bodies sunk it by degrees below the water level which ran under us on the skin. But we concluded it was best to lie still and keep the water warm that was about us for if we stirred we let in the cold water and if we removed our bed

we were more likely to find a worse instead of a better place as it rained very hard all night.

And so it went for a couple of weeks until they hobbled into Fort Laramie, where they were treated with contempt by the man in charge but given a few ratty blankets and a warm place to sleep.

LOST CABIN

Here, at the turn of the century, a Wyoming millionaire who had worked his way up from penniless cowboy to real estate tycoon built a huge mansion and a village to go with it. His name was John Broderick Okie and he named the village Lost Cabin. The first floor of the mansion was built with native stone, the second with lumber hauled to the site. Okie threw big parties, hired gardeners to tend his extensive lawns, stocked the grounds with peacocks, and lit the town with carbide lamps. He died shooting ducks in a nearby reservoir. The town, abandoned and decaying, now stands on a private ranch.

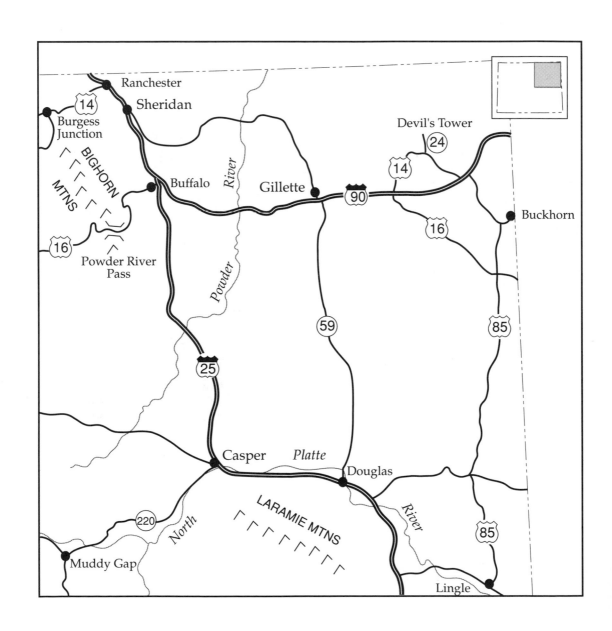

POWDER RIVER COUNTRY

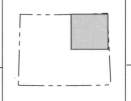
On an autumn day in 1823, Jedediah Smith was leading a group of trappers through the scrubby badlands of the Powder River country. Suddenly a grizzly bear charged down out of the hills, swatted him to the ground, and wrapped its jaws around his head. Smith's companions drove it away, but not before it nearly ripped his scalp clean from his skull. A little frontier surgery and a ten-day rest put Smith pretty well to rights, and soon the trappers went on their way.

It is a small item of brutality, but telling nonetheless, because blood laces the history of Powder River country. In fact, most of the notable violence in Wyoming history broke out in this part of the state.

Here, during the 1860s, war smoldered and flared between whites traveling north to the Montana goldfields and Plains Indian tribes defending their last great hunting ground—the Powder River country. Emigrant wagon trains were attacked along the Bozeman Trail that ran through the region, but army troopers and members of the Lakota, Cheyenne, and Arapaho tribes did most of the dying in fights near army forts and Indian villages. The sites dot Powder River country. Near Ranchester in 1865, an army column attacked an Arapaho village of fifteen hundred that had not been hostile until then. The next year, at Fort Phil Kearny near modern Story, eighty-one soldiers were killed during one of the most successful Lakota ambushes in history. Several months later, troops at Phil Kearny managed to beat back a strong Indian attack in what

POWDER RIVER COUNTRY

A portrait, painted around 1830, of the mountain man Jedediah Smith. Not a bad crop of hair for a man who had his scalp torn off by a grizzly bear. *(University of Wyoming American Heritage Center)*

would be called the Wagon Box Fight. The sites of other clashes turn up near Casper, Kaycee, and along Crazy Woman Creek. The war ended in 1868 with a treaty that ceded to the Lakota, or Sioux, tribe the entire Powder River country—all of the land east of the Big Horns and north of the North Platte River.

The peace lasted eight years, time enough for prospectors to discover gold in the Black Hills (also Indian land) and for the U.S. government to break the 1868 treaty. This second war ended after just a year, and most of the pivotal battles were fought outside Wyoming, including Custer's Last Stand in Montana. However, an army campaign fizzled miserably in Powder River country during the winter of 1876, and the last battle of the war was fought west of Kaycee. Information about events leading up to both wars can be found on pages 79–83.

With the opening of the Black Hills to prospectors, a new chapter began in the history of Powder River country—that of the Cheyenne and Black Hills stage line, which skirted the eastern boundary of the state from Fort Laramie on the North Platte to present Buckhorn in Crook County.

John Bozeman, who blazed a trail from the North Platte in Wyoming to the goldfields of central Montana in the early 1860s. This road, which became known as the "Bloody Bozeman," crossed the Powder River country, which the Lakota regarded as their last great hunting ground. The road, the whites traveling it, and the forts built to protect it kicked off a major war with the Plains Indian tribes in the middle 1860s. The Indians, under the Lakota chief Red Cloud, won the war, and the United States government signed a treaty forbidding whites from crossing into northeastern Wyoming and the Black Hills. The treaty kept the peace until whites discovered gold in the Black Hills in the 1870s. *(University of Wyoming American Heritage Center)*

Prospectors, land speculators, gamblers, bank presidents, and prostitutes could step off a Union Pacific train in Cheyenne and make the Hills two days later by stagecoach. Along the way, they could knock back drinks with such colorful characters as Mother Feather Legs and Dangerous Dick, or get held up at gunpoint by outlaws on horseback. Most of this stage-coach history can be found along U.S. 85.

War in Powder River country did not stop after the tribes were forced onto reservations. With the Indians gone, the whites fought among themselves for control of the land. These range wars divided into two types: big cattle ranchers against small cattle ranchers, and cattle ranchers in general against those who wanted to raise sheep. Both conflicts got plenty of people killed around the turn of the century, but it was the range war between cattle interests that came to a head in Powder River country. Called the Johnson County War, it was the most dramatic confrontation between the two factions. It involved a private army operating outside the law on behalf of the big cattle interests, and it was played out between Kaycee and Buffalo, in territory now traversed by I-25 (see page 65). The sheep vs. cattle conflict came to its grisly climax in the Big Horn Basin.

Not all of the history in Powder River country revolves around violence. Here, on land where Indians hunted among the vast herds of buffalo, cowboys rode among immense herds of cattle, helping to establish one of Wyoming's most enduring industries and one of Hollywood's most enduring romantic legends. Busy little towns blossomed near coal mines at the turn of the century, and today colossal deposits of clean-burning low-sulphur coal near Gillette fuel an economic boom.

This is a beautiful region of the state, where the red stone and pine forests of the Big Horn Mountains rival the appeal of the more famous Tetons to the northwest. Much of the land is lonely, broken, and severe, but only those with a narrow view of beauty can fail to appreciate its allure.

As it makes its way from Casper to the eastern slopes of the Big Horn Mountains, I-25 passes through land where many of the pivotal events in Wyoming history took place. The oil fields north of Casper have fueled that city's boom-and-bust economy since the turn of the century, and they even played a part in a national political and financial scandal, Teapot Dome. Farther north, the road strikes into territory where violent competition between big-time ranchers and newcomers boiled over in the Johnson County War of 1892. It runs past Hole-in-the-Wall, perhaps the most storied hideout for outlaws in the American West. The road also runs through country where Indians ambushed wagons bound for the goldfields of Montana during the 1860s, and passes within several miles of the site where they fought the last battle of the war for the Black Hills during the 1870s.

CASPER: NAMESAKE

Poor Caspar Collins. Not only did the Indians make a pincushion of the young cavalry officer in 1865, but those who sought to enshrine him geographically misspelled his first name.

The battle that made him famous started July 26, 1865 on the plains a few miles northwest of the present city. A military supply train had been traveling toward the fort at Platte Bridge Station, located on the north bank of the river. Soldiers at the fort knew that a large force of Lakota and Cheyenne (some estimate about three thousand) had gathered in the area. Collins, who had arrived at the fort only the night before, rode out with twenty-five men to warn and protect the approaching wagons. Soon they were ambushed by an overwhelming number of Indians. Fighting hand-to-hand, the troopers began making their way back to the fort. Five, including Collins, were killed. All the survivors were wounded.

Meanwhile, another portion of the Indian

W. H. Jackson's drawing of the July 1865 battle at Platte River Bridge, in which young Caspar Collins lost his life. *(University of Wyoming American Heritage Center)*

force attacked the supply train. Three of five scouts made it to the fort. The other two, as well as all the men who fought by the wagons, were killed. When the fighting at both sites ended, a total of twenty-six soldiers and an estimated sixty Indians had been killed. (For details about the background of the 1860s and 1870s wars between whites and Indians, see pages 79–83.)

Three months after the battle, the army managed to get Lt. Collins's first name spelled right when it changed the name of the outpost from Platte River Station to Fort Caspar. The misspelling occurred about twenty years later, when the railroad laid track through the valley and platted the town of Casper on the south bank of the river. The military abandoned the post in 1867 and the Indians immediately burned it. In 1938 the old fort was reconstructed at its original location and now serves as a historic site and excellent pioneer museum.

The museum not only commemorates the 1865 battle nearby but also celebrates the vast migration west of the hundreds of thousands of emigrants who passed this way between 1840 and 1868. To get to the museum, take the State 220 exit and follow the signs. (For more about the emigrant traffic itself, see page 31.)

Fort Caspar, in which the army spelled Caspar Collins's name correctly when they renamed the Platte River Station after him. Unfortunately, the city fathers of the town of Casper committed a spelling error that endures to this day. *(University of Wyoming American Heritage Center)*

CASPER: CATTLE

Although hundreds of thousands of whites passed through the Casper area, few settled here until the late 1870s, after the Wyoming tribes had been forced onto reservations. Then, the first big cattle outfits moved into the Platte River Valley, and Wyoming's most enduring industry began to thrive. In less than ten years, the explosive growth of the ranching industry encouraged the Chicago & North Western Railroad to announce plans for extending a branch line into the heart of central Wyoming's cattle country. The end of the line was Casper, platted in 1888. A sparsely populated cow town, Casper stayed quiet most of the time. But it came to life every month for a few days when the ranches paid their cowboys and the hands came to Casper to spend it fast on whiskey and calico queens.

CASPER: OIL

During the 1890s, rumors of gold and copper in the hills around Casper boosted hopes for a boom, but both metals disappointed the town. Instead, Casper's booms (and busts) would come from oil of surprising quality discovered in enormous pools close to the ground's surface and within easy reach of early drilling equip-

ment. Through the years, the richest field north of Casper produced more than a half-billion barrels of crude. All the oil activity boosted the city's population, touched off a furious local trade in stock speculation, led to the construction of extensive oil-production facilities, and even forced the resignation and imprisonment of a U.S. cabinet secretary.

Drilling started with a small cluster of wells forty-five miles north of town that produced enough oil to justify building a small refinery in Casper in 1894. Oil was shipped to the refinery by horse and wagon. In 1908, the state's first gusher came in on the Salt Creek field, about forty miles north of town. That well, and the huge reserve of oil in the Salt Creek field, led the Midwest Oil Company to lay pipe to the west side of Casper, where it built a new refinery. Then Standard of Indiana moved in in 1913 and built a cracking plant. The First World War kicked up demand; more pipelines were built and a boom was underway.

Stocks for the various oil companies were traded in the lobby of the Midwest Hotel, where a volume of $500,000 a day was considered pocket change. When trading was fast, the crowd often spilled out onto the street. The boom continued through the 1920s, ending with the 1929 crash and the imprisonment of Interior Secretary Albert B. Fall for crimes connected with the development of a small oil field north of Casper named Teapot Dome.

It's been boom and bust ever since for Casper, with local prosperity tied closely to the world oil market. When World War II broke out, the oil industry boomed and so did Casper. But when OPEC's control over the world market collapsed in the 1980s, Casper's economy withered along with the per-barrel price of crude oil. In 1991 Casper took a body blow when Amoco shut down a large refinery there. Although Casper's refining capacity thus shrank considerably, oil continues to play a large role in the city's economy.

JUNCTION WITH 220

From Casper, State Route 220 heads southwest, loosely following the Oregon Trail route used by Indians, mountain men, and emigrants to cross the state (see page 31).

JUNCTION WITH 26

Highway 26 crosses the North Platte and continues northwest over a classic high plains landscape, through the Wind River Indian Reservation, and up the Wind River Valley to Grand Teton National Park (see page 56).

TEAPOT DOME

East of I-25 and just off State 259 stands Teapot Dome, the physical epicenter of a scandal that shook the presidency of Warren G. Harding. The dome is a saucer-shaped formation that once contained a large reserve of crude oil. It was named after Teapot Rock, a rounded sandstone formation on which a column and arch, which resembled the handle and spout of a teapot, once stood.

In 1912 President Taft prohibited private development of the large deposit of oil discovered near Teapot Rock and set it aside for the future use of the navy. However, control of the field passed from the navy to the Department of the Interior in 1921, after President Harding came to power. The following year, Interior Secretary Albert B. Fall secretly leased the field to oilman Harry F. Sinclair without offering other oil companies a chance to bid for it. For his trouble, Fall took a $100,000 bribe. Between 1922 and 1927, Sinclair's Mammoth Oil Company drilled eighty-seven wells at Teapot Dome, including the largest gusher ever opened in Wyoming. The wells pumped an average of 273 barrels a day by 1923.

Later, a Senate investigation led to the criminal prosecution of Fall and Sinclair. Both were sentenced to prison terms.

KAYCEE

The town got its name from the KC brand, owned in 1884 by Peters Alston. The town was established in 1900.

Today, the little town lies in the center of a wide region of sheep and cattle ranches. It's a quiet place, with little to indicate that a small war erupted here about a hundred years ago.

The Johnson County War

Before dawn on a chilly April morning in 1892, a group of roughly fifty armed men quietly surrounded a small cabin on the southern edge of modern Kaycee. Concealed among the scrub brush and gullies, they prepared to strike the nastiest blow yet in a broad struggle between Wyoming's large cattle barons and a growing number of small ranchers who were interfering with the barons' control of the state's livestock industry. The violence that commenced just after daybreak and continued for five days would become known as the Johnson County War.

As wars go, this one was a relatively bloodless affair. In spite of all the bullets that flew near Kaycee and elsewhere in Johnson County, only four men were killed. Many others would have died, however, had it not been for poor marksmanship, bad organization, and the timely intervention of government troops. The historian T. A. Larson ranks the war as "the most notorious event in the history of Wyoming."

Sponsored, planned, and executed by some of the most powerful men in the state, the Johnson County War was nothing less than an invasion of north-central Wyoming by a small private army operating entirely outside the law. The men who stole into position around the cabin south of Kaycee represented big ranchers who owned vast herds and who had enjoyed unchallenged command of the state's cattle business for years. But by the late 1880s, they felt threatened by narrowing profits, by rustling that often went unpunished in the courts, and by the encroachment of settlers on a public range already overstocked and overgrazed.

Through the Wyoming Stock Growers Association, they had tried different ways to retain their grip on the state's cattle industry. Most of their efforts were advertised as measures to crack down on rustling, a growing problem. But the measures also had the effect of making it very difficult for newcomers to break into the field. For instance, big cattle interests tightly controlled the registration of all brands and all roundups throughout the state. If a newcomer could not get a brand and could not participate in the official roundups, he had trouble making a living.

Getting a brand was essential. Everybody ran their cattle on the open range, and herds from different ranches invariably mixed together. If they were unbranded, a newcomer's cattle would be treated as strays during the official roundups and would be divided among ranchers who had brands. Getting a brand sounds simple: dream up a new design and hire a blacksmith to whack together a set of irons. However, to be valid, the brand had to be registered. A person caught using an unregistered brand could be accused of rustling. Also, stock inspectors at major shipping points kept a sharp eye out for cattle bearing unregistered brands. Such cattle were sold and the proceeds were turned over to the Wyoming Stock Growers Association.

Though they shouted loudest about their outrage over rustling, the big cattle interests were also deeply concerned about losing control of the public range. Various ill-conceived land laws had prevented most western cattlemen from claiming title to more than a fraction of the land necessary to support a reasonable number of cattle. Instead, they grazed their herds on the veritable sea of public land that surrounded their homesteads. The system worked in the early days, but after the range became overstocked in the mid-1880s, big ranchers were often severely aggravated to find a new homesteader staking out a claim in the middle of what the rancher had come to regard as his own best pasture. Big ranchers often tried to intimidate the newcomers by prohibiting them from using vast tracts of the public land.

Of course, newcomers resented the big cattlemen's control of the industry. They had a perfect right to settle on public lands and to raise cattle without getting their competitors' permission to do so. In the late 1880s they started to speak up for themselves and to organize against the big-time ranchers. Sometimes they paid a hefty price, usually after they were branded as rustlers. No one has ever proved that Jim Averell and Ella "Cattle Kate" Watson were rustlers, but they clearly annoyed the big cattle interests because they were lynched near Independence Rock in 1889 by large cattle ranchers (see page 34).

In Johnson County, three other violent incidents preceded the outbreak of the war. On November 1, 1891, a handful of gunmen burst in on a cabin in the Hole-in-the-Wall country west of Kaycee and tried to kill Nate Champion, who may or may not have rustled cattle. It was a botched attempt. Champion fought them off and lived to die another day. Later that same month, two other small ranchers were ambushed in separate incidents outside Buffalo and shot to death. A stock detective and former sheriff of the county was accused of the murders, but the charges were dropped.

At about the same time, the small cattle ranchers of Johnson County organized themselves under the banner of the Northern Wyoming Farmers and Stock Growers Association and announced they would hold a roundup of their own a month in advance of the official roundup. This act may have been what finally convinced the big cattle interests that something drastic had to be done up in Johnson County.

For several years, the large cattlemen had regarded the area as a hotbed of opposition to their influence, a center for rustling and a place where you could not get a jury to convict a rustler no matter how damning the evidence. Now, on top of everything else, it had become a region where small-time outfits had the audacity to organize themselves. Some of the big-time cattle ranchers decided to teach Johnson County a lesson, and in so doing scare the bejesus out of anyone else who might think of opposing them. The big cattlemen had been discussing such plans since the summer of 1891, when rancher Frank Wolcott suggested to the president of the Wyoming Stock Growers Association that they hold a "lynching bee." String up enough of the "rustlers" and opposition would fade.

So, egged on by the announcement of an unsanctioned roundup in Johnson County, the big cattlemen drew together a force of roughly fifty men and headed north from Cheyenne by train in early April 1892. Among their number were nine large-ranch owners, thirteen ranch foremen, five private stock detectives, and twenty-two Texas mercenaries. They intended to occupy Buffalo, raid the outlying settlements, and kill upwards of twenty Johnson County men who may or may not have rustled cattle from the big owners' far-flung herds. Some accounts of the war say the hit list included Red Angus, sheriff of Johnson County, his deputies, and the mayor of Buffalo. Some, including historian

T. A. Larson, say the acting governor, Amos Barber, and both Wyoming U.S. senators, Joseph Carey and F. E. Warren, probably knew about the plan in advance.

On April 6, the Invaders, sometimes called the Regulators, got off their special train at Casper, the end of the line, and hurried on toward Buffalo by horseback. About forty miles north of Casper the foreman of a large ranch met them and said a group of about fifteen rustlers was spending the night at the KC ranch, just eighteen miles away. They decided to ride over there, surround the cabin, and knock off the rustlers before galloping on to Buffalo. They arrived before dawn and took their positions.

Instead of the fine brace of rustlers they expected to bag, just four men snoozed inside the cabin. They included two trappers and two men on the hit list—Nick Ray and Nate Champion, who was about to wake to his second ambush in just five months.

Shortly after dawn, one of the trappers opened the door of the cabin and walked over to the bank of the river that runs along the southern edge of modern Kaycee. Some of the Regulators jumped him, kept him quiet, and tied him up. A while later, the other trapper wandered out looking for his buddy. He got the same treatment. When Ray stepped out of the cabin, he got a warmer reception. The surrounding riflemen opened fire and dropped him. Champion rushed to the doorway, fired back, then ran out and dragged Ray inside while bullets slammed into the ground and the log walls of the cabin.

Thus began a seige that would last the rest of the day. Champion edged around the window frames, shooting at whatever looked like a person scrambling around outside. The Regulators blasted away at whatever shadow they saw make a promising move. Sometime during the day, Ray died. But the fight was a standoff. The

Group portrait of the Invaders, the small private army that rode into Johnson County in 1892 to kill so-called rustlers who were threatening the interests of large cattle ranchers. *(University of Wyoming American Heritage Center)*

Regulators would not rush the cabin, and Champion clearly could not make a run for it.

During lulls in the shooting, Champion is said to have written a brief account of the day's action. Serious questions have been raised about the authenticity of Champion's diary, but it is part of the legend, so here are portions of it:

> Boys, there is bullets coming in like hail. Them fellows is in such shape I can't get at them. They are shooting from the stable and river and back of the house. Nick is dead, he died about 9 o'clock. I see a smoke down at the stable. I think they have fired it. I don't think they intend to let me get away this time . . . Boys, I feel pretty lonesome just now. I wish there was someone here with me so we could watch all sides at once.

At about 2:30 P.M., a neighboring rancher named Jack Flagg stumbled across the gun battle. He was riding a horse about fifty yards behind a wagon driven by his stepson. He later described the action to a newspaper reporter:

> When the wagon hove in sight, the murderers jumped up and ordered the boy to halt, but he urged up his horses and drove for the bridge. When they saw he would not stop, one of them took aim on the corner of the fence and fired at him. The shot missed him and scared his team, which stampeded across the bridge and on up the road.

Several of the Regulators jumped on horseback and rode after Flagg, by now hightailing it after his stepson.

> When the men behind the stable saw me, they jumped for their guns, which were leaning up against the fence, and called on me to stop and throw up my hands. I did not comply with their order, but kept straight for the bridge. When I got to the nearest point to them—47 steps—a man whom I recognized as Ford, stepped from the crowd and,

taking deliberate aim at me with his Winchester, fired. Then they all commenced firing. I threw myself on the side of my horse and made a run for it. The seven horsemen followed me. When I overtook my wagon, which had my rifle on it, I told my boy to hand it to me, which he did. I then told him to cut one of the horses loose and mount him. The seven horsemen were following me, and when I stopped, were 350 yards behind, but as soon as they saw I had a rifle, they stopped. I had three cartridges for my rifle, and did not want to fire any of them unless they came closer, which they did not seem inclined to do.

Flagg and his stepson got away and rode for Buffalo, raising the general alarm. Their escape, and the Paul Revere ride to Buffalo, would give the town time to defend itself and send out a large posse in opposition to the Regulators (see page 84).

Recognizing that Flagg could easily spoil their surprise attack on Buffalo, the Regulators knew they had to polish off Champion in a hurry. To do that they needed to flush him out. So they loaded Flagg's abandoned wagon with hay, wood, and pine pitch, rammed it against the house, torched it, and waited for Champion to make a run for it. Meanwhile, Champion's diary goes like this:

> Well, they have just got through shelling the house like hail. I heard them splitting wood. I guess they are going to fire the house tonight. I think I will make a break when night comes, if alive. Shooting again. I think they will fire the house this time. It's not night yet. The house is all fired. Goodbye, boys, if I never see you again.

He never did. Champion made his break in broad daylight, sprinting south with a Winchester in his hands and a revolver on his belt.

"[He] emerged from a volume of black smoke that issued from the rear door of the house and started off across the open space sur-rounding the cabin into a ravine, fifty yards south of the house," wrote Sam Clover, a reporter for the *Chicago Herald* who had accompanied the Regulators. "The poor devil jumped square into the arms of two of the best shots in the outfit, who stood with leveled Winchesters around the bend waiting for his appearance. Champion saw them too late, for he overshot his mark just as a bullet struck his rifle arm, causing the gun to fall from his nerveless grasp. Before he could draw his revolver a second shot struck him in the breast and a third and fourth found their way to his heart."

With Champion dead, the Regulators mounted their horses and spurred toward Buffalo. But there would be another detour and siege before they reached the town, and this time, the Regulators would be the ones keeping clear of the windows (see page 73).

The site of the Kaycee gun battle is marked with a sign south of town. Take the main street through Kaycee and over the bridge that spans the river. The cabin stood in what is now a flat pasture on the west side of the road.

THE DULL KNIFE BATTLE

Despite a treaty signed in 1868 guaranteeing that no whites would so much as pass through what is now the northeast quarter of Wyoming, gold in the Black Hills prompted the U.S. government to go back on its word and seize the territory from the Indians. In 1876, the government ordered three army groups to converge on the Powder River country and smash the power of the Lakota, Cheyenne, and Arapaho tribes. It was during this campaign that Lt. Col. George Armstrong Custer and about 265 of his men were killed in what is now southern Montana. (For more details about events leading up to the war, see page 81).

The final battle of the war was fought about

Dull Knife, the Cheyenne chief who fought the last battle of the war that erupted over the U.S. government's seizure of the Black Hills in 1876. Dull Knife's village was attacked on the slopes of the Big Horn Mountains in late November 1875 by army troops. The Cheyenne fought the troops to a standstill and then retreated to Crazy Horse's village on the Powder River. *(University of Wyoming American Heritage Center)*

twenty-five miles west of Kaycee, on the slopes of the Big Horn Mountains. At dawn on November 25, Col. Ranald Mackenzie and his force of 750 cavalrymen and 400 Indian scouts and auxiliaries attacked a village of about 1,400 Cheyenne led by Dull Knife and Little Wolf. The

army troops overran the village, burned the lodges, and captured the pony herd. The women and children fled into the surrounding mountains while Dull Knife's warriors fought Mackenzie's force to a standoff. The army lost one officer and six men. The Cheyenne lost about twenty men and virtually all of their belongings. Left destitute in the winter mountains, Dull Knife's people retreated and were taken in by the Lakota. The following spring the Cheyenne surrendered. They eventually accepted a reservation in southeast Montana.

With the end of the war, the Powder River country opened up not only to prospectors, but also to cattle ranchers, settlers, rustlers, and stagecoach robbers.

HOLE-IN-THE-WALL

A haven for rustlers of cattle and horses and later for the robbers of trains, banks, and stagecoaches, Hole-in-the-Wall is the most celebrated spot of its kind in the West. It is a notch in a steep red cliff sixteen miles southwest of Kaycee. It leads into a wide broken country that made an excellent hideout for criminals on the run. Butch Cassidy once boasted that the notch was such a fine defensive position that twelve men could keep one hundred from passing through. While that assertion may be an exaggeration, it is true that a dozen outlaws on the run could easily lose one hundred deputies in the grassy mountain pockets, hidden canyons, and great rolling foothills that stretch for miles beyond the cliffs.

Hole-in-the-Wall offered tremendous strategic benefits to any bandit. It was close to the Bozeman Trail, not far from the Cheyenne-Deadwood Trail, and just a couple of days hard riding from the Union Pacific tracks. Once through the Hole, the way was open to the Big Horn basin and routes that led to Montana, Idaho, Utah, and Colorado.

In the summer of 1897, Bob Devine, the foreman of a large ranch, wrote an open letter in the *Casper Tribune*. He announced that he and his crew of men, accompanied by crews from two other big ranches and the sheriffs of Natrona and Johnson counties, would hold a roundup in the Hole-in-the-Wall country in order to recover some of the cattle stolen from their ranches. Soon after his letter appeared, a reply was printed, signed by the "Revenge Gang":

> Bob Devine you think you have played hell, you have just begun . . . There is men enough up here to kill you. We are going to get you, or lose 12 more men. You must stay out of this country if you want to live . . . We want one hair apiece out of that damned old chin of yours. You have give us the worst of it all the way through and you must stay out or die. You had better keep your damned outfit out if you want to keep them. Don't stick that damned old head of yours in this country again if you do not want it shot off.

Devine did stick his old head in that country, but nobody shot it off. He and his outfit gathered their cattle and skirmished with halfhearted outlaws.

In 1899, Butch Cassidy and the Wild Bunch robbed a Union Pacific train at Wilcox Siding, southeast of modern Medicine Bow. Afterward, several of the outlaws streaked north toward Hole-in-the-Wall country. They included the Sundance Kid, Harvey Logan, and George "Flat Nose" or "Big Nose" Curry. Curry earned the sobriquet by his malformed nose, the result of a horse kicking him in the face. In early June the trio made camp west of Kaycee along the Red Fork of the Powder River, not far from today's State 190. As they sat down to a meal, Converse County Sheriff Joe Hazen rode up with a posse. The outlaws drew their guns. Logan killed the

The Hole-in-the-Wall Gang in 1900. Harry Longabaugh, the Sundance Kid, sits on the left; Robert Leroy Parker, known as Butch Cassidy, sits on the right. Other members of the gang are Ben Kilpatrick, sitting center; William Carver, standing left; and Harvey Logan, known as Kid Curry, standing right. This photo was taken shortly after the gang robbed a bank in Colorado. They sent a copy of the portrait to the owner of the bank and thanked him for the money to buy their new clothes. *(From the original photograph by John Swartz. University of Wyoming American Heritage Center)*

sheriff with a shot to the stomach, then the outlaws leaped into the river and escaped.

Having killed sheriffs in Wyoming, Utah, and Arizona, Logan became one of the most wanted criminals in the West. He was killed in 1904 when a train robbery went awry. Flat Nose Curry didn't last that long. A Utah posse tracked him down in 1900 and killed him for rustling. The Sundance Kid was killed in Bolivia in 1909. Some say Cassidy died with him, others that he lived to old age and died of cancer in the 1930s in Seattle.

Cassidy owned a ranch ten miles northwest of Hole-in-the-Wall on Blue Creek. His cabin still stands and is in good condition, but it is not open to the public.

A RUDE AWAKENING

Some accounts of the Johnson County War paint him as a talented rustler, others as a hero of the small-time ranchers in the struggle against Big Cattle. What was probably more important to Nate Champion's longevity, or lack thereof, was that powerful ranchers considered him a rustling kingpin who needed killing.

On November 1, 1891, Champion and a friend were sleeping in a shack near the Hole-in-the-Wall country southwest of Kaycee. Suddenly, someone kicked open the door and shouted for Champion to give up. A chaotic burst of gunfire followed. The shooting was so close that Champion got a powder burn, but it was also so dark that no one could really see what they were doing. Champion managed to fight off his attackers and later said he thought there were four of them and that he had grazed one and hit another in the side.

This was the first of two attacks on Champion. The second and fatal one came five months later, during the Johnson County War (see page 65).

FORTS CONNOR AND RENO

Forts Connor and Reno were built in the mid-1860s, during the first phase of warfare between white and Indian societies. They were built about twenty-eight miles east of Kaycee to protect emigrants traveling north on the Bozeman Trail to the Montana goldfields.

Fort Connor was built by General Patrick E. Connor as a supply base for his largely unsuccessful expedition against the Lakota. A year later, Fort Connor was abandoned in favor of Fort Reno, which was built about a mile west and offered defenders better fields of fire.

Both forts lay on an imaginary line drawn by the great Lakota leader Red Cloud, who warned that if troops moved north of Fort Connor they would touch off a war. After building and garrisoning Fort Reno in 1866, Col. H. B. Carrington marched beyond Red Cloud's line and built two more outposts: Fort Phil Kearny, northwest of modern Buffalo; and Fort C. F. Smith, in southern Montana.

As Red Cloud promised, war followed. Fights broke out up and down the Bozeman Trail, but the most important battles were joined at Fort Phil Kearny, near the modern town of Story, where the Lakota sprang one of its most successful ambushes in western history. The fighting ended with the Fort Laramie Treaty of 1868, in which the government agreed to shut down the Bozeman Trail, abandon the forts, and forbid whites from setting foot north of the North Platte River and east of the Big Horn Mountains.

When the troops pulled out of Fort Reno, warriors burned the place to the ground. Red Cloud had won, but only for a while. In just eight years the Black Hills gold rush would sweep away the treaty and the tribes. (For more about the 1860s conflict, see page 79).

LOST CABIN LEGEND

Mining regions all over the West are thick with stories about prospectors who find a fabulous lode of precious metal and then, after announcing its presence, promptly forget where in the heck they stumbled across the stuff. In Wyoming there are at least three versions of the Lost Cabin Mine Legend, and for some reason they all have their roots in the eastern slopes of the Big Horn Mountains.

According to one version, seven Swedish prospectors returned to Wyoming from the Black Hills in the summer of 1865 (about ten years before the big gold rush). While knocking around in the streams of the Big Horns, they stumbled across a deposit of placer gold so rich that they managed to pan, sluice, or snatch off the ground seven thousand dollars worth in three days. However, a band of Indians interrupted their lucrative activity, reduced the venture's partnership by five souls, and drove the survivors out of the country. In all the confusion, the two remaining Swedes could not remember where they found the gold.

CRAZY WOMAN CREEK

During the mid-1860s, Indians trying to shut down the Bozeman Trail often chose the Crazy Woman Creek crossing as an ambush site. The creek is also about as far as John Bozeman got with the first wagon train of emigrants to travel his road in 1863. Bozeman's train was camped on a tributary of Crazy Woman Creek when a band of 150 Lakota and Cheyenne arrived and peacefully but firmly insisted that the group of emigrants turn around. Dorothy Johnson, in her excellent book, *The Bloody Bozeman*, says one of the chiefs present explained the order this way:

> You can't go on in the direction you are going. You are going into our country, where we hunt. This is the only good big hunting ground left for us. Your people have taken the rest or scared the game away.
> We won't let our women and children starve. This is where we make meat, and we will keep this land.
> Along the great road to the south [the Oregon Trail], white men have driven away all the buffalo and antelope. We won't let you do that here . . . If you go on into our hunting country, our people will wipe you out.

After more than a week of hemming and hawing, the emigrants did turn around. However, subsequent trains rolled north of Buffalo, and the traffic kicked off several years of bloody fighting.

TA RANCH

By sunset on April 9, 1892, the invading cattlemen had finally done their dirty work in the first battle of the Johnson County War (see page 65). Nate Champion lay dead in a ravine near a small cabin south of modern Kaycee. The cabin he had defended all day was in flames, and inside lay the roasting body of his friend, Nick Ray. The group of roughly fifty "Invaders" mounted their horses and rode hard for Buffalo, where they still hoped to kick off the second battle of the war with a surprise attack on the town. Instead, at least two reports of their fight with Champion had reached Buffalo, giving residents time to grab their guns and organize for the defense of their homes.

The Invaders rode within eight miles of Buffalo before a sympathizer warned them that two hundred men stood ready and eager to shoot them from their saddles if they approached the town. Knowing now that they had lost the element of surprise and that they were badly outnumbered, the Invaders doubled back to the TA Ranch, about a dozen miles southeast of Buffalo on the banks of Crazy Woman Creek. There they prepared for a siege.

They spent April 10 setting up positions in the ranch house, barn, and icehouse—all of which were made of stout hewed logs. They also dug rifle pits and built log breastworks around the house. Thus fortified, they could hold off rifle attacks indefinitely. Their enemies would need either to starve them out or blow them out with a cannon.

The small ranchers of Johnson County thought of both tactics. They captured the Invaders' supply wagons, leaving them only what food they could rustle up at the TA. They also dropped by Fort McKinney, just southwest of Buffalo, and asked to borrow a cannon. When the fort's commander denied their request, the settlers soon found an alternative. The Invaders' supply wagons contained not only food but dynamite.

By the morning of April 11, small ranchers and settlers from throughout Johnson County and parts of Sheridan County had converged on Buffalo. They were deputized and sent off to lay seige to the TA Ranch. Estimates of how many men showed up vary, but two hundred men, eager to pump lead at the Invaders, is a conservative count. Under the leadership of Sheriff Red Angus, who some say was on the Invaders' hit list, these men surrounded the ranch house, dug rifle pits, and built breastworks of their own.

On the morning of the eleventh, the besieged Invaders opened fire. Bullets cracked through the air from both directions, slamming harmlessly into the log walls of the ranch house and kicking up dirt around the settlers' rifle pits. The shooting would continue for two days with little to show for all the noise except that it pinned down the Invaders. However, the settlers used the time to build a siege wagon — a log wall on wheels that they meant to use as a shield so they could approach the ranch house safely and blow it up with the dynamite they had captured. The siege wagon's business end was made of a double thickness of eight-inch logs that stood six feet high. This they attached to the back ends of a couple of wagons. Five men could move the contraption slowly, fifteen made the going easy, and it could protect as many as forty.

While the settlers built their siege wagon and the Invaders bickered inside their defenses and both sides blasted away with their rifles, the outside world finally got word of what was happening in Johnson County. The news was very late in coming, thanks to the Invaders. When they had ridden north from Casper, they had made sure that the telegraph line was cut between Buffalo and Douglas in order to prevent the settlers from calling for help. This precaution almost doomed the Invaders when they found themselves besieged at the TA and in need of rescue.

The line was repaired the afternoon of the twelfth, however, and supporters of the Invaders soon contacted the acting governor, Amos Barber, who immediately telegraphed President Benjamin Harrison.

"An insurrection exists in Johnson County, in the state of Wyoming . . . against the government of said state," Barber wrote. "Open hostilities exist and large bodies of armed men are engaged in battle . . . I apply to you on behalf of the state of Wyoming to direct the United States troops at Fort McKinney to assist in suppressing the insurrection. The lives of a large number of persons are in imminent danger."

Harrison cut the orders. During the early

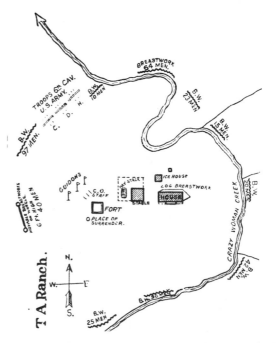

A map of the TA Ranch, near Buffalo, where the Johnson County War fizzled to its anticlimactic end. *(University of Wyoming American Heritage Center)*

morning of the thirteenth, Col. J. J. Van Horn and a cavalry force set out from Fort McKinney for the TA. If they had marched just a few hours later, they might have spent the day digging graves for the Invaders.

By sunrise, the settlers had finished building their siege wagon and had begun to move it toward the house. Also during the night, they had constructed a breastworks within three hundred yards of the house. The dynamite they planned to use would have killed some Invaders, blown a big hole in their defenses, and probably flushed some of them out where the settlers' rifles could polish them off.

But Van Horn's force arrived shortly after sunrise, and the shooting immediately stopped. The colonel, accompanied by Sheriff Angus, approached the house under a flag of truce and asked for the Invaders' surrender. The leader of the Invaders said he would surrender to Van Horn but never to Angus. Van Horn took charge of the Invaders and moved them to Fort McKinney, where they would be out of the reach of Johnson County's angry citizens while they awaited trial for the deaths of Champion and Ray. Ten days later they were transferred to Fort Russell, near Cheyenne, and eventually released, with all charges dropped (see page 85).

BOZEMAN TRAIL

About ten miles south of Buffalo, I-25 picks up the route of the Bozeman Trail and runs parallel with it to the vicinity of Banner and Story. From this point, a dirt road runs off to the southeast, shadowing the trail across Crazy Woman Creek to the Powder River.

FORT MCKINNEY

Located three miles west of Buffalo on U.S. 16, Fort McKinney was built in 1877 as a supply depot and became a permanent post five years later in anticipation of future wars with the Plains Indians. The fort never played a crucial role in an Indian war, but it did house the troops that defused the Johnson County War.

JUNCTION WITH I-90

Interstate 90 continues north from Buffalo through country dense with the history of warfare between whites and Indians. Many of the most important battles in the 1860s war over control of the Powder River took place between Buffalo and Sheridan. On I-90, too, readers will find the story of how the town of Buffalo responded to the Johnson County War.

As it dips through the northeast corner of Wyoming, I-90 crosses a region where bitter fights for the land erupted throughout the latter half of the nineteenth century. At first the battles were fought between whites and Indians, then between rival factions of white settlers. History along I-90 focuses mainly on the wars fought during the 1860s and 1870 between whites and several Plains Indians tribes, principally the Lakota (often called Sioux), the Cheyenne, and the Arapaho. Several of the most important sites of the 1860s conflict lie close to the road—near Story and Ranchester.

However, history along I-90 also deals with the dawn of Wyoming's cowboy era, when most of the cattle were owned by foreign investors and when most people thought cowpunchers were about as romantic as ditch water. Buffalo was a center of the range conflagration known as the Johnson County War.

SUNDANCE

Named for the nearby mountain, Sundance got its start in 1879 as a supply center for neighboring cattle ranches. It is also the town that gave outlaw Harry Alonzo Longabaugh his famous nickname: the Sundance Kid. Here the young Longabaugh was convicted in 1887 of stealing horses. Since the territorial prison was booked solid, Longabaugh served his time in the Crook County jail.

The mountain got its name from a ceremonial dance the Lakota held on its slopes every year. Whites called it the "Sun Dance." This important religious ceremony was practiced then by at least two dozen tribes of Plains Indians and is still practiced by many today. The ceremony is understood as an act of the whole tribe, an expression of their oneness as a people and of the paramount importance of the common good.

Different tribes perform the ceremony in different ways, but it generally follows this form: A cottonwood tree is chosen, cut down, trimmed, decorated with religious emblems, and erected as the center of a pole enclosure. Within it, a buffalo skull, facing east, rests on an altar. At the proper time, men who have pledged themselves begin four days of dancing and blowing eagle-bone whistles. Throughout the four days of the ceremony they neither eat nor drink.

The Sun Dance is famous for the gesture of self-scourging, in which some dancers permit skewers to be passed under the skin of their chests or backs. The skewers are then attached to a pole with leather thongs and the dancer rips them out by leaning out against the thongs. Not all tribes accepted self-scourging, and some forbade it. The practice horrified missionaries and Indian agents, who banned the ceremony for a time. Today the dance, and sometimes the self-scourging, continues.

JUNCTION WITH 585

About ten miles south of Sundance, George Armstrong Custer camped in July 1874 on the eastern slopes of Inyan Kara Mountain, on his illegal gold-seeking mission to the Black Hills (see page 81).

SIDE TRIP: DEVIL'S TOWER

Visible from as far away as one hundred miles, this six-hundred-foot stump of volcanic rock with fluted sides served as a landmark for Indians, soldiers, and settlers. The Lakota called it Bear Lodge. One of their legends explains the odd geological formation this way: Three young girls were out picking wildflowers one day when a group of bears attacked them. The girls jumped on top of a large boulder and, as the bears climbed after them, the gods took pity on the

Devil's Tower, the country's first national monument, and the root of several Indian legends. *(University of Wyoming American Heritage Center)*

WINTER 1887

The winter of 1886–87 was a disaster for most of Wyoming's cattle ranchers, but the bitter cold, deep snows, and freezing rain hit ranchers in Crook County the hardest. Here, assessors estimated that about forty-five percent of the cattle died from dehydration and cold.

Although losses were lower elsewhere in Wyoming, the winter brought to an end the easy prosperity stockmen had known since they started grazing large herds of cattle on the state's grasslands in the early 1870s. Common wisdom held that cattle turned loose on the rich grass could more or less take care of themselves. All that was required was to round them up once in the spring to brand and castrate the new calves, and then to round them up once again in the fall to send the fattened animals to market.

Until the winter of 1886–87, that pattern held true. Investors from the East Coast and the British Isles bought enormous tracts of land, usually from the railroads, and ran tens of thousands of cattle over the open range. At the crest of the cattle boom, the Swan Land & Cattle Company owned land from Oglalla in Nebraska nearly to Rawlins and laid claim to 123,400 of the roughly 1.5 million cattle grazing in Wyoming. The absentee owners made plenty of money. Their success led them to push more and more cattle onto the limited amount of grassland available on the high plains. By the winter of 1887, the Wyoming range was crowded and overgrazed. In a sense, the early success set up the failure that followed.

In the aftermath of the harsh winter, many of the large cattle combinations went out of business. Even Swan went bankrupt, but it soon reorganized and continued in business until 1947. Generally, though, those that led the industry's recovery tended to be smaller operations run by owners on the scene who could pay better

girls. They made the rock grow bigger and bigger. The bears kept climbing, digging their claws into the rock face, but eventually they fell and died. The girls then braided their wildflowers into a rope and descended to the valley.

Geologists say Devil's Tower was formed about 20 million years ago from a huge blister of upwelling lava. The polygonal columns, mostly five-sided and about six feet thick, formed as the lava cooled under special conditions.

In 1906, President Theodore Roosevelt designated Devil's Tower as the country's first national monument. Today the tower is a mecca for rock climbers, who follow in the footsteps of Bill Rogers, a local rancher who made the first recorded ascent in 1893 by driving wooden pegs into a system of cracks as a sort of ladder.

attention to the care and feeding of their herds than did absentee investors.

SHEEP VERSUS CATTLE

After the fatal winter of 1886–87, cattle ranchers across Wyoming began to take a violent dislike to the presence of sheep on public grazing lands. The sheep—which were often called "woollies," "hoofed locusts," or "maggots" by the cowboys—had come through the winter in much better shape than had the cattle. Now, after the winterkill had opened voids on the range, sheep began filling in where cattle once grazed in large numbers. The struggle for control of the limited amount of pasture made for bad blood between sheepmen and cattlemen. Tempers flared and masked men started raiding sheep camps all over Wyoming. They burned wagons, whipped herders with ropes, and sometimes killed them. They ran the sheep off cliffs, tossed dynamite into sheep pens, clubbed thousands to death, and scattered thousands more to be devoured by coyotes and mountain lions. In Wyoming, the violence reached its height during the first decade of the twentieth century. All told, the conflict killed ten Wyoming sheepmen, one cattleman, and about sixteen thousand sheep.

Here in Crook County, a handful of cattle ranchers swore in 1908 to drive two sheep companies out of the country. The cattlemen agreed that if anyone betrayed the others, he would be killed. In August, they attacked one of the sheep ranches on Kara Creek. There, they shot up a herder's wagon in which a man and his son happened to be sleeping. The boy was grazed by a bullet, but he and his father managed to skip out of the wagon before either was seriously injured. The raiders tied them up, torched the wagon and the ranch buildings, and then rode away. During the following two months the cattlemen struck several more times, burning wagons and hay, cutting miles of fences, and destroying ranch buildings.

The two sheep companies then took a leaf out of the cattlemen's book. During the years when the cattlemen were at their strongest, they had employed range detectives to uncover rustlers. Now the Wyoming Wool Growers Association hired some of the West's finest detectives to track down the culprits. One of the detectives was Joe Lefors, who had built the case that hung the gunman Tom Horn for murdering a sheepman's son in 1901. Soon two men were arrested. They implicated seven others. Before the case came to trial, however, the cattlemen settled out of court for more than twenty-five thousand dollars and a promise never again to harass sheep camps.

MOORCROFT

Established in 1891 with the arrival of the railroad, Moorcroft became an important shipping point for livestock. Today it is a center for bentonite production. Bentonite is a clay used primarily in oil drilling but also in the manufacture of many other goods, including paper, toothpaste, and cosmetics.

GILLETTE

A billboard outside Gillette refers to the city as "America's answer to OPEC," and no wonder. It stands on an immense deposit of low-sulphur coal that underlies virtually the entire northeast quarter of the state and includes some veins as thick as three hundred feet. Geologists estimate the region contains about a trillion tons of coal. During the 1980s the coal lands around Gillette became the hottest coal-mining region in the nation, kicking off an economic boom and boosting Wyoming past Kentucky and West Virginia into first place among the coal-producing states. The area is home to the seven largest mines in the country.

This coal boom swelled Gillette's population tenfold, to twenty-one thousand by the early 1990s. In addition to the mines, several demonstration plants have been built that convert the low-sulphur coal to fuel oil. Demand for Wyoming's low-sulphur coal increased after passage of the 1990 Clean Air Act, which tightened sulphur dioxide emission standards at coal-fired electric power plants.

The presence of coal around Gillette has been obvious for many years. In the early 1800s, Indians and trappers reported seeing at least one coal deposit on fire, presumably ignited by lightning. In the 1930s, as many as thirty such fires burned near Gillette, some of them large enough to glow at night.

While coal is the major energy resource around Gillette today, oil and gas discoveries in the area also have contributed to its growth.

The city is named after Edward Gillette, chief of the surveying crew that laid out the route for the Burlington Northern railroad through northeast Wyoming. The tracks reached the town in 1891, and Gillette soon became a major shipping point for cattle and sheep from ranches as far away as Buffalo. In 1911, the tracks hauled in the first airplane ever flown over Wyoming. It was assembled in Gillette, and daredevil George Thompson was paid thirty-five hundred dollars to fly it.

JUNCTION WITH STATE 59

State 59 runs directly south through Wyoming's rich coal fields, connecting I-90 with I-25 (see page 103).

POWDER RIVER

The Indians in the area are said to have named the river Powder because of the fine sand that sifts into the water from the surrounding hills, obscuring and dirtying the water. The river is often said to be too thick to drink and too thin to plow.

POWDER RIVER WAR

Most of the violence between whites and Indians in Wyoming hinged on control of the Powder River Valley. This vast stretch of broken grassland was the last great hunting ground of the Plains Indians. Loss of the territory would deal the death blow to a way of life that had been eroding since the first whites moved into the area. Without the land, the tribes would have to find an entirely new way to feed and clothe themselves. The Indians fought to preserve the Powder River country in the 1860s and again in the 1870s.

During these wars, white society's interest focused not so much on the Powder River land itself but rather on what lay beyond it: gold. In the 1860s, Montana gold drew whites up the Bozeman Trail, which led from the North Platte (near modern Douglas) through the precious Powder River country. In the 1870s, gold in the Black Hills prompted the U.S. government to seize the Black Hills and secure a route north from the Union Pacific tracks at Cheyenne through Powder River country.

During the 1860s, the tribes worried that the Bozeman Trail would not only disrupt the hunting as whites rolled through but also that the road would encourage whites to settle there.

"They began to perceive clearly, as it affected them, the significance of the ancient, continuing, universal search for grass," wrote Struthers Burt in his book, *Powder River: Let 'er Buck.* "If enough white men went up the Bozeman Trail, pretty soon some of them, seeing the lovely valleys at the foot of the Big Horns, would want to settle, and the buffalo herds, the life-blood of the Sioux, would go."

To white civilization, the presence of the Indians along the Powder River was a threat not only to the Bozeman Trail but also to the major transcontinental road, the Oregon Trail.

The Lakota had been trying to shut down the emigrant trails since 1862, when their cousins in Minnesota had rebelled, killing eight hundred whites and suffering retribution in return. The western Lakota, knowing that the U.S. Army often failed to distinguish between different groups of Indians when it was out for blood, had decided to strike before the army came looking for them. They were joined in their raids by Cheyenne and Arapaho warriors who had seen white miners pour into Colorado lands that had been promised to their tribes. Violence had accelerated after the 1864 Sand Creek Massacre in Colorado, in which troops slaughtered a Cheyenne village that had been promised protection by the government. As long as the Civil War continued, the army could do little to protect emigrants in the far-flung West.

Expedition of 1865

After Lee surrendered to Grant in 1865, the U.S. government could finally dispatch enough troops to smash the power of the tribes on the Powder River and make the region safe for white travel and settlement. Or so the whites thought.

The plan was to march into the Powder River country, whip the tribes, and build a strong post to enforce the peace. The expedition was led by Gen. Patrick E. Connor, who was supposed to head north with three thousand men through the Powder River country and meet two other columns on the Rosebud River in southern Montana. The two additional columns, with a total of two thousand men, would march in from the east by way of the Black Hills.

When he issued the following order, Connor left little doubt in the minds of his subordinates about what he intended to accomplish during the expedition: "You will not receive overtures of peace or submission from Indians, but will attack and kill every Indian male over 12 years of age."

Connor got just a third of the men he thought he needed and only half of the supplies and horses. To make matters worse, many of the troopers were on the verge of mutiny. They had joined the army to fight the Civil War, and the Civil War was over. They figured it was high time to go home. But rather than getting mustered out, here they were in some godforsaken corner of the world, fixing to fight Indians.

Meanwhile, more than three thousand warriors of the Lakota, Cheyenne, and Arapaho tribes had gathered in the Powder River country and had marched south, where they attacked Platte Bridge Station (later renamed Fort Caspar), just west of modern Casper (see page 63).

Far from punishing the Lakota and forcing them to accept the will of the government, Connor's Powder River Expedition degenerated into a dark comedy of errors, a tragic farce. A late start, lousy weather, bad morale, rotten guiding, the strange country, and clever hit-and-run tactics by the Indians led to eternal confusion and frustration.

The two columns that were supposed to converge from the east never found Connor. The Indians dogged them as they blundered across northeastern Wyoming, running off their horses and occasionally killing a few soldiers. A sleet storm in early September killed six hundred mules and horses. Worse, the soldiers completely lost their way in the badlands. Cold, hungry, many without shoes, the men straggled south and eventually stumbled across a Pawnee scout who guided them back to a fort that Gen. Connor had built near modern Kaycee.

Red Cloud, the principal leader of the Lakota during the war over control of the Powder River country in the mid-1860s. *(University of Wyoming American Heritage Center)*

Connor's column fared better than the other two. He marched straight through the Powder River country, skirmishing occasionally with small bands of Indians. Near Kaycee, while the troops built Fort Connor, the column's Pawnee scouts killed twenty-four Cheyenne. Then, at Tongue River near modern Ranchester, Connor attacked an Arapaho village of some fifteen hundred people who had not been hostile before. The soldiers killed about sixty warriors and destroyed the lodges and winter supplies (see page 101).

Connor's disappointing expedition led the U.S. government to begin negotiating a new treaty with the Indians. Red Cloud and other Indian leaders were willing to call a halt to hostilities, but only if the government would promise

to keep whites out of the Powder River basin. While the two sides negotiated this point at Fort Laramie in 1866, Col. Carrington marched past the proceedings with seven hundred troops bound for the Powder River. The Indians broke off the talks, and Red Cloud warned that if any whites moved north of Fort Connor (near modern Kaycee), the war would resume.

Carrington built two forts north of Red Cloud's line, and the war continued for two more years. The conflict included a major defeat of Carrington's troops at Fort Phil Kearny (see page 85), as well as skirmishes up and down the Bozeman Trail.

When the two parties finally made peace, the terms of the treaty stipulated that the government would shut down the Bozeman Trail, abandon the forts the army had built along the road, and forbid whites to pass through the northeast quarter of Wyoming. The treaty set aside the Powder River country as an Indian hunting ground and created a reservation for the Lakota composed of the entire western half of modern South Dakota. That reservation, "set apart for the absolute and undisturbed use and occupation of the Indians," included the Black Hills.

Expeditions of 1876

Because the territory included the Black Hills, the 1868 treaty didn't last long. Just six years later, in the summer of 1874, George Armstrong Custer led twelve hundred men into the Black Hills and found gold in large quantities. Recognizing that the Indians owned the land, the U.S. government spent almost two years trying to negotiate legal entry. The government at first offered to buy the land for $6 million, but the Lakota made a counteroffer: $600 million and a promise to feed and clothe the tribe for seven generations. Too much, the government said. How about a $400,000-per-year lease for the right to mine the gold? This the Indians refused. With legal remedies at a standstill, the government simply ordered the Indians to abandon the Black Hills and the Powder River country by January 31, 1876. If they did not leave, they would be considered hostile and open to attack. In short, the government was saying, Get off your land or we'll kill you. Thus began the last of the big Indian wars in the mountain West.

After the government's deadline passed, the army argued for a crushing winter campaign in the Powder River country. Proponents of the plan argued that the tribes could bring together no more than five hundred warriors and that winter was the best time to strike because their ponies would be weak from lack of forage.

On March 1, 1876, Gen. George Crook, with about one thousand men, marched north from Fort Fetterman in bitter cold. At night, temperatures plunged to forty degrees below zero. The men suffered terribly from the weather but reached the Powder River in southern Montana by March 17. There, Crook came across a mixed village of Lakota and Cheyenne and ordered Col. J. J. Reynolds to attack with six companies of cavalry. The fight lasted five hours. Reynolds's men captured the village, burned the tipis, and corraled the pony herd. But Crazy Horse counterattacked, drove them away, and managed to recapture most of the village's ponies. Crook, low on supplies, his men tormented by the cold, turned south and returned to Fort Fetterman.

This was not the smashing victory the army had envisioned. In the summer, the generals tried again, this time with a campaign strategy very similar to the one used by Connor in 1865. Like Connor, Crook marched north into the Powder River country, intending to link up with two other columns that would converge on the same area from the east and the west. The eastbound column was commanded by Col. John Gibbon. Brig. Gen. Alfred Terry commanded the westbound column, which included the Seventh

General George Crook in 1876. Crook's winter campaign against the Lakota in 1876 was a failure. *(University of Wyoming American Heritage Center)*

Cavalry under Lt. Col. George Armstrong Custer. It was going to be a rough summer for the whites in the Powder River country.

On June 17, Crook's command stopped for coffee on the banks of Rosebud Creek in southern

The legendary Lakota chief Sitting Bull, who foresaw defeat of the white forces at the Battle of the Little Big Horn, in 1876. *(University of Wyoming American Heritage Center)*

Montana. Suddenly, several hundred Lakota and Cheyenne warriors descended on the troops. The battle lasted six hours before the Indians withdrew, leaving Crook shaken and bloodied but in possession of the field. However, because of the large number of wounded men, Crook withdrew and called for reinforcements.

The Indians then moved on to the Little Big Horn where, on June 25, they surrounded and wiped out Custer and about 210 of his command as Custer prepared to attack their village. The Indians also killed fifty-three other soldiers from a second column that had attacked the village and been turned away.

The Indians broke up their camp after Custer's defeat, apparently believing that their great victory would be enough to convince the whites to leave them alone. However, during the rest of the summer, the fall, and the following winter, the army defeated the various bands one by one. Gen. Miles chased Sitting Bull across the Canadian border. Col. Ranald Mackenzie defeated Dull Knife near Hole-in-the-Wall country west of Kaycee, killing about thirty Cheyenne. (These Cheyenne walked through the snow, many of them naked or barefoot, seventy miles north to Crazy Horse's village on the Powder and were taken in.) By the spring of 1877, band after band returned to their reservation agencies to surrender. The war was over.

COWBOYS

After the Lakota, Cheyenne, and Arapaho had been cleared out of the Powder River country, cattle ranchers poured into the region and began to report astonishing profits. "Here was all the space of Texas with luxuriant grass and abundant water thrown in," wrote Struthers Burt in *Powder River: Let 'er Buck.*

> All you needed was a ranch house, a couple of bunkhouses, a few corrals, a field

or two of wild hay to cut for your work stock in winter. As for the rest of it, the horizon much farther than you could look was yours. You turned your cattle loose and saw them only twice a year: at the spring roundup when you branded your calves; at the fall roundup when you branded what had been missed in the spring, and cut your beef and shipped it. And, miraculously, each spring your herds had almost doubled.

By 1884, there were twenty big cattle companies on the North Platte and Powder rivers capitalized at $12 million. Half of them were owned by Scottish or English investors, often the second sons of dukes and lords or members of rich East Coast banking or industrial families. They came in on the Union Pacific in the early spring and spent a glamorous week or two hobnobbing with their chums in Cheyenne before riding out to their ranches for the spring roundup. During the summer they lounged around the Cheyenne Club drinking, dining, and playing tennis. In the fall they went back to their ranches for the second roundup and to hunt. Then it was back to Cheyenne for one more round of parties before taking off for the winter.

One absentee investor who made the grand tour was an Englishwoman named Rose Pender. She and her husband, James, went West in 1883 to have a look at the cattle operation they had invested in. They didn't like the look of the cows much, and the cowboys even less:

> I did not like the cowboys. They impressed me as brutal and cowardly, besides being utterly devoid of manners or good feeling . . . When we began to put up our tent, a work of much labor, as the ground was so hard and the pegs took so much driving in, not a man offered to help me. I mention this because we hear so much of the chivalrous cowboy and his great admiration and attention to everything in the shape

of a woman, or "lady," I ought to say. Well, I can only say that in England, Scotland or Ireland, the humblest laborer, gillie or lounger that walks would have come forward to offer at any rate to help a woman as a simple matter of courtesy.

CRAZY WOMAN CREEK

Two possible accounts of the naming of this creek include the story that a trader's wife went crazy after seeing her husband killed next to the stream and scalped by Indians. The other story tells of a surviving woman who witnessed the destruction of her Indian village.

Indians trying to close down the Bozeman Trail during the 1860s considered Crazy Woman Creek an excellent ambush site. They skirmished repeatedly with army troops about fifteen miles south of the interstate, where the Bozeman Trail crossed the creek (see page 73).

BUFFALO

Founded by cattlemen in 1879, the town was named when five early residents tossed their nominations into a hat and drew the hometown of a man from Buffalo, New York.

They weren't the first whites to consider making a living in the area. Perhaps the very first to do so was a French Canadian named Francois Laroque, who led an expedition into Wyoming in 1805 for Canada's North West Company. Though he intended to return to the Powder River country the following year, his employers had other ideas. They decided to concentrate on the Canadian fur trade instead and never sent Laroque back.

Unlike Laroque's superiors, American fur trappers did not neglect the Powder River and its tributaries. Besides offering an abundance of beaver, the country became a favorite wintering ground for the mountain men because there was plenty of game to shoot and eat—especially buffalo—as well as plenty of forage for their horses.

The Plains Indian tribes cherished this portion of the Powder River country and fought for several years to keep whites off its lush grasslands. One of the gentler attempts to convince whites to stay away took place near Buffalo. There, a trader named H. E. Palmer built a sod hut in 1866 and unloaded four wagonloads of goods. Within a week, a band of Cheyenne paid him a visit and gave him a choice: Leave the Powder River country or die. Palmer agreed to leave and so lived to watch the Cheyenne dismantle his hut and lay the sod back onto the prairie, grass side up. The Indians explained that the ground was virgin buffalo country and that no one had a right to tear it apart.

When the Indians were forced out of the Powder River region for good in the late 1870s, ranchers moved in to raise cattle, sheep, and more than a little hell.

BUFFALO AND THE JOHNSON COUNTY WAR

On April 9, 1892, Terrence Smith rode into town with startling news of a gun battle taking place at the KC Ranch, just south of modern Kaycee. Sheriff Red Angus swore in a twelve-man posse and galloped down to have a look but arrived long after the Invaders' private army of fifty men had killed Nate Champion and Nick Ray and burned down the cabins. When Buffalo got word of the killings and heard that the Invaders were heading north, it got ready to defend itself. Robert Foote flung open the doors of his general store to feed, arm, and clothe whatever men were willing to oppose the Invaders. Soon, men guarded all of the approaches to town and reinforcements kept arriving as news of the invasion spread throughout the county. The presence of these men convinced the Invaders to forgo their attack on Buffalo and instead fortify themselves at the TA Ranch a dozen miles south of town (see page 73).

While the fight went on at the TA, a large force was held in reserve at Buffalo because of rumors that a second band of Invaders might sweep down on the town. There was no second band, but after the surrender of the Invaders down at the TA there were still plenty of rumors to keep Buffalo mouths moving.

"Here in Buffalo all was excitement and unrest," a Buffalo newspaper reported. "Rumors of all descriptions, preposterous, ludicrous and probable, pervaded the atmosphere. No two men could start a conversation but what a crowd would soon gather around. Knots of men could be seen on all street corners, earnestly speculating on the outcome."

By then, the outcome in question was what would be done with the Invaders. Would there be a trial in Buffalo to hold them accountable for the murders of Champion and Ray, or would the Invaders' powerful friends manage to get them off the hook?

Two of the Invaders were arrested by Sheriff Angus and placed in the Buffalo jail. He tried to have the rest of the Invaders transferred from Fort McKinney to Buffalo in order to stand trial, but acting governor Amos Barber denied his request, saying the safety of the defendants could not be ensured. Barber then ordered Angus to turn over the two men in the Buffalo jail to the commander at Fort McKinney and asked that all the prisoners be shipped to Cheyenne. There would be no trial in Buffalo for the Invaders.

There was barely even a trial in Cheyenne, where feelings in favor of the Invaders ran high. The cattle lobby hired the best lawyers in the West, including Willis Van Devanter, who would

one day serve on the U.S. Supreme Court. The two trappers who had witnessed the shootings at the KC Ranch were spirited out of the state and hushed up. Because Johnson County was not paying the costs of room and board for the prisoners, the judge ordered them released. Nearly half of them were Texas mercenaries, and they caught the first train out for the Lone Star State, never to be seen here again. The trial was postponed once, and when it finally got underway, more than one thousand people were examined before a jury was selected. At that point, the prosecuting attorney from Johnson County threw in the towel. The case was dismissed.

FORT PHIL KEARNY

This fort was one of three built in 1866 to protect the Bozeman Trail. Its presence, in the heart of Powder River country, intensified the warfare that began in the early 1860s between whites and the Plains Indian tribes. Troops garrisoned here suffered in 1866 what would be the greatest defeat for the army in the West until

A sketch of Fort Phil Kearny as it appeared in 1866 during the war with Red Cloud and the Lakota over control of northeastern Wyoming. *(University of Wyoming American Heritage Center)*

General H. B. Carrington, who planned and built Fort Phil Kearny in 1866. The construction of that fort and others was supposed to protect travelers along the Bozeman Road. *(University of Wyoming American Heritage Center)*

Custer and his men were wiped out at the Little Big Horn ten years later. To reach the site of the fort, where an excellent visitors center now stands, take the 87/193 exit and follow the signs.

In 1866, Red Cloud, a renowned Lakota leader, had warned that if whites came north of Fort Connor, the Indians would oppose them. Red Cloud made good on his word. As soon as Col. Henry Carrington's troops staked out Fort Phil Kearny in July 1866, Indians began raiding it. They stampeded some of the fort's horses and killed two men in the force that rode out in hot pursuit. Before the month was out, they killed eighteen emigrants and other civilians within the territory that Carrington was supposed to protect with forts Phil Kearny and Reno. At Phil Kearny, the Indians probed and attacked and maneuvered. Troops frequently galloped off, to the relief of isolated lookouts and parties felling trees for the continuing construction of the fort. Sometimes the rescuers were too late. In mid-September, two members of a timber crew were killed and a third—wounded several times by arrows—dragged himself a half-mile before he was rescued, only to die the next day.

All in all, Carrington's position was tenuous. He was short of soldiers, and those he had were short of ammunition and armed with obsolete weapons, including muzzleloaders. By the end of autumn the Indians had run off with half of his horses, and there were so many warriors in the hills that men considered it suicidal to ride out from the fort alone.

Carrington bided his time. Experience fighting Indians had taught the army that winter was the best time to attack, when the tribes had settled in to wait out the cold weather and when their ponies were weak. Carrington wanted to spend the autumn building his fort and gathering supplies before striking out once winter fell.

What Carrington did not know was that the winter of 1866 was going to be very different. The Lakota and Cheyenne warriors had no intention of putting their feet up while the snow piled high around their lodges. They figured that if they allowed the whites to stay in the valley the game would disappear and winters from then on would be very tough indeed. They meant to fight all winter, and fight they did.

On December 6, they attacked a wood train. A rescue party rode out and relieved the train, but lost two men in the process. This skirmish was alarming because it came so late in the season. But it proved to be small beer compared with the battle that followed on December 21.

The Fetterman Fight

Capt. William J. Fetterman, a recent arrival to Fort Phil Kearny and the West, must have regarded the frequent violence around the fort as rinky-dink scuffling. He had fought in the Civil War, after all, facing a well-armed opponent commanded by some of the finest military minds of the century. He had risked his neck in engagements involving tens of thousands of men. No wonder he bragged that if given the command of eighty men he could ride unscathed through the Lakota country.

On December 21, 1866, Fetterman got the chance to make good on his boast. A wagon

William Judd Fetterman, the hotheaded army officer who galloped into one of the most successful Lakota ambushes in history. *(University of Wyoming American Heritage Center)*

train pulled out of the fort around 10:00 A.M. to bring in the last of the wood the troops needed to finish building the fort. About an hour later, a lookout signaled that the train had been attacked and that the wagons had been corralled. Fetterman took charge of an eighty-one-man relief force. As the men departed, Carrington ordered Fetterman not to proceed beyond Lodge Trail Ridge. The men galloped off into what would be the most successful Lakota ambush in history until Custer's Last Stand.

Throughout the Indian Wars, a favorite tactic of the Lakota was to detach a small decoy party to attack a superior force. The decoy party, apparently having made a horrible mistake, would then make a fighting retreat. The enemy, eager to exploit its apparent advantage, would follow the decoy party into an ambush where an overwhelming number of Lakota would rise and annihilate them. This is exactly what happened to Fetterman.

As Fetterman's force approached the beleaguered wagons, the decoys withdrew up Lodge Trail Ridge. Disobeying orders, Fetterman chased them over the crest. Soon, intense firing was heard from the other side of the ridge. The fort's commander, notified that the wagon train

had broken corral and that Fetterman had trotted over the ridge, sent out a second detachment of men to see what had happened. A rider soon came back with the message that the valley beyond the ridge was thick with Indians and that there was no sign of Fetterman's command.

They were all dead. Later that day, soldiers came across the site of the debacle and returned to the fort with forty-nine of the eighty-one bloody, mutilated bodies. The wood train returned safely, and the fort closed up for an anxious night.

Convinced that the Indians would soon attack the fort itself, Carrington paid a civilian three hundred dollars to make a perilous 236-mile ride to Fort Laramie in order to notify the army of what had happened and to carry a dispatch pleading for more troops and guns. The civilian, John "Portugee" Phillips, made it to Fort Laramie in time to break up the post's cheery Christmas party.

Meanwhile, Carrington led a large force over Lodge Trail Ridge to recover the rest of the bodies. The small number of men left guarding the fort were given chilling instructions on what to do with the women and children should the Indians attack and overwhelm the defenses: put them in the armory among the containers of gunpowder and shot and then blow them all up rather than allow them to be captured.

There was no attack. The women and children lived to see their husbands and fathers buried. There would be no winter campaign. There would be no major fight for months. The weather got so bad that snow drifted to the height of the fort's stockade and had to be shoveled away to keep the Indians from simply dropping in. The relief column from Fort Laramie did not start for more than a week, thanks to the intense cold and snow, and on the two-week march north one man froze to death.

Today, signs lead from the visitors center to

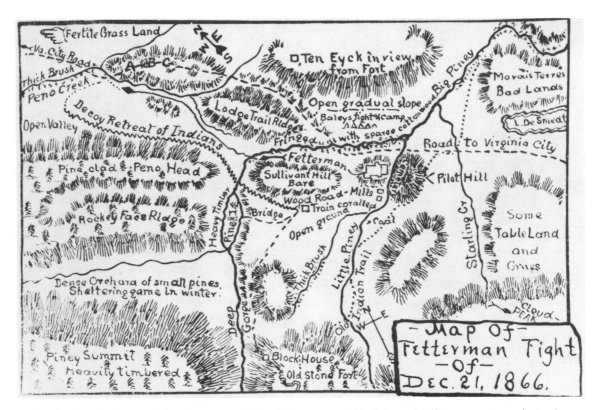

A sketched period map of the Fetterman Fight. Fetterman and his force of eighty-one men rode to the left of Fort Phil Kearny and followed a decoy party of Lakota over a ridge, where they were wiped out by an overwhelming force of Indian warriors. *(University of Wyoming American Heritage Center)*

the site of the Fetterman Fight. The monument, exhibit, and a fine interpretive trail lie on the fatal side of Lodge Trail Ridge.

THE WAGON BOX FIGHT

By the summer of 1867, Red Cloud and his Lakota, along with the northern Cheyenne, had strangled the Bozeman Trail. The truth of the Fetterman Fight would have been enough to discourage the most determined emigrants, but newspaper accounts of the battle were even more horrifying than the actual event. Emigrant traffic on the Bozeman Trail dried up. Those bound for Montana now took the long way around on the Oregon Trail through Idaho, pre-

ferring to arrive in Montana several weeks later rather than risk not arriving at all.

The forts along the trail, including Phil Kearny, remained occupied, but the soldiers in them went on the defensive. At Phil Kearny, the Indians constantly harassed the wood and hay crews that ventured from behind the stockade and that labored under heavy guard. In late July, one of the fort's officers, Capt. James Powell, fortified a position close to the camp of a wood crew working near the present town of Story. Powell built his barricade by lifting the boxes off of sixteen wagons and arranging them in a rough oval. At night, the livestock were kept in this corral. In case of an attack, everyone had orders to take cover behind the wagon boxes and fight until relief could be sent from the fort.

Although the Fetterman Fight had been a disaster for the garrison at Fort Phil Kearny, it had expedited the arrival of much-needed relief supplies. Six new companies of soldiers had marched through its gates during the winter, along with plenty of ammunition and repeating rifles. The new rifles were to prove their value shortly.

On the morning of August 2, a combined force of Lakota and Cheyenne attacked the wood crew near Story and the soldiers protecting it, splitting the whites into two groups. Some could not make it back to the wagon-box corral, so they hightailed it to the fort. Most made it. Meanwhile, the Indians concentrated their attack on the thirty-two men, mostly soldiers, who had holed up behind the wagon boxes.

In the past, Red Cloud's warriors had learned to stagger their attacks between volleys from the soldiers, whose muzzleloaders took time to reload. But the steady fire from new breech-loading rifles tore through the Indian ranks and broke up their charges. The battle continued through the morning. Three of the defenders were killed. So was an unknown number of Indians. Early in the afternoon the Indians shifted tactics. Rather than charge in waves, they rallied for a mass attack. Several hundred pounded up the hill in a wedge. The defenders fired away and dropped many of their foes, but not enough to stop the advance. The Indians kept coming and it looked as if they would overrun the position. Then a field howitzer opened fire on them, and the defenders could see a large relief force from the fort hurrying toward them. The Indians turned and ran back down the hill.

All together, six men from the fort were killed—three in the corral, three more in the initial attack or on the run back to the fort. No one knows how many Indians were killed. The defenders, who shared just one thousand rounds of ammunition, thought they had been attacked by as many as three thousand and that they had killed hundreds.

The Indians continued to raid along the Oregon Trail and also attacked Union Pacific workcrews. The federal government did not have the troops to protect the railroad line—its top priority—in addition to the Bozeman Trail. Troops were also needed to enforce the Reconstruction laws Congress had passed to bring the conquered Confederacy back into the Union. On top of all that, the Bozeman Trail would be obsolete as soon as the railroad opened its line through Wyoming.

Rather than continue to fight, the government decided to negotiate a settlement. In return for peace, it promised to abandon the three forts it had built to protect the Bozeman Trail, and it agreed to prohibit whites from setting foot north of the North Platte River and east of the Big Horn Mountains. This treaty, signed in 1868 at Fort Laramie, effectively turned over what is now the northeast quarter of Wyoming to the Indians. Red Cloud's warriors delighted in burning down the forts, but their joy would be short-lived. Just eight years later the government would seize the Black Hills and order the Indians out of Powder River country (for details, see page 81).

STORY

This summer resort town was named for either a Sheridan newspaper editor or for the celebrated Montana cattleman Nelson Story, who drove the first herd of Texas longhorns north through Wyoming in 1866. Nelson Story also drove cattle up the Bozeman Trail in 1867, a year when no one else dared to travel the trail other than heavily guarded army supply wagons.

SHERIDAN

Named by a settler in the early 1880s after the Civil War commander Gen. Phil Sheridan, the city did not grow much until the Chicago, Burlington & Quincy Railroad hammered tracks through the area in 1892.

Combined with nearby coal deposits, the railroad made it possible for Sheridan to become a coal production center. Its original and most enduring industry, though, was ranching. After the Plains Indians were forced out of the region in the 1870s, vast herds of cattle and then sheep poured into the Powder River country. Sheridan had its share of large cattle outfits that eventually clashed with the interests of small cattle ranchers and those who raised sheep. The same tensions that lay at the heart of the Johnson County War (see page 65) existed here but never came to such a furious boil. However, tensions between cattle and sheep interests did degenerate into violence near Sheridan.

The root of the problem was control of the open range. Cattle ranchers contended that sheep ruined grazing lands for cattle. Sheep ranchers argued that they had just as much right to graze their animals on the public lands as did cattle ranchers. In many areas of the state cattlemen declared wide areas of the public range off-limits to sheep. If sheep crossed the boundaries, raiders in the employ of the cattlemen often slaughtered the animals and occasionally killed those who tended them.

The first man killed in Wyoming's range war died near Sheridan on June 7, 1893. Cattleman John Adams ordered sheepman William Jones to keep his sheep off ranges near the Adams ranch. Jones refused to be bullied, a gunfight followed, and the sheepman killed the cattleman. Jones was tried for the killing, convicted of second-degree murder, and sentenced to twenty-two years in prison.

The range war between cattlemen and sheepmen would continue throughout Wyoming until 1912 and result in the deaths of eleven men and sixteen thousand sheep. The climax of the struggle came in 1909 on the other side of the Big Horn Mountains, near Ten Sleep (see page 156).

Some of the high life of the great cattle boom of the 1880s is preserved for the public at Trail End, a mansion built by John B. Kendrick, one of Wyoming's most powerful cattlemen, who went on to become governor and a U.S. senator. Main Street in Sheridan, with its well-preserved examples of prairie architecture, is listed on the Register of Historic Places.

CONNOR BATTLEFIELD

Located south of Ranchester, the battlefield marks the spot where soldiers under Gen. Patrick E. Connor surprised an Arapaho village in late August 1865, killing between thirty-five and sixty people (see page 101).

U.S. 85 breaks away from Interstate 25 several miles north of Cheyenne and runs across dry, broken country to the North Platte River. From there, it skirts the state's border north to Buckhorn. The stretch from Lingle to Buckhorn traverses a region crisscrossed by thousands of stagecoaches during the Black Hills gold rush of the 1870s and 1880s. In addition to threading its way through that legacy, U.S. 85 also turns up stories about cowboys, coal miners, outlaws, and the range war between sheep and cattle interests.

THE STAGE LINE

From 1876 to 1887, the highly skilled drivers of the Cheyenne and Black Hills stage line guided their four-horse teams from the relatively cosmopolitan streets of young Cheyenne to the raucous and bawdy clamor of the Black Hills boomtowns of Custer and Deadwood, South Dakota. The route led almost directly north from Cheyenne, where miners, prospectors, and the riffraff that fed off their labors could step off the Union Pacific line and book passage for the Black Hills. The first leg of the stage route to Fort Laramie followed a well-worn path that had been in use for years before the gold rush began. It is now traced by I-25 as far as Wheatland. From there, it struck northeast along the banks of the Laramie River to the old fort. North of the fort, various routes branched off into a network of trails that ran almost as far north in Wyoming as modern Sundance. Indian attacks, holdups by bandits, swollen rivers, blizzards, and other conditions influenced the route taken at any given time. In the early days, when the prospecting, gambling, and drinking centered around Custer, most of the wagons crossed the Wyoming border northeast of Lusk. Later, when the excitement shifted to Deadwood, the wagons pushed farther north in Wyoming before heading east. Much

of the latter route lies close to U.S. 85, beginning at Lusk.

The early wagon routes from Cheyenne to the Black Hills were blazed by the miners themselves and then improved upon and modified by bullwhackers—the drivers of large freight wagons who hauled supplies north for the gold diggers. Bullwhackers ran wagons to Custer during the winter of 1875–76. The first passenger coach left Cheyenne on January 27, 1876, under the banner of the Cheyenne and Black Hills Stage, Mail and Express Line. It was the first of a stream of fast coaches that plied the rough country between Cheyenne and the goldfields for the next eleven years.

GOLD AND SILVER TONGUES OF THE FORKED VARIETY

The story of the Cheyenne and Black Hills stage line starts about eighteen months before the departure of that first coach—in the summer of 1874, when Custer's expedition found large quantities of gold in the Black Hills. For white civilization, Custer's announcement came as tremendous news. It gave thousands of hopeful prospectors a solid chance to strike it rich. It gave traders of all classes—from bank presidents to whores—a good shot at sweeping some of the new wealth into their own pockets. And it pumped new life into the shaky frontier economies of communities along the transportation routes to the Black Hills, especially Cheyenne's.

To the Plains Indians, Custer's news was about as welcome as a smallpox epidemic. They knew what gold, and the whites' appetite for the metal, could mean to their way of life. Already, gold strikes in California, Colorado, and Montana had brought waves of miners and settlers to the West. Their presence had disrupted and then largely destroyed the buffalo herds that the Plains Indians depended on for food. Gold had

Lieutenant Colonel George Armstrong Custer. *(University of Wyoming American Heritage Center)*

pushed Indians off lands that by tradition and even by treaty belonged to them. In Wyoming just ten years earlier, it had touched off a major war over the Bozeman Trail, which had been built through prime hunting lands as a shortcut to the Montana goldfields. That war, sometimes called the First Sioux War, had smoldered until 1868. It ended in a victory for the Indians and a treaty that forbade whites from the Powder River country and the Black Hills.

After the 1874 discovery of gold, prospectors poured into the forbidden lands, squatting on and working their claims and even building log cabins in the Custer area. The prospectors, like the men in Custer's expedition, were clearly trespassing and the government did make some effort to keep them out. Gen. Phil Sheridan issued an order to all military posts on the approaches to the Black Hills to stop any prospect-

ing party that ventured onto Indian land, arrest the group's leaders, and burn its wagons and supplies. The order did not do much to keep miners out of the Black Hills, however.

When the U.S. government failed to negotiate legal entry to the goldfields, it simply disregarded the treaty it had signed and sent in troops to kick the Indians off the land. Thus was the path cleared for the Cheyenne and Black Hills stage line. (For more about the conflict of the 1870s, see page 81.)

THE COACHES

Shortly after the first coaches began making the run between Cheyenne and the Black Hills, the stage line's superintendent, Luke Voorhees, supplemented his fleet of vehicles with thirty of the finest overland stagecoaches available. Built by the firm of Abbot and Downing of Concord, New Hampshire, these fine examples of nineteenth century craftsmanship arrived in Cheyenne just six weeks after Voorhees placed the order.

One of the Concord coaches that made the trip along the Cheyenne and Black Hills stage route in the 1870s and 1880s. *(University of Wyoming American Heritage Center)*

Painted a cheerful red with yellow running gear and ornamental scrollwork, each Concord had three cushioned seats and enough room for nine passengers. Two more passengers could sit next to the driver on the bench out front and, if traffic was especially heavy, as many as nine more could travel on the coach's rooftop. Luggage was stacked onto the back of the coach and protected by a canvas tarp.

The Passengers

For the 250-mile run between Cheyenne and Custer, first-class passengers paid twenty dollars, second-class fifteen dollars, and third-class ten dollars. The trip usually took about forty-eight hours in good weather and from sixty to seventy-two hours in bad. Every eight miles or so the coach stopped to change horses. Every forty miles or so it stopped to change drivers. At many of the stations, and at roadhouses along the way, passengers could buy a meal, spend the night, get liquored by the bartender, shellacked by a professional gambler, comforted by a hooker, and maybe knocked senseless by a local cowboy.

Through the years, passengers of all descriptions stepped aboard in Cheyenne. There were miners, of course, with supplies and gear they may have bought in Cheyenne. But there were also doctors and lawyers, land speculators and sheriffs, prostitutes and gamblers, gunfighters and grocers, bartenders, bouncers, pimps, faro dealers, bankers, and butchers. Many rolled into Deadwood or Cheyenne with tall tales about shoot-outs and confrontations with robbers.

Outlaws

Bandits were thick on the road between Cheyenne and Deadwood, especially during the early years of the stage line and especially north of Fort Laramie. Their targets were fat, easy to hit, and the scene of their crimes lay far away from the nearest outpost of law and order.

Sometimes the take seemed pretty meager. Only thirteen dollars could be scraped off the passengers of one northbound coach in the summer of 1877. Competition among the robbers also led them well past the point of diminishing returns. The gangs got so thick in 1877 that some coaches were stopped two and even three times en route.

The bandits were not without a sense of humor. At the height of their power, they sent Luke Voorhees a request to stop locking the strongboxes into the coaches. The locks merely hindered the process of plundering and wasted much valuable time and trouble for both robbers and robbed. Also, could Voorhees please send them a gold scale? Dividing the stuff by spoon wasn't always satisfactory.

RAWHIDE BUTTES

As U.S. 85 makes its way north from the isolated town of Jay Em, the eastern slopes of Rawhide Buttes swing into view, forested hills to the northwest that look nearly black against the golden grasses of the prairie. They were long favored as a camping area by Indians and fur trappers.

According to local legend, the name dates from the great wave of westward migration. Sometime during that era a particularly rabid emigrant rolled into view, vowing to kill the first Indian he saw. Unfortunately, the first to cross his path was a woman. True to his word, however, the man drew a bead on her with his rifle and shot her dead. The act so enraged his companions that they made no objection when the woman's friends and relatives came for revenge. Rather than shooting the man outright, the Indians skinned him alive and stretched his hide on a nearby hillside. Thus Rawhide Buttes.

Though this story is no doubt apocryphal,

some wagon trains did travel under the stated policy of shooting any and all Indians on sight, no matter how peaceful they appeared to be.

Mormon leader Brigham Young blamed this sort of policy for touching off the very Indian depredations that worried emigrants. Wrote Young, in 1857:

> A company of some three or four hundred returning Californians . . . travelled these roads last spring to the eastern States, shooting at every Indian they could see. Hence the Indians regard all white men alike as their enemies, and kill and plunder whenever they can do so with impunity, and often the innocent suffer for the deeds of the guilty. It is hard to make an Indian believe that the whites are his friends and the Great Father wishes to do them good when, perhaps, the very next party which crosses their path shoots them down like wolves.

LUSK

Although Lusk wasn't founded until the railroad arrived in 1886, plenty of activity had swirled around the site for about twenty years before that. Hundreds of thousands of Texas longhorn cattle had passed by on the Texas Trail, just three miles east of town, on their way to open range in northern Wyoming, the Dakotas, and Montana. The Cheyenne and Black Hills stage line also ran through the Lusk vicinity, hauling thousands of people to and from the goldfields.

Not all the miners who rolled north out of Cheyenne had their sights set on the Black Hills. Some prospected in the Lusk area and produced a short-lived, though robust, boom in silver. The mines were dug into Silver Cliff, just west of town, and eastern money built a mill here. But it wasn't long before the eastern money dried up, paychecks started to bounce, and the venture failed.

With so many cowboys, miners, bullwhackers, gamblers, and the like either passing through or taking up residence, dustups inevitably broke out. One of the most serious boiled over in January 1887 after the local newspaper speculated that a recently arrived cowhand named Bill McCoy might actually be an outlaw wanted in Texas for murder. McCoy naturally took offense. He complained bitterly and drunkenly until the sheriff finally told him to get out of town. McCoy heeded the sheriff's advice, but not before he shot the sheriff in the head.

During World War I, oil was discovered north of Lusk. It kicked off another boom and pumped the town's population to ten thousand before the wells dried up and Lusk went back to its more stable status as a livestock center.

FEATHER LEGS GRAVE

In 1876, just as the Black Hills gold rush hit its stride, a woman named Mom Shephard opened a saloon along the Cheyenne-Deadwood Trail, about ten miles southwest of Lusk. She ran the place with a man named Dangerous Dick Davis, and both were reputed to be outlaws who had fled vigilantes in Louisiana. Shephard got her colorful nickname, "Feather Legs," from a pair of bright red pantalettes that tied off at the ankles and ruffled furiously in the wind when she galloped her horse across the flats. One wag said it made her look like a feather-legged chicken, and the term stuck.

In 1879, a neighbor found Mother Feather Legs shot to death. Dangerous Dick and Feather Legs's money were gone. Later, vigilantes caught up with Dangerous Dick in Louisiana. Just before they strung him up, he supposedly confessed to the Feather Legs shooting. A monument to Mother Feather Legs stands at the site of her old roadhouse, several miles south of U.S. 20/18 on a gravel road. Ask locally for directions.

Built in 1868 as a military outpost, Hat Creek Station became a stop on the Cheyenne and Black Hills stage line during the Black Hills gold rush of the 1870s and 1880s. Located about fifteen miles north of modern-day Lusk, this stage station stood at the edge of the most dangerous portion of the route. Bandits routinely robbed stagecoaches that ran north of this point. *(University of Wyoming American Heritage Center)*

SPANISH DIGGINGS

Farther west of Lusk, in quarries that eventually hollowed out an area ten miles wide by forty miles long, prehistoric people dug what could be called Wyoming's first strip mine. Starting about five thousand years ago, they came from great distances to excavate a distinctive type of purplish quartzite particularly well suited for making the points of spears, arrows, knives, and so forth. Those who came for it probably lived elsewhere and stayed only as long as it took them to collect what they needed. They were the first in a long line of people who came to Wyoming to extract something of value and then headed back home. Their quarries are known as the Spanish Diggings because the cowboys who found them in the 1870s believed the pits had been dug by Spaniards looking for gold.

Most of the quarries lie on private ground. Ask locals for directions to accessible sites.

HAT CREEK STAGE STATION

About fifteen miles north of Lusk a paved road runs due east for about six miles, picking up the Cheyenne-Deadwood stage route and crossing Sage Creek just a few miles north of the site of Hat Creek Stage Station.

The station was established first as a military outpost in 1868 by soldiers ordered to enforce the Fort Laramie Treaty of 1868, which prohibited whites from entering the northeast quarter of present Wyoming. After the U.S. government reneged on its treaty commitments and seized the Black Hills, this outpost became a station on the Cheyenne and Black Hills stage line. The soldiers were supposed to build their fort on Hat Creek, in modern Nebraska, but they got lost and built it here on Sage Creek instead.

During the stagecoach era, Hat Creek Station stood at the edge of the most dangerous section of the road. From here north, bluffs and broken country concealed bandits and funneled stagecoaches into predictable paths where they were easily ambushed and from which it was difficult for them to escape.

NICKNAMES

In these parts, nicknames flew as thick as bullets in a bungled stagecoach robbery. The Dunc Blackburn gang, which committed many of the holdups near Hat Creek Station, included Lame Johnny and a fellow named Wall. Persimmons Bill shot and killed a stock detective named Stuttering Brown in 1875. Sourdough Dick worked as a stock tender at the stage station on Old Woman Creek. And all of these gentlemen could have ridden down the road for a drink with Dangerous Dick and Mother Feather Legs.

REDBIRD

During the twenty years that straddled the turn of the century, violent conflicts between cattle ranchers and sheep ranchers flared all over Wyoming. It was a range war, fought to decide which animal would graze on land that at least in theory belonged to everybody.

One incident in the general struggle took place about five miles north of Redbird in March 1903. Seven masked men tied up a herder, burned his wagon, killed his horses, and slaughtered five hundred sheep. The range war between the sheep and cattle factions continued until 1912 and killed a total of eleven men and sixteen thousand sheep (see page 149).

MULE CREEK JUNCTION

Northwest of town, at the confluence of Lance Creek and the Cheyenne River, stood a stage station that became a favorite target of bandits. The river crossing there, with steep banks on both sides, made it a terrific place for outlaws to hide and wait for stagecoaches fording the river. People called it Robbers' Roost.

One night in the autumn of 1877, Jack Bowman was riding shotgun on a northbound stage that was stopped by the Dunc Blackburn gang near Robbers' Roost. He later recalled the incident:

> The night was dark and we could see no one . . . George didn't pull up quick enough, and we heard the gun locks click. They halloed to George to "make that man get down." I at once recognized the voice of Blackburn, as he used to work for me, so I replied, "Oh, no. You don't want me to get down." They came up to the coach and inquired who in — I was, and ordered me to get down. I laughed at Dunc and he recognized me. They pulled off their masks, and passed up a flask of whiskey, and then wanted to know if they [the passengers] had any money. I said "No," but told them I had some. They replied, "Oh —, we don't want your money."

Before riding into the night, members of the gang complained about how the profits from holdups had dropped off lately and said they were thinking about giving up the bandit's life. Blackburn and one of his accomplices were later captured near Green River.

MORRISEY: GHOST LIGHTS

Fanciers of UFOs might be interested to know that, during the 1930s, motorists in the Morrisey area ran off the road to avoid hitting vivid tumbling lights. The "ghost lights" were said to roll across the ground like tumbleweeds.

NEWCASTLE: JUNCTION WITH U.S. 16

As the center of an anthracite-coal mining area before the turn of the century, Newcastle was an important terminus on the Chicago, Burlington & Quincy Railroad (see page 99).

FLYING V RANCH

About seven miles north of Newcastle the highway passes the Flying V Ranch, where an imposing stone building stands as a monument to those who discovered the anthracite-coal deposits at Cambria. Built from granite blocks, the building stands at the bottom of a hill on the east side of the road. It looks a bit like an English estate home where an ambitious do-it-yourselfer has run amuck. However, it was the site of much lavish entertaining in the 1890s, and it still feeds summertime visitors.

CAMBRIA

The coal mines at Cambria, about two miles west of the Flying V Ranch and accessible by foot, thrived for nearly four decades. A ghost town today, Cambria drew miners from a wide variety of ethnic backgrounds, including Austrians, Italians, and Swedes. In the thirty-nine years that Cambria's mines were in operation, they dug out 12 million tons of high-grade anthracite coal—an unusual variety in this part of the country, where soft, low-sulphur bituminous coal is the rule. Much of Cambria's production was converted into coke and shipped to a reduction plant in South Dakota.

CANYON SPRINGS ROBBERY

In the autumn of 1878, five robbers held up an armored stagecoach that had stopped at a sleepy stage station called Canyon Springs, about five miles east of modern Four Corners on Beaver Creek. The coach contained twenty-seven thousand dollars in gold dust, ingots, and cash. It was the biggest and most daring robbery in the history of the Cheyenne and Black Hills stage line.

Plagued by bandits, the stage company had built an ironclad coach to make the weekly treasure run from Deadwood to Cheyenne in 1878. Locals soon dubbed it "The Monitor," after the ironclad Civil War gunboat. All that iron made for a heavy coach. To keep the weight down, the makers refrained from lining the roof with metal plates. This was not such a great idea, as it turned out.

On the afternoon of September 26, 1878, the iron coach hove into the yard at Canyon Springs in order to change horses. Usually the stock tender, William Miner, stood waiting to make the seven-minute change. But on this day he was being held captive in the grain room of the stable by five men who had knocked the chinking from between the logs of the building and were now training their rifles on the stage.

When Miner did not answer the driver's calls, one of the stagecoach men stepped down and prepared to block the rear wheels of the coach. A volley of gunfire erupted from the stable, and the man, Gale Hill, was struck in the arm and chest and fell to the ground—but not before he managed to wound two of the robbers.

The gunfire continued and a bullet ripped through the unlined roof of the coach, dazing one of three guards traveling inside. Try as they might, the other two could not get a good shot through the portholes at any of the robbers. So they opened the door and fled across the road toward a tree. One of them, Hugh Campbell, did not make it. He was shot dead in the road. The other, Scott Davis, made it to the tree and kept firing.

One of the robbers ordered the driver down and, using him as a shield, advanced on Davis at the tree. Seeing that he could not kill the robber without killing the driver, Davis ran off into the woods and went for help.

The robbers tied up all of the stage men and broke into the safe with a sledgehammer and a cold chisel. They escaped with twenty-seven thousand dollars in gold bullion, cash, and jewelry, but several suspects were lynched later. The beaten-up safe is on display at the museum in Lusk.

Along this meandering route across northern Wyoming, army troops marched during the 1870s to seize land that belonged by treaty to Indians. Outlaws held up stagecoaches. A Newcastle hotelier drilled the mayor with a forty-five for trying to clean up the town. The road runs intermittently from the South Dakota border through the Powder River country and over the Big Horn Mountains. The first leg slants up to Moorcroft, where it joins I-90 to Gillette and then strikes off in a wide curve that eventually intersects again with I-90 at Buffalo. From there, the drive over the Big Horn Mountains is one of the most appealing alpine journeys in the state.

WHOOPUP CANYON

This canyon, whose name has a distinct cowboy ring to it, lies about three and a half miles west of the border and about a mile south of the road. Cowboys did in fact name the canyon for the spring floods that came a-whoopin' through the narrow passage. Indian petroglyphs depicting a hunt mark the canyon's soft sandstone walls, which are also pocked with caves and fissures.

In the canyon lies a branch of the Cheyenne and Black Hills stage line. The canyon's tight walls made it a natural place for bandits to ambush the coaches that traveled back and forth from the Dakota goldfields. (For more about the Cheyenne and Black Hills stage line, see page 91.)

STOCKADE BEAVER CREEK

Close to where Highway 16 crosses Stockade Beaver Creek, a government geologist named Walter P. Jenney built a log cabin and a stockade in 1875 while surveying the Black Hills area for gold. Jenney's party, as well as several bands of prospectors, had trespassed on

land the government had ceded to the Lakota (often called Sioux) in the Fort Laramie Treaty of 1868. Gold fever and the government's ultimate unwillingness to recognize a treaty just six years old kicked off the last of the big wars with the Plains Indians (see page 81).

Jenney's stockade was moved in 1933 from its site on the creek to the courthouse in Newcastle. It is a national historic site.

TUBB TOWN

Abandoned now, Tubb Town got its start about eight miles from the border in 1888 when De Loss Tubbs of Custer, South Dakota, built a store here. Another man built a saloon nearby, starting with the essential feature first—the bar—and then enclosing the altar to demon rum with walls and a ceiling. The bartender apparently had a firm grasp on the sentiments of his flock. The town's first ordinance provided for a toll upon strangers "sufficient to set 'em up to the bunch."

Residents abruptly abandoned Tubb Town the following autumn when the first lots went up for sale in Newcastle, which was right on the railroad tracks.

NEWCASTLE

This town was established in 1889 as a terminus for the Chicago, Burlington & Quincy Railroad (now the Burlington Northern) and is named for the famous English coal port. The name was appropriate, because coal mining played a big part in the early development of the Newcastle area. Frank Mondell, then a railroad employee, discovered rich deposits of anthracite coal nearby while helping to determine a route for the new tracks. The railroad changed its course to take advantage of the coal and soon began mining in Cambria, about ten miles northwest of Newcastle.

In its early days Newcastle was a rowdy place, combining the raucous clamor of a railroad boomtown with the hard-nosed revelry of miners and cowboys on the loose. Frank Mondell, the town's first mayor and later a U.S. representative, described early Newcastle as "the banner wide-open frontier town" of its day.

Mondell came in for a large measure of its frontier violence when he tried to tone the place down a bit in 1890. He and the city council gave the marshal a list of twenty people to run out of town within twenty-four hours. But a hotelkeeper objected. He wanted Mondell and the marshal to wait to kick them out until several gamblers on the list won enough to pay off their hotel bills. The hotelkeeper got so riled up about the impending departure of his undesirable guests that he shot Mondell with a .45 caliber pistol. Mondell survived the attack but carried the slug near his spine for most of his life.

MOORCROFT

For information on Moorcroft or to pick up the I-90 route at this point, see page 78.

GILLETTE

From Gillette, Highway 16 runs north and then west through country where the Lakota, Cheyenne, and Arapaho tribes fought army troops in two major campaigns—one in 1865 and one in 1876 (see page 79).

ARVADA: FIREWATER

An early cow town, Arvada once bragged an artesian well that tapped both water and natural gas. The materials bubbled up through a pipe, and locals enjoyed thrilling passing tourists by igniting the "water" and drinking from the pipe.

BUFFALO

Founded in 1879 by cattle ranchers, Buffalo soon gained a reputation as the rustler's capital of Wyoming and became the target of an invasion by a private army financed and directed by some of the most powerful cattle ranchers in the state (see page 84).

As it approaches the Big Horn Mountains, U.S. 14 passes the site of an important 1865 battle between whites and Indians over control of the Powder River Valley. After climbing through the Big Horns, the road empties out onto the plains of the Big Horn basin and eventually leads through Cody and connects with the roads of Yellowstone National Park.

RANCHESTER: THE CONNOR BATTLEFIELD

On August 28, 1865, army troops and Arapaho Indians clashed on the north bank of the Tongue River, just a half-mile south of the present town of Ranchester. This battle was the only major confrontation between whites and Indians in a poorly coordinated three-pronged attack that Gen. Patrick E. Connor launched that year in Powder River country.

In the Battle of Tongue River, Connor surprised an Arapaho village of fifteen hundred people who had not been hostile before. His men killed between thirty-five and sixty warriors, destroyed the village and all of the Indians' winter supplies, and captured their herd of some five hundred horses. Eight of Connor's men were killed.

A few days later, as Connor made his way down the Tongue River into Montana, he received word that a road-building crew had been attacked just a few miles from the site of the battle. He sent back a relief party. The road-builders, often called the Sawyer Expedition, had lost three men while corraled but were brought through safely to Montana.

Connor's Powder River Expedition was a disappointment to everyone but the Indians who opposed it. The fizzled campaign was one of several major failures to enforce the U.S. government's will on the tribes during the years 1865–68. In the end, it helped to convince the

government to seek a negotiated settlement. (For more about the Powder River expeditions of 1865 and 1876, see pages 79–83.)

DAYTON

In 1887, the good citizens of Dayton banished an obnoxious drunk from their presence and in so doing kicked off a brief Indian scare in the neighboring town of Sheridan. Once outside the warm embrace of his favorite Dayton saloon, the drunk had to find another way to fend off the cold. Fortunately, he came across a haystack, which he set on fire, and then he sat back to enjoy the soothing effects of the blaze. The flames lit up the sky and could be seen from quite a distance. A group of travelers making their way toward Sheridan saw the glow and concluded that the fire could mean just one thing: that the Crow Indians had ridden down from their reservation in southern Montana and were in the process of razing Dayton and scalping its inhabitants. Naturally, their news alarmed the citizens of Sheridan, who turned out in their pajamas for a defense of the town. They barricaded public buildings and made sure families from the outlying ranches got word of the impending Indian raid and were brought to town safely. Nothing happened, of course, except that the drunk probably got more sleep than anybody in Sheridan.

In 1911, Dayton put another feather in Wyoming's feminist cap by electing Susan Wissler mayor. For a while, locals bragged her up as the world's first woman mayor.

BURGESS JUNCTION

Here, U.S. 14 splits. Regular old U.S. 14 heads southwest over Granite Pass and down the Shell Canyon to Greybull. Alternate U.S. 14 loops across the northern perimeter of the Big

Horn basin and runs through the ranching and farming communities of Lovell, Byron, and Powell before rejoining the main branch of the highway at Cody. The alternate route passes the site of Heart Mountain Relocation Center, where Americans of Japanese descent were confined during World War II. It also leads past a stone monument called Medicine Wheel, an archeological mystery (see page 160).

State 59 connects I-25 with I-90 and runs through the most productive coal lands in Wyoming. It also crosses land where some of the state's first ranchers raised their cattle, and where one of the biggest names in the fur trade happened upon a grizzly bear that tore his scalp to shreds.

DOUGLAS

A cow town and supply center for some of the earliest ranches in the state, Douglas's history revolves around cowboys and the soldiers who lived at nearby Fort Fetterman.

One of the earliest cattle ranchers in the state, John Hunton, spent much of his life in the vicinity. During the Civil War he had fought for the Confederacy. After the war, Hunton moved West to bullwhack freight trains between Nebraska City and Fort Laramie and ended up buying the S O herd. When the army pulled out of Fort Laramie in 1890, he bought the place and lived there for many years.

BURLINGTON NORTHERN RAILROAD

This 126-mile stretch of Burlington Northern Railroad that sometimes runs beside the highway was built during the 1970s to carry low-sulphur coal out of the vast strip mines that were established south of Gillette in the wake of the OPEC oil embargo.

SHEEP-CATTLE CONFLICT

Throughout Converse County during the years 1893–94, cattlemen and sheepmen fought several skirmishes over who would control the range. The cattlemen marked boundaries on public land that sheep were not to cross, but the sheepmen disregarded these so-called deadlines. Raiders wearing gunnysack masks swept down in retribution, shooting or clubbing sheep to death and sometimes wounding and killing those who tended the flocks.

The most serious altercation in this area involved cowboy Virgil Turner, who argued with a sheepherder out on the range. The sheepherder grabbed a rifle and ran behind a rock, whereupon Turner charged on horseback and killed him. Turner was acquitted on the grounds of self-defense, which goes to show what sort of clout the cattle interests had in the 1890s.

BILL

This little town was named for four men, all Bills, whose homesteads came together more or less at this point.

About twenty miles north of Bill, and long before there were any towns in Wyoming, Jedediah Smith was out front of a small group of mountain men heading toward the Powder River. As they pushed through the thick brush and narrow ravines, a huge grizzly bear charged down the slope of a ridge, slammed Smith to the ground, and bashed him around before the others could drive it away. The bear had broken some of Smith's ribs and cut up his head pretty badly. James Clyman, a fellow trapper, described Smith's inuries in his 1823 journal: "The bear had taken nearly all his head in his capacious mouth close to his left eye on one side and close to his right ear on the other and laid the skull bare to near the crown of the head . . . One of his ears was torn from his head out to the outter rim."

Clyman repaired this ear by stitching it back in place, or as near to back in place as possible, after "laying the lacerated parts together as nice as I could with my hands."

It took Smith about ten days to heal up and feel ready to travel.

WRIGHT

Wright is a coal-mining town that sprang up during the coal boom of the 1970s and still lies at the center of Wyoming's production of low-sulphur coal. Demand for Wyoming's coal swelled during the 1970s in the wake of the OPEC oil embargo and the clean-air legislation passed in 1977. After a droop in the 1980s, demand surged again with passage of the 1990 Clean Air Act, which tightened standards for sulphur-dioxide emissions from the nation's coal-fired electric power plants.

There are rich coal fields throughout the Powder River basin, but the strippable deposits lie in an arcing ribbon roughly sixty miles long and five miles wide. The nation's seven largest mines operate along that black ribbon, strip-mining the mineral from veins that run as thick as seventy feet.

Environmentalists are concerned that the companies have destroyed vast tracts of grassland habitat for elk and deer and that the mining could threaten the quality of groundwater. The coal companies, though, say they comply with federal regulations that require them to save and replace the topsoil and rocks they remove to get at the coal.

GILLETTE: JUNCTION WITH I-90

The presence of coal in the Gillette area has been apparent for many years. Occasionally, deposits near the surface of the ground have caught fire. For information on Gillette or to pick up the I-90 route at this point, see page 78.

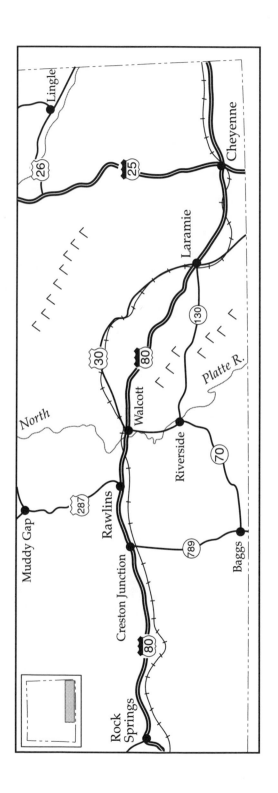

UNION PACIFIC COUNTRY

UNION PACIFIC COUNTRY: INTRODUCTION

From Pine Bluffs in the east to Evanston in the west, a crucial event dominates the history along Wyoming's southern highways: the construction of the nation's first transcontinental railroad, the Union Pacific. As the building crews shoveled, blasted, and hammered their way over the mountains and across the desert in the late 1860s, they not only graded the land, spanned gorges, and set track, they played the central role in three of the most exciting years of Wyoming's past. They drew a flock of lowlifes, saloon-keepers, gamblers, and whores that followed them across the state like gulls behind a fishing boat. In their wake they left a short but lively history of shootings and lynchings, garrotings and druggings, riots, brawls, broken noses, and gouged eyeballs. As this motley collection of hell-on-wheels characters made its way across the state, Wyoming's first towns and cities sprang up. Some, such as Cheyenne and Laramie, survived and prospered. Others fell back into the alkaline dust. After the railroad's construction ended in 1869, the state's population had increased eightfold (to a not-so-whopping 8,100) and the groundwork had been laid for the livestock, mining, and lumber industries. These tracks, and the branch lines that grew from them in later decades, lie at the heart of Wyoming's development as a territory and a state.

THE CREW

When construction of the Union Pacific began outside Omaha in 1863, the railroad employed only about 250 construction workers and

A construction supervisor stands on the freshly laid track bed of the Union Pacific Railroad. The ties, hewn flat on one side, have not yet been packed with dirt. *(University of Wyoming American Heritage Center)*

failed to lay a single rail in eighteen months of labor. By the time the crew had reached Wyoming, four years later, its ranks had swelled to several thousand and laying track had developed into a highly efficient process that routinely pushed the railhead forward a couple of miles a day. Following the route laid out by surveyors, the graders moved ahead of all the other crews. They blasted out rock where they had to, filled in depressions, and cut through the hills with picks, shovels, and wheelbarrows. Next came the ties—heavy timbers cut from the neighboring hills and mountains and hewed or sawed flat on one side—which were set into place on the roadbed. The track-layers came last, busily hammering down rail after rail.

If you could have been at the very end of the line in 1867 to watch the men set rails into place, you would have seen a light horse-drawn car clatter up to the crew with a small load of rails. Two men would grab the end of a rail and start dragging it off the wagon while others fell in behind, each taking a share of the burden until the entire rail cleared the car. Then the men would run forward and set it in place. The gaugers, spikers, and bolters followed, fastening each rail to the ties with spikes. One newspaper correspondent who witnessed the process wrote that three blows sunk each spike. Since there were ten spikes to the rail, four hundred to the mile, and eighteen hundred miles to San Francisco, the sledgehammers would have to swing 21 million times before the line would span the continent.

Many of the men were Irish, and most had fought during the Civil War on one side or the other. One in four laid track. The others were graders, teamsters, herdsmen, cooks, bakers, blacksmiths, bridge-builders, carpenters, masons, and clerks. They made about three dollars a day— good wages for the time.

Jack Casement was the boss. A former army general who had commanded a Union division during the Civil War, Casement had worked in Michigan and Ohio on track-building gangs. He was a short man, just over five feet tall, but he cut an impressive figure all along the line. He had a full black beard, and in cold weather he liked to wear a cossack cap and fur-trimmed coat and to carry a bullwhip.

The track-laying crew lived and worked out of an eighty-car train that crept along behind the men. A flatcar at the head of the train carried their tools. There was a forge for blacksmithing and a complete feed store and saddle shop for those who worked with horses. In another car, butchers processed cattle from herds driven alongside the lengthening track. The cuts were prepared in the train's kitchen car and served up in a dining car where the plates were nailed to the table to prevent theft. The men sopped up the gravy with bread baked in the bakery car and slept in three long passenger cars crammed with triple-decker bunks. Some men escaped the stifling bunks by pitching tents on top of the cars, and some even built small wooden shacks up top that looked like doghouses. The entire outfit was pushed forward by three wood-burning locomotives.

HELL ON WHEELS

As the work crews made their way west, towns sprang up every fifty or sixty miles at sites where railroad supervisors identified a railhead. Virtually overnight, gamblers, land speculators, saloon-keepers, thieves, pimps, and their charges pulled up stakes at the previous railhead and moved forward, some by rail and some by wagon. By the time the rowdy track-layers caught up with them, these mobile entrepreneurs would be

By the time the Union Pacific crews reached Wyoming, track-laying had developed into a highly efficient process that routinely pushed the railhead forward a couple of miles a day. Many of the crew members were Irish, most were Civil War veterans. They made good money for the times—three dollars a day. *(University of Wyoming American Heritage Center)*

all set to shuffle the deck for three-card monte, pour shots of 100 proof tonsil oil, or stand ready to help some of the gents out of their trousers. Newspapers printed up the sordid details of bar fights, shootings, and suicides. Dry-goods merchants pulled up in their wagons, broke open their boxes, and sold right from the street. There were dogfights, cockfights, and boxing matches. The men drank hard and went on the prowl for trouble. Some towns reported daily stranglings and robberies. Bartenders sometimes drugged customers and lifted their wallets while they slept it off. Oddly enough, considering the dangers of building a transcontinental railroad on a tight schedule, more railway workers died while amusing themselves in these wild towns than in construction accidents.

"These settlements were of the most perishable materials—canvas tents, plain board shanties, and turf-hovels—pulled down and sent forward for a new career, or deserted as worthless at every grand movement of

The main drag in Bear River City in 1868, when it was a railhead for the Union Pacific and one of the many hell-on-wheels towns that sprang up all along the line. *(University of Wyoming American Heritage Center)*

the railroad," wrote Samuel Bowles, in his account of an 1869 journey in the West. "Restaurant and saloon keepers, gamblers, desperadoes of every grade, the vilest of men and women made up this 'hell on wheels,' as it was most aptly termed."

Soon, the railroad blew the whistle for the next "grand movement," and the hell-on-wheels crowd pulled out. Often nothing remained after they left but tawdry memories and a bit of trash to be blown out onto the prairie. But in some places, people who managed to put down roots were relieved when the scum had floated by. The last such town east of the present Wyoming border was Julesburg, Colorado. The next would be Cheyenne.

As it bends across the southern regions of Wyoming topping the mountains and crossing deserts, Interstate 80 roughly traces the same course charted in 1867 by surveyors of the Union Pacific. More than any other road in Wyoming, I-80 plunges into railroad history and follows the subsequent developments that the Union Pacific tracks made possible. Here one finds not only riotous tales from the hell-on-wheels days but also stories about the communities that survived after all the construction commotion died away.

PINE BLUFFS

Located a half-mile inside the Wyoming state line, Pine Bluffs was once the center of an enormous hunting area shared by the Arapaho, Cheyenne, Ute, Lakota, and Blackfeet Indians.

The town, named for the scrub pines that grew on the nearby bluffs, was little more than a tent, a shed, and a shack with a stone chimney in 1868. However, its location on both the Union Pacific and the Texas Trail helped the town grow tremendously during the cattle boom of the 1870s and 1880s. Cattle came up from Texas through Pine Bluffs, fattened on the nutritious Wyoming grass, and then rolled east through Pine Bluffs on the Union Pacific. By 1884 Pine Bluffs was the largest cattle-shipping point on the Union Pacific Railroad.

BURNS

Like Carpenter south of the road, Burns on the north was settled by Iowans. This bunch arrived in 1907 and, being largely German Lutherans, they decided to name their town Luther, after the founder of their church. However, Union Pacific officials apparently had greater regard for one of their division engineers named Burns than for the father of Protestantism. The town went by two names until 1910, when the railroad preference finally prevailed.

HILLSDALE

Hillsdale, which lies about four miles north of the interstate along the Union Pacific tracks, was named for a railroad engineer, Lathrop Hills, who was killed near the present-day town by Indians on June 11, 1867, while leading a survey party. Indians made just one other fatal attack on railroad workers in Wyoming. They killed three members of another survey crew the same summer, farther west near Bitter Creek.

The following year, Jack Casement's track-laying crew came prepared for trouble. The men traveled with one thousand rifles slung in racks under the ceilings of their railroad cars. No serious trouble developed.

CHEYENNE

Wyoming's capital and the largest city in the state, Cheyenne got off to a rip-roaring start in the summer of 1867 when the Union Pacific's chief engineer, Grenville Dodge, laid out the streets. It thrived first as a rude and bawdy railroad construction camp and then settled down to a more permanent existence as a major division point on the Union Pacific line. Traffic of all sorts moved through Cheyenne. When gold was discovered in the Black Hills during the 1870s, all the usual boomtown riffraff poured into Cheyenne on the railroad and then headed north for Deadwood, South Dakota. At about the same time, the western livestock industry surged to life, and Cheyenne became one of its most important centers. It served not only as a shipping point for cattle and sheep but also as a civilized meeting place and base of operations for the millionaires who owned practically all of the cattle.

"I had been led to understand Cheyenne was still quite outside the pale of civilization," wrote the Englishwoman Rose Pender when she and her husband visited the West in 1883 to inspect their cattle operation. "However, I found this a decided mistake . . . Mr. R— introduced the men of our party at the Cheyenne Club, and there everything was very nice—in fact, quite luxurious."

Back in July of 1867, though, there was nothing luxurious about the place at all. Three days after Dodge platted the streets, the first lot sold for $150. By November, when the tracks arrived, lots sold for $2,500, reaping a nice profit for land speculators.

In the intervening months, Cheyenne had become your basic slap-together hell-on-wheels town flushed with the kind of arrogant frontier logic that said if the ground is under your feet, it belongs to you. Many squatted on railroad land and denied that the Union Pacific was entitled to anything more than a right of way for the tracks and a bit more ground for a depot, some switches, and sidetracks. Army troops from nearby Fort Russell (now Warren Air Force Base) threw them out.

People slept where they could. Many spent nights under canvas or beneath their wagons. Soon frame buildings began to rise, and by autumn Cheyenne boasted two hundred buildings and a couple of thousand residents. There were two newspapers, some stores, restaurants, warehouses, gambling halls, and even some hotels. When the French traveler Louis Simonin arrived in October, he checked into one, the Dodge House, where he was shown into a room that had thirty beds, two men to a mattress. "The democratic customs of the Far West permit this nocturnal fraternity," he wrote. "The American endures it with very good grace."

Not the Frenchman. Simonin insisted on sleeping alone. He could afford to be philosophical about the sleeping arrangements, but he was disgusted by the sharing of brushes, combs, and towels in the communal bathroom.

Out in the street, Simonin and others of a civilized temperament could find plenty more to be disgusted about. There were robberies, assaults, shootings, thefts, and plenty of prostitution. Drunks brawled and gamblers gathered in their chips with a smile. Large crowds of men assembled in the streets to bet on which dog would rip the other to shreds, and a couple of boxers were said to have lasted 126 rounds during one prizefight. When things got out of hand, there was no jail where the rowdies could sleep off their liquor and bad attitudes. At first, the roughest of the so-called rough element were confined in chains. Later, a one-room cabin was commandeered as a jail, but it filled quickly and had to be emptied periodically by running the inmates out of town.

When the tracks arrived on November 13, 1867, the saloons cleared long enough for residents to cheer Jack Casement's crew as it pushed steadily through town laying rail after rail. The first passenger train arrived the next morning bearing the diehards of Julesburg's hell-on-wheels contingent, as well as much of Julesburg itself. On the flatcars lay many of the prefabricated buildings that had given that Colorado town its hell-raising reputation. There were storefronts, wooden sidings, dancehall floors, entire roofs, and plenty of tents. One man is reported to have stepped off the train and said to the crowd of onlookers, "Gentlemen, I give you Julesburg."

With the baser elements of Julesburg now under its belt, Cheyenne got wilder. In early 1868 vigilantes lynched five men. One was a saloon-keeper named Charles Martin who, after being acquitted of killing his partner, promptly threatened to kill the prosecuting attorney. There were seventy places you could buy a drink, including one, McDaniel's, where you could also enjoy a museum, live theater, and a zoo that included apes, snakes, porcupines, and parrots. Brothels were inevitable, but the number necessary to meet demand amazed upright citizens, including the editorial writers of the *Cheyenne Leader:* "We think if there ever was a city on the face of this sinful sphere that was well supplied with bawdy houses, that village is ours."

Complain though it did about the hell-on-wheels gang, the *Leader* sounded awfully nervous the following spring when the next railhead was declared at Laramie and roughly three-fourths of Cheyenne cleared out. "At no time since the founding of Cheyenne has there been more universal gloom and doubt pervading the minds of our citizens," the paper wrote in May 1868.

The paper need not have worried. Oliver Ames, president of the railroad, made a special visit to Cheyenne the following month to assure residents that the Union Pacific would make the town a major base of operations. The railroad began a branch line from Denver to Cheyenne and built a hotel as well as machine shops and a twenty-four-locomotive roundhouse. Cheyenne wasn't about to dry up and blow away. By midsummer the town had twenty-five grocery stores, sixteen clothing stores, nine liquor wholesalers, eight hotels, seven lawyers, and six doctors. There were three daily newspapers and four weeklies. You could buy a meal for ten cents, a bath for a buck, and have two shirts cleaned and pressed for twenty-five cents. The laundryman, Yee Jim, entertained kids by squirting water through his teeth on the clothes he was ironing, and he sometimes delivered narcissus bulbs with a clean load of linens.

Gold Rush

Life bubbled along and Cheyenne grew,

establishing itself as the capital of the spanking new Territory of Wyoming. Then, in 1874, George Armstrong Custer led a prospecting expedition north to the Black Hills. This act directly violated the 1868 treaty with the Lakota that forbade whites from setting foot in the northeast quarter of present Wyoming. The ensuing gold rush was a disaster for the tribes, but it ushered in a tremendous era for Cheyenne.

Because Cheyenne was one of the Union Pacific towns closest to the Black Hills, flocks of prospectors, laborers, bankers, merchants, and all variety of boomtown substrata crowded into the city. It was hell-on-wheels all over again, except this time it looked more like a parade than an invasion. Most of the traffic jumped off the tracks at Cheyenne, got outfitted, and quickly headed north to Deadwood, three hundred miles away. Most of those who didn't set off in their own wagons rode north on the Cheyenne and Black Hills Stage, Mail and Express Line. Stages departed every day, taking about two days to make the trip during good weather. When the four- and six-horse coaches returned to Cheyenne, they pulled in with gold for the city's banks and big spenders for the city's shops, restaurants, theaters, saloons, and bordellos. The first passenger coach pulled out of Cheyenne on February 3, 1876, and the line continued ferrying passengers and freight for the next eleven years. Then most of the traffic shifted to the Chicago and Northwestern Railroad, which completed its line between Chadron, Nebraska, and Rapid City in 1886. (For more about the Cheyenne-Deadwood Trail, see page 91.)

One of the most colorful entourages to roll through Cheyenne during the Gold Rush belonged to Madame Vestal, who had earned a reputation in Denver's Tenderloin district as the finest blackjack dealer west of the Missouri. In the spring of 1876 she closed up her gambling hall and headed north to Deadwood with her entire staff. She traveled in a secondhand yellow carriage outfitted with a bed, cookstove, curtained windows, and a shelf of books. Her maid and staff traveled in a separate wagon behind her. Two more wagons followed, bearing the personal effects of the staff, gambling paraphernalia, and a huge tent. Born into an upper-class southern family, Madame Vestal spied for the Confederacy during the Civil War under the name La Belle Siddons.

Gambling was big business in the West, and Cheyenne was no exception. In 1877, a writer for *Leslie's Weekly* noted that the town had twenty gambling saloons and reported that "gambling in Cheyenne, far from being merely an amusement or recreation, rises to the dignity of a legitimate occupation – the pursuit of nine-tenths of the population, both permanent and transient."

Miriam and Frank Leslie, publishers of *Leslie's Weekly,* had gathered a clutch of writers and artists to travel cross-country in a special excursion train and sample trackside life in the West. In Cheyenne, the Leslies visited a saloon theater. Miriam wrote:

> The auditorium departs from the conventional horseshoe pattern, and is shaped rather like a funnel. It is so narrow that we, leaning out of one box, could almost shake hands with our opposite neighbors. The trapezes through which the wonderful Mlle. Somebody is flying and frisking like a bird, are all swung from the stage to the back of the house, so that her silken tights and spangles whisk past within a hand's breadth of the admiring audience, who can exchange civilities, or even confidences with her in her aerial flight. Below, the floor is dotted with round tables and darkened with a sea of hats. A dense fog of cigar smoke floats above them, and the clink of glasses rings a cheerful accompaniment to the orchestra, as the admiring patrons of the variety business quaff brandy and "slings,"

and cheer on the performers with liberal enthusiasm.

Everything about Cheyenne brightened up during the gold-rush era, even the whorehouses. Ida Hamilton ran the classiest joint. Known as the House of Mirrors for the two large floor-to-ceiling mirrors in the front hall, her two-story brick house at 209 West 18th Street was a handsome structure. When workers finished it in 1878, Ida threw a big celebration party. She sent engraved invitations to all the prominent men in Cheyenne and imported the best liquor and horizontal laborers for their amusement.

Livestock

Handfuls of cattle had been grazed in the Cheyenne area well before the railroad provided a reason for building the town. But it wasn't until after the Union Pacific tracks came through that cattle appeared in great numbers. The presence of the railroad suggested the possibility of driving herds north from Texas to the high plains, where the cattle would fatten up, multiply, and then board trains to the East for slaughter. John Iliff brought a herd of Texas longhorns into the Cheyenne area in 1868 to supply military garrisons along the Union Pacific route. Hi Kelly sold the first carload of cattle to be shipped east from Cheyenne. After slaughter some were shipped to Europe, where they were eaten by French Army troops during the Franco-Prussian War.

The high-plains cattle did well. The grasslands had been virtually untouched for years because so many buffalo had been slaughtered. The new grazers thrived on the rich native grasses, which proved high in nutritive value and cured beautifully for winter forage.

Word spread that tremendous money could be made with little effort. Cash poured in from investors in the East and from the British Isles. Soon many herds grazed near the tracks in western Nebraska and eastern Wyoming. The largest operation belonged to the Swan Land & Cattle Company, which, at the height of the 1880s boom, owned a 600,000-acre spread that stretched from Oglalla, Nebraska, to Fort Steele, near Rawlins.

Cattle weren't the only form of livestock grazing on the Cheyenne plains. Many sheep were there, too. In 1871 the Durbin brothers brought fifteen hundred to the Cheyenne area. The following year they had enough spare woollies to ship a few carloads to the East. Others followed suit, including F. E. Warren, Wyoming's first governor and a U.S. senator.

At the time there was enough grass for everybody. Later, as ranchers and sheepherders overstocked the range, competition for the limited amount of grazing land touched off violent encounters between cattle ranchers and sheepherders, and between the big cattle outfits and the small.

Tom Horn

One man deeply involved in the conflicts between the cattle barons and their challengers was Tom Horn, a stock detective who was hanged in Cheyenne on November 20, 1903, for the murder of a sheep-rancher's son.

Horn was a hired gun. "Killing is my specialty," he once said. "I look at it as a business proposition, and I think I have a corner on the market." He was methodical. He studied the habits of his victims, picked his time and place, and then fired from ambush with a high-powered rifle. He picked up the shell casings and left as his calling card two stones under the victim's head. His targets were those whose activities encroached on the interests of the big cattle outfits: rustlers, homesteaders, and sheep growers.

Horn had been a cowboy, miner, army scout, deputy sheriff, and Pinkerton agent when,

in the 1890s, he was employed by various members of the Wyoming Stock Growers Association to hunt and kill suspected rustlers. When war broke out between Spain and the United States, he went to Cuba as a mule packer. He returned to Wyoming after the war and went back to work, rousting out undesirables for large cattle outfits in Colorado and northwest of Cheyenne.

In 1901, suspicion centered around Horn when Willie Nickell, son of an aggressive sheepman, was murdered while wearing his father's coat and hat (see page 137). A detective named Joe LeFors posed as an agent for a large Montana cattle baron looking for a tough man to clear rustlers out of the area. Horn leaped at the opportunity and agreed to meet with LeFors at the U.S. marshal's office in Cheyenne. There he bragged about his prowess as a liquidator of rustlers and admitted that it was he who had killed Willie Nickell. Horn did not know that LeFors had concealed a stenographer and a witness within earshot of their conversation. He was arrested the following morning and charged with the murder.

Horn said he had not shot Nickell, that he was drunk at the meeting with LeFors and had bragged up the shooting only because he wanted to impress a potential client. LeFors said Horn had been drinking but that he clearly was not drunk.

After a lengthy trial, Horn was convicted in 1903 and sentenced to hang. Awaiting execution in the Cheyenne jail, he and a fellow inmate jumped a deputy, took his revolver, and rushed outside. With no horse in the vicinity, Horn tried to flee on foot. But Cheyenne citizen O. A. Aldrich shot at him and wrestled him to the ground. Lucky for Aldrich, Horn couldn't figure out how to release the safety on the deputy's gun before Aldrich managed to get it away from him.

A few months later Horn was hanged at the corner of Pioneer and 19th after some of his friends sang a favorite ballad and watched T. Joe Cahill, the county clerk, lead him up the scaffold. Horn's last words were to Cahill: "Joe, they tell me you are married now. I hope you're doing well. Treat her right."

The Club

During the fat, happy days of the early livestock industry, Cheyenne lay at the center of the business. In early summer, the big absentee land owners from the East Coast and the British Isles gathered here. Some arrived in private trains, then set out to inspect their holdings and see how their operations had fared during the annual roundup. Back in the city they got together with the resident millionaire cattlemen at The Cheyenne Club, an opulent place with the air and furnishings of an English gentleman's club.

It was the center of the city's uppercrust social life, where old money from the old country hobnobbed with the rags-to-riches rabble of the new frontier. According to author Jack Gage,

It was a glass knocker on a hen house door that insisted upon being used. It boasted fine appointments, fine furnishings, fine china, snow-white linens, sterling silver, crystal glassware, and a world renowned wine cellar. There were men servants about the place that had been imported for the service, who knew there were such things as classes and accepted the idea. It is easy to understand that no ex-roundup cook could quite fill the bill in such an establishment, where the names of the dishes on the menu might well have sounded like insults to him.

Rules at The Cheyenne Club prohibited profanity, drunkenness, fighting, tipping, cheating at cards, the smoking of pipes, betting, and games on Sunday, but club members managed to have fun anyway. In 1895, John C. Coble got smashed and shot up a painting of a Holstein bull.

Mansions

Most of Cheyenne's millionaires, whether they made their fortunes in cattle or otherwise, built their mansions on Ferguson Street (later renamed Carey Avenue). Residents included officials of U.S. Steel, a member of the English Parliament, and members of some of the most powerful families in the United States and Europe. They hired Italian artisans to paint frescoes on their ceilings. They bought hand-carved doors, stained-glass cathedral windows, and French wallpaper. They built ballrooms, turrets, and conservatories and covered the floors with Oriental carpets.

Just as at The Club, however, the rough-and-tumble of the frontier sometimes intruded upon the stuffed-shirt elegance of Millionaire's Row. One morning, for example, a horse thief was found dangling from a cottonwood tree in front of the Jim Moore mansion.

Entertainment

The Union Pacific brought some of the best road shows of the day to Cheyenne, as well as some of the biggest names in entertainment. They performed in a thousand-seat opera house replete with ornamental scrollwork, velvet-draped boxes, and a huge crystal chandelier. The English actress Lillie Langtry appeared in *Pygmalion* at the Opera House in 1884. Ladies got satin souvenir programs in honor of the occasion and the house was decorated with fresh flowers. A hard-boiled local reviewer said her performance never rose above "the dead level of mediocrity."

Buffalo Bill Cody brought his Wild West Show to Cheyenne twice, but he didn't impress the locals. They were very well schooled in the finer points of riding, roping, and shoot-em-up.

Besides, by the time Cody came back in 1898, Cheyenne had already kicked off its own version of the Wild West Show called Frontier Days. It's still an annual summer event.

WARREN AIR FORCE BASE

This military post was originally established on July 4, 1867, to protect railroad construction crews. Times change; in 1963 it became an important intercontinental ballistic missile site, with two hundred Minuteman silos within a 150-mile radius of the city.

JUNCTION WITH I-25

Interstate 25 heads north along the Cheyenne-Deadwood stagecoach line, picks up a portion of the Oregon Trail, and then runs north to Montana (see page 136).

UNION PACIFIC ROUTE

Between Cheyenne and the pass leading over the Laramie Mountains, I-80 closely follows the original roadbed of the Union Pacific. This stretch of track was so difficult to build that the railroad was allowed to charge double its normal per-mile construction rate in order to lay track over what was then called Sherman Hill. Construction was complicated not only by the elevation of the pass, about 8,250 feet where the tracks crossed, but also by the necessity of spanning a deep gorge on the western slope at Dale Creek.

Most of the emigrants who passed through Wyoming in covered wagons from 1841 to 1868 preferred the lower, gentler crossing of the Rockies at South Pass. The railroad decided on the more arduous route for three major reasons. First, following the Oregon Trail along the North Platte and Sweetwater rivers would have meant laying forty extra miles of track. Second, the southerly route lay closer to Denver and the Colorado mining camps. Third, the railroad picked up mineral rights with its land grant, and it had found richer coal deposits along the southerly route.

Sherman Summit

After months of struggling up the eastern slope of the Laramie Mountains, Union Pacific track crews finally topped the summit of Sherman Pass on April 16, 1868. This pass marked the highest point along the Union Pacific: about 8,250 feet. The point is marked by a big limestone pyramid built in 1881–82 as a monument to Oliver and Oakes Ames for their achievements as principals of the Union Pacific Railroad. (Take the Vedauwoo exit and follow the signs to reach the site.)

One of their achievements, through the Credit Mobilier of America, was to fleece the Union Pacific out of $13 to $16 million while the road was being built.

Credit Mobilier contracted with the Union Pacific to oversee construction of the road and then routinely overbilled for the work it did and often for work that was never done. The overbilling was not challenged by the railroad because the railroad's top officials were in on the scheme. Credit Mobilier's founders, Oakes Ames and Thomas C. Durant, were both inner stockholders of the Union Pacific. Ames's brother, Oliver, was president of the railroad. They and other controlling officers of the Union Pacific had a financial stake in Credit Mobilier. By allowing Credit Mobilier to overbill, they milked the railroad for cash to enrich themselves.

Because the federal government was subsidizing the Union Pacific through land grants and loans, it had an interest in making sure Credit Mobilier did not overbill. So, to forestall congressional investigations and interference, Ames (himself a member of the House) gave stock in Credit Mobilier to other influential members of Congress.

Charles Francis Adams picked up on the scandal during the late 1860s and tried to expose it in the *North American Review:*

> Who then constitute the Credit Mobilier? It is but another name for the Pacific Railroad ring. The members of it are in Congress. They are trustees for the bond-holders. They are directors. They are stock-holders. They are contractors. In Washington they vote the subsidies. In New York they receive them. Upon the Plains they expend them. And in the Credit Mobilier they divide them.

By the time the scandal broke, in 1872, politicians holding Credit Mobilier stock included the vice president, the vice president-elect, chairmen of important committees in the House, a dozen Republican Party leaders of both House and Senate, the Democratic floor leader of the House, and James Garfield, who would shrug it all off later and become president.

Congress investigated itself over the matter and censured two of its own, including Oakes Ames.

Lincoln Monument

Also on the summit of Sherman Pass, right beside the interstate, stands a 12.5-foot bust of Abraham Lincoln, who dreamed of linking the country east to west with a transcontinental railroad. He laid much of the groundwork for the project during the Civil War but did not live to see much progress. When he was assassinated in the spring of 1865, the Union Pacific was floundering near Omaha. Four years after his death the last spike was driven at Promontory, Utah, where the Union Pacific finally met up with the eastbound Central Pacific track gangs.

Sherman Hill

During the spring of 1868, construction crews camped on the pass while graders smoothed the western slope for the track-layers and bridge-builders. One evening just before dinner a camp cook returned to her kitchen and found a large black dog gnawing on the roast she meant to serve to a crew of hungry workers. The woman, who weighed in at over two hundred pounds, picked up an ax, whacked the animal over the head with the flat side of the blade, and chased it out of camp. When the men arrived for dinner she told them there wasn't much left. The camp hunter grabbed a rifle and set off to shoot the dog so the crew wouldn't go hungry another night. When he returned with the dead animal, the cook nooded and said "Yup, that's the dog, all right." The men looked at her with new respect. The animal was not a dog but a bear.

Passenger Service

After the railroad was completed, passengers reached Sherman Summit at midmorning on the second day out of Omaha. The train often stopped here for longer than the usual water-tank stop to give people a chance to walk around and enjoy the high alpine scenery. Most were pleased to get such a fine view of the famous Rocky Mountains, but the altitude bothered some of them and even caused an occasional nosebleed. After a brief stop at the pass the train barreled down the western slope into Laramie. There, passengers bought lunch before rolling toward the Medicine Bow Range and then out across the plains. Darkness fell by the time they reached Wyoming's Red Desert, which was just as well, because most people were bothered by it. At sunrise the train stopped at Green River for breakfast.

The whole trip, from Omaha to Sacramento, took four to five days of traveling at what seemed like amazing speeds during the 1870s: ten to thirty-five miles per hour. A first-class ticket cost one hundred dollars, plus four dollars a day for a berth in one of the luxurious Pullman Palace cars. Pullman passengers got a sofa, a light, and a table to themselves. In the evening a porter would come and convert the sofa into a bed. A second-class ticket cost seventy-five dollars, and emigrants, who had to sit on planks, paid forty dollars.

In the early days there were no dining cars. The trains stopped at depots for meals that sound hearty enough to the modern ear but that passengers still found time to complain about in their diaries. Mostly what bothered them was the sheer monotony of it: breakfast resembled lunch, which resembled dinner. Mainly they ate steaks—beef, buffalo, or antelope—along with bread, biscuits, potatoes, and coffee or tea. Sometimes a person could get fried ham, fried eggs, cornmeal, and pancakes. Some stations stood out for their superior cuisine. Laramie gained a reputation for its beefsteaks, Green River for its hot biscuits, and Evanston for trout. One station tried to vary the menu with prairie-dog stew, but it didn't go over very well.

On board, passengers entertained themselves with cards, songs, and conversation. When things got quiet they watched for wildlife: antelope, prairie dogs, elk, wolves, bears, and coyotes. And when just watching the wildlife got too dull, they sometimes opened the windows and squeezed off a few shots with their guns.

Brakemen

While barreling down the west slope from Sherman Summit, modern drivers only have to touch a pedal to slow their cars. Braking a transcontinental train on this steep downhill run into Laramie was a much more complicated, much more dangerous undertaking before the turn of the century. In the early days the trains were braked by hand. Men leaped from roof to roof on the boxcars, turning hand brakes as the train began to pick up speed. It took balance, nerve, timing, and coordination, and it had to be done in the rain, sleet, and snow, no matter how treacherous the footing. While passengers sat inside the cars admiring the fierce thunderstorms and blizzards of the high plains, the brakemen climbed up top to do their work. If they didn't slow the line of cars evenly the train could break apart and careen on down the tracks. The brakemen did their job well here—no major crackups. In 1872 George Westinghouse perfected an air brake that simultaneously braked each car when the engineer pulled a lever in the locomotive. But the brakemen continued their dangerous line of work for fifteen to twenty more years because the railroads were slow to adopt the innovation.

LARAMIE

The present-day city of Laramie takes its name from one of the pioneers of the Wyoming fur trade: Jacque LaRamee. There are several spellings of the man's name, but little is known about him except that he trapped beaver in what is now southeastern Wyoming and died in 1821 at the hands of Arapaho Indians along the banks of the river that now bears his name. Several other landmarks in the area were also named after him: the mountain range between Laramie and Cheyenne, and Laramie Peak, northwest of Wheatland.

Settlers did not arrive at Laramie until 1868, when the impending arrival of the Union Pacific tracks gave fly-by-night operators of all descriptions good reason to set up shop. Land speculators made a killing when rumors spread that the division shops and locomotive roundhouse planned for Cheyenne would in fact be built in Laramie. About four hundred lots sold in the space of a week, all at exorbitant prices. Then, when the tracks were laid to Laramie, about three-quarters of Cheyenne's population bugged out and came to the new town.

Even more than Cheyenne, Laramie was a classic hell-on-wheels town. Gangs preyed upon the citizenry. Robbery and garroting were daily events, and those empowered to put an end to the violence were often no better than the outlaws.

One of these so-called lawmen was "Big Steve" Long, who had picked up a job as deputy marshal. He seemed to regard his badge as a license to kill over the slightest provocation. In the best of western traditions, a fistfight had broken out in a local saloon between a bunch of cowboys and some new men from Illinois. Big Steve yelled at them to stop. But when nobody paid any attention to him, he drew his pistols and began shooting into the fray. He killed five. Then, a few months later, a pair of drunks at the Baby Doll Saloon annoyed Big Steve. They were arguing over who should buy the next round of drinks. Big Steve told them to shut up. When they protested his order, he drew his guns and blazed away, killing three men and wounding a fourth.

In Laramie, the lawless element organized itself to oppose both the legitimate local government and any vigilante committee that might form. It forced the provisional government to resign just a few weeks after its officers had been sworn in, and then it cowed a tentative vigilante committee that retreated after lynching just one outlaw. However, by autumn the vigilante force rebounded to five hundred men. They secretly plotted simultaneous raids on several of Laramie's principal gambling halls on October 29, 1868. The coordinated attack failed, but a big gun battle erupted at a dance hall called Belle of the West. There, five men were killed and fifteen people were wounded. The dead in-cluded an outlaw, a vigilante, and a musician. Four of the outlaws surrendered and were lynched at the Union Pacific depot. They included none other than Big Steve, the justice of the peace, and a gambler who seems to have been christened at birth for his career: Con Wager.

Many of the outlaws then joined the vigilante committee and, while professing to revere law and order, took control of both the committee and the second provisional government. Under color of law they continued their nefarious deeds. Finally, the Dakota legislature (Wyoming then being a part of Dakota Territory) revoked Laramie's charter and placed the town under jurisdiction of the federal courts. There Laramie would remain until 1874, when the Wyoming territorial legislature incorporated it. In the meantime, things finally settled down.

Taking Root

The railroad, which had attracted the hell-on-wheels crowd, soon brought a taste of civilization to Laramie. A month after the first train pulled into town, a large hotel stood beside the tracks. The dining room had white tablecloths, polished silver, china, gleaming woodwork, chandeliers, and imitation marble columns. While not quite the Ritz, it was a far cry from the dirt-floor road ranches that stagecoach passengers had to endure.

The Union Pacific also built an enormous windmill here to pump scarce water for its locomotives. It hauled stone fifty miles from Rock Creek to assemble a twenty-stall roundhouse and machine shop. This demonstrated another settling influence of the railroad: the easy transportation of substantial building materials. Train passengers and the Union Pacific weren't the only ones to benefit from this change. Structures of all types for all classes of people improved.

The tracks made it possible to fetch stone for the state capitol from quarries in Fort Collins and Rawlins. The railroad made it feasible to build the mansions on Cheyenne's Millionaire Row. Houses for those of more modest means could be prefabricated in Chicago and shipped West by rail. Saloons were delivered by flatcar complete with carved bar, hardwood tables, beer cooler, and piano.

Laramie's economy, like Cheyenne's, also benefited from the burgeoning livestock industry during the 1870s and 1880s and from periodic excitement about precious metal discoveries. Efforts at mining produced more ghost towns than ingots. Various industries did catch hold during the 1880s in Laramie, though, including a flour mill and a glass plant. During the 1920s, two oil refineries were built in Laramie to process crude pumped out of the Rock Creek field. One of the most enduring props in Laramie's economy is the university, established in 1886.

Women's Rights

Wyoming women in 1869 became the world's first to win the vote. And in the general election of 1870, Laramie resident Elza Swain became the first woman to exercise that right.

The same year, Laramie women were the first in the world to serve on grand and petit juries. Eastern newspaper editorials of the time expressed skepticism about the women's abilities. But Wyoming's foremost judge, Chief Justice J. H. Howe, praised their dignity, decorum, conduct, and intelligence and said they deserved the admiration of every fair-minded citizen of the territory. Historian T. A. Larson wrote that they took their work more seriously than did men:

> Some of the male jurors had been known to spend more time over whiskey

and cards than pondering the guilt or innocence of the accused . . . In a day when many men in the West carried sidearms and when men accused of murder regularly pleaded self-defense, the women were less ready to accept such pleas without substantial supporting evidence.

The Pattee Swindle

For a year, Laramie served cheerfully as the base of operations for James M. Pattee, an unabashed swindler who ran a nationwide lottery that never paid a jackpot. At the time, Wyoming had no law forbidding a lottery, so Pattee blithely advertised monthly drawings for a $50,000 prize and quarterly drawings for $100,000. Tickets cost a buck. He mailed his ads throughout the nation and soon the money poured into Pattee's pockets. He made no enemies in Laramie because the tickets were not sold locally. Instead, Pattee made a lot of friends. He employed fifteen clerks, paid the two newspapers well to print his advertising circulars, and gave generously to local churches and philanthropic organizations. The lottery generated so much mail that the post office rose to first-class status and the postmaster got a nice fat raise.

Pattee made no bones about what he was up to. If people wanted to be humbugged, he once said, it was his business to oblige. However, the scheme collapsed in 1876, when Congress passed a law against using the mails to defraud.

FORT SANDERS

Built a few miles south of modern Laramie in 1866, Fort Sanders protected railroad workers as well as emigrant and stagecoach traffic on the Overland Trail. It was also the site of a crucial showdown in 1868 between feuding officials of the Union Pacific Railroad. The railroad's vice

General Grenville Dodge as an older man. Years before this picture was taken, Dodge had laid out the route of the Union Pacific Railroad. *(University of Wyoming American Heritage Center)*

president, Thomas C. Durant, and his associate Silas Seymour had been altering the routes laid out by Grenville Dodge, the railroad's chief engineer. Durant's purpose in rerouting the tracks and changing Dodge's other plans was to make some quick money. For instance, he has been credited with touching off the wild speculation in Laramie lot sales by ordering that the major machine-shop facilities planned for Cheyenne be transferred to Laramie. Dodge countermanded that order, but not before the price of lots spiraled. Durant and Seymour were also responsible for surveying the wide, winding northwest curve in the tracks that commences at Laramie. Their purpose, states author Dee Brown in *Hear That Lonesome Whistle:* "Add 20 miles to the railroad . . . [and] bring almost two million easy dollars into the pockets of the railroad's builders."

By the time Dodge learned of the rerouting,

too much of the preparatory grading and filling had been done for him to change the route back to his original survey. He called a meeting during the summer of 1868 at Fort Sanders that was presided over by Ulysses S. Grant, the shoo-in candidate for president that year. Durant accused Dodge of wasting the railroad's money by needlessly building across rough country. Dodge threatened to quit the road if Durant or anyone else meddled with his routes. Grant backed Dodge and Durant backed down.

JUNCTION WITH 30/287

Here Highway 30/287 heads north, paralleling the Union Pacific tracks and the Durant detour mentioned above (see page 140).

TIE SIDING

As the name suggests, this outpost alongside the Union Pacific rail line supplied the heavy timber ties that undergirded the rails.

At this gathering at Fort Sanders in 1868, Ulysses S. Grant, then candidate for president, settled a crucial feud between officials of the Union Pacific Railroad. Grant is to the left of center with his hands on the picket fence. The man in the center of the picture with his jacket over his arm is another famous Civil War general, William T. Sherman. *(University of Wyoming American Heritage Center)*

During 1868, ties cost thirty-five to sixty cents apiece to produce and were sold to the railroad's construction company for a dollar to a dollar-thirty. Demand for the ties continued after 1868 while the Union Pacific rebuilt some of its track and while it and other railroads established branch lines throughout the region.

Tie drives down the Laramie River were often large and exciting. On June 29, 1870, 80,000 ties and 2 million feet of logs floated down the Little Laramie. In 1875 an estimated 350,000 ties and 2 million feet of lumber were cut out of the forests around Laramie.

JUNCTION WITH STATE ROUTE 130

State Route 130 heads west across the Laramie plains and climbs through the Medicine Bow Range, where stories of quashed mining hopes abound (see page 145).

OVERLAND TRAIL

From Laramie, I-80 heads across the plains, skirting the Medicine Bow Mountains along roughly the same route traveled by emigrant wagons and stagecoaches on the Overland Trail. Most of the emigrants who passed through Wyoming followed the Oregon Trail through the central portion of the state. However, the Overland Trail was heavily used from 1862–68 when Indian attacks on the Oregon Trail drove many, including Ben Holladay's stagecoaches, to the south. In spite of the presence of the railroad, the trail was used to some extent as late as 1900. It led northwest across the Laramie plains, crossed the North Platte at Saratoga, and then reached straight across the bottom of the state to Fort Bridger.

At Arlington, on Rock Creek, travelers can visit the remains of an important stagecoach way station on the Overland Trail.

LARAMIE PLAINS

During the 1870s, the plains west of Laramie were part of an enormous open range stretching between Evanston and North Platte, Nebraksa, which the Union Pacific described as the finest place in the United States to raise cattle. Railroad officials had an interest in saying so, of course, since their tracks ran through the heart of the region and provided the link to eastern markets. Still, major cattle dealers were quoted as saying herds could thrive in the area, roaming freely with little tending and minimal loss. Texas cattle could be delivered to the area for $9.50 a head and appreciate in value $6 a year while fattening up on free grass. Ranch managers were willing to do all the work for one dollar a head per year.

Numbers like that attracted plenty of investors and lots of cattle. Some of the biggest investors were members of wealthy British families.

In 1867, perhaps five hundred head of cattle could have been found in the vicinity of Laramie. By 1880 there were more than 90,000 cattle, 85,000 sheep, and 3,000 horses and mules grazing within forty miles of town on some of the best grasslands in North America. The livestock was worth about $2.25 million.

The railroad, profiting enormously from shipping cattle east, did its best to make sure production remained high. It decided not to bother stockmen squatting on its lands and, early on, sometimes chose not to sell land to those who wanted to buy. The railroad feared that if some cattlemen gained a monopoly on the grass and water in certain areas, fewer cattle would be raised and shipped to market. During bitter winters when it looked like the ranchers would lose large numbers of cattle, the railroad would ship feed at near cost rather than risk losing the freight the following season.

In 1886–87, a disastrous winter finally caught up with everyone involved in the cattle industry. Hurricane blizzards, deep snow, and lots of sleet killed off about one-third of the cattle on the high plains. Most of the animals died of thirst rather than want of food. The rivers and streams had frozen over and then disappeared under the snow. Wyoming, with losses averaging about fifteen percent, made out better than Montana and Dakota. Laramie County reported losses of just five percent, but northeastern Crook County lost forty-three percent. The winter bankrupted many and drove most of the foreign investors out of the country.

ARLINGTON

Here, in 1865, Cheyenne Indians attacked a train of seventy-five wagons making their way along the Overland Trail. They carried off two young girls named Fletcher: Mary, thirteen, and Lizzie, two. The Indians killed their mother, wounded their father, and chased off their three brothers. Mary herself was wounded with arrows but managed to pull them out. After the kidnapping, Mary was separated from her sister and spent the winter with the Cheyenne. In the spring, a white trader paid sixteen hundred dollars, a rifle, and a horse for her release. She spent the next year making her way back to her father in Salt Lake City.

No one heard a thing about Lizzie for thirty-five years. Then a white woman raised by Arapahos turned up in Casper with Indians from the Wind River Reservation. Mary read about the appearance, traveled to Wyoming, and identified the woman, Lizzie Brokenhorn, as her sister. But Lizzie preferred her life among the tribe and refused to leave the reservation.

JUNCTION WITH 72

State Route 72 runs up to the coal-mining community of Hanna, where mine explosions in 1903 and 1908 killed hundreds (see page 143).

FORT STEELE

The remains of Fort Fred Steele lie on the north side of the interstate shortly beyond the crossing of the North Platte River. It was established in 1868 to protect railroad workers.

In 1879, thirteen soldiers from the fort were killed and forty-three wounded in the Battle of Milk Creek, in Colorado. A force of 150 had ridden south to quell an Indian uprising among the Utes on the White Pine Agency. The Ute agent, Nathan Meeker, had tried to convince the Indians to take up farming by threatening to cut off rations promised them by treaty. The Utes naturally objected. They killed Meeker and six of his assistants, burned the agency, and attacked the column of approaching soldiers from Fort Steele. The Utes' chief, Ouray, managed to arrange a truce, but the tribe lost the reservation.

LAND SALES

To encourage the Union Pacific to build the transcontinental railroad, the federal government agreed to grant it a checkerboard of land twenty miles wide on either side of the tracks. These serpentine swaths were divided between the railroad and the federal government: the railroad owned the odd-numbered sections, the government the even-numbered sections. In Wyoming the railroad picked up 4,582,520 acres. By the time Fort Steele was abandoned in 1886, the Union Pacific had sold most of its Wyoming holdings except for what lay west of the fort. The big cattle outfits bought large blocks

Fort Fred Steele as it appeared in 1868, shortly after it was built to protect railroad workers. Today the remains of the fort can be seen north of Interstate 80 after the road crosses the North Platte. *(University of Wyoming American Heritage Center)*

for a dollar to a dollar-fifty an acre. The Swan Land & Cattle Company picked up 425,000 acres near Fort Steele for fifty cents an acre, then made a quick profit on some of it when the Union Pacific realized it had sold valuable coal deposits and bought it back. The arid land west to Evanston eventually sold for less than a dollar an acre.

BENTON

About three miles south of Sinclair the end-of-track community of Benton sprang to life during the summer of 1868. Named for Senator Thomas Hart Benton, the place had very little going for it other than its status as the first rail-head west of Laramie. Water had to be hauled in from three miles away and cost a dollar a barrel. Alkali dust blew through the town, covering the streets, buildings, animals, and people. John Hanson Beadle, a newspaper correspondent, reported that the dust was eight inches deep the day he arrived and that "a new arrival with black clothes looked like nothing so much as a cockroach struggling through a flour barrel."

RAWLINS

Valued by Union Pacific construction workers for a freshwater spring south of the present town, Rawlins was established in 1868 and named for Gen. John A. Rawlins, commander of the troops protecting the railroad crews. By 1870, Rawlins was an important embarkation point for the mines of South Pass, where a gold rush, ultimately disappointing, had started in the late 1860s.

As a railroad town, Rawlins was susceptible to railroad sorts of trouble, including train robberies. In June 1878, a couple of bandits loosened some of the track on a curve east of Rawlins and lay in wait for a payroll train to derail. They went by the colorful names of "Big Nose George" Parrot and "Dutch Charlie" Burris. Some say that Frank James, of the infamous Missouri gang of Frank and Jesse James, waited with them and may have acted as the guiding hand in their apprenticeship to big-time crime. While they hid in some bushes, a Union Pacific section chief happened to come down the line inspecting the tracks. He noticed the freshly drawn spikes and immediately understood their significance but had the presence of mind not to pause. Without indicating in any way that he knew robbers must be near, the inspector proceeded nonchalantly until he rounded the curve, then hightailed it and flagged down the approaching train.

Soon, a posse rode after the would-be robbers, who fled east to Rattlesnake Pass near Elk Mountain. Two members of the posse, Henry Vincent and Bob Widdowfield, tracked them up the pass. There the lawmen were shot dead.

Parrot and Burris escaped, but not for good. Burris was arrested in Montana several months later and lynched in Carbon (see page 143). Big Nose George was arrested, tried, and sentenced to hang. While awaiting execution in Rawlins, Parrot secretly filed through the chains that bound his ankles. His escape attempt failed and a mob lynched him from a telegraph pole to make sure he didn't try again.

A local physician made a death mask of Parrot's face and removed a portion of his skull, which he gave to his female assistant as a souvenir.

As cattle and sheep poured into Wyoming during the 1870s and 1880s, Rawlins became a center for sheep and cattle ranchers. Rawlins resident John Candlish made the western shepherd's life a bit easier in 1884, when he started building sheepherders' wagons. Sheepherders (they are not called shepherds in the West), unlike cowboys, had to follow their animals all year no matter what the weather. Until Candlish came up with his bunkhouse on wheels, they slept out on the ground and occasionally froze to death in winter storms. Candlish built a bed

across the back of a round-topped wagon. A table pulled out from under the bed. The grub box beneath the wagon could be reached from inside, and there was a stove for cooking and warmth. Wagons like those Candlish built are still seen all over the West.

When the Wyoming legislature divvied up the territory's institutions in the late 1880s, Cheyenne got the capital and Laramie got the university. Rawlins got the prison, built in 1898, and an inmate riot in 1912. Twenty-seven prisoners escaped. One killed a Rawlins citizen.

Not all crime in Rawlins was so direct. During Prohibition, speakeasies here stayed open by paying fifty dollars each to the state law enforcement commissioner.

JUNCTION WITH 287

State Route 287 leads north to Muddy Gap and then slants northwest to the Wind River Valley (see page 41).

GREAT DIVIDE BASIN

From Rawlins to Table Rock, I-80 passes through the southern edge of the Great Divide Basin. Here the Continental Divide draws a large, rough circle around a bleak landscape that drains into itself. It is the sort of country that kept emigrants moving through Wyoming, anxious to put the state behind them as soon as possible. "Barren in the extreme," is how William Anderson described it while traveling with a party of mountain men in 1834: "It is sand and nothing but sand . . . a true American Sahara." Those who traveled through it later sent back equally discouraging reports, thus contributing further to Wyoming's reputation as being part of The Great American Desert, even though wild horses gallop through the sand dunes here.

The region's whiskey disappointed early travelers almost as much as the landscape did. The newspaper publisher Horace Greeley, a teetotaler, wrote in 1859 that he had not tasted it himself, "but the smell I could not escape, and I am sure a more wholesome potable might be compounded of spirits of turpentine, aqua fortis [nitric acid], and steeped tobacco."

JUNCTION WITH 789

State Route 789 runs down to the little towns of Baggs and Dixon (see page 147).

TIPTON

Butch Cassidy and the Wild Bunch robbed a train on August 29, 1900, at Tipton, now a ghost town on the Union Pacific line halfway between Rawlins and Rock Springs.

Farther east on the tracks, one of the gang slipped aboard the train behind the tender car. When he saw a bonfire kindled by the rest of the gang near Tipton, he climbed forward to the locomotive and forced the engineer to stop the train. Some of the outlaws kept the passengers' heads down by shooting around the cars while others dynamited the Wells Fargo safe. Varying accounts of the robbery place the take at fifty-four, forty-five, and fifty-five thousand dollars.

The exploits of Butch Cassidy, the Sundance Kid, and the Wild Bunch took them all over Wyoming. West of Hanna the gang robbed another train. Near Kaycee they often hid out in the Hole-in-the-Wall country of the Big Horn Mountains. In Baggs and Dixon they celebrated raucously. Cassidy owned property near Jackson Hole, spent a winter in Star Valley, and served time in the Lander jail. Harry Longabaugh got his nickname while serving time in the Sundance jail.

BITTER CREEK

The Union Pacific was built in haste. Track crews routinely laid miles of rails every day and even succeeded once in slamming down ten miles in a single day. After the tracks were joined with those laid by the eastbound Central Pacific crews, the results of hasty construction showed. Hundreds of miles of track had to be relaid. Ties were unballasted, the roadbed in some places just dirt. The joints between rails and ties were sloppy, trestles flimsy. The space between ties varied from fifteen inches to twenty-six, and the ties themselves had been made of soft pine when construction standards clearly called for hardwood. Embankments had eroded. Sharp curves needed straightening. Rough grades needed smoothing. One government inspector said the Union Pacific's western track was the worst he had ever seen and declared that many bridges were unsafe and tunnels too narrow.

Here, along Bitter Creek in 1869, the soft sandstone abutments of a bridge over the creek crumbled under the pressure of a train. The locomotive, tender, and express car fell off the track into the creek. One passenger was killed. More might have died except that a beam of the bridge caught the passenger car and held it back. Just the day before the bridge had been inspected and declared unsafe.

POINT OF ROCKS

Named for high sandstone cliffs that jut eleven hundred feet over Bitter Creek, Point of Rocks was a relay station for stagecoach traffic on the Overland Trail, which crosses the interstate here and then runs close by all the way to the Utah line.

After the Union Pacific laid tracks through the state, Point of Rocks was the railroad station closest to the South Pass goldfields. It was a busy

One of the many deep cuts the Union Pacific's grading crews shoveled out to prepare the way for the railroad's track-laying crews. This cut was made near Bitter Creek in southwestern Wyoming. *(University of Wyoming American Heritage Center)*

terminal, where those who came to seek their fortunes in the mining camps got off the train and headed north by wagon. Wells Fargo & Company ran daily stagecoaches between Point of Rocks and South Pass.

DIAMOND HOAX

Gold wasn't the only precious commodity to stir interest in this part of Wyoming. In 1872, prospectors Philip Arnold and John Slack touched off a flurry of lucrative speculation when they leaked their discovery of a rich gem field south of the Union Pacific between Rawlins and Rock Springs. Cousins from Kentucky, the pair had turned up in San Francisco and had tried quietly to deposit a bag of uncut diamonds in the Bank of California. This act caught the eye of the bank's director, William Ralston, who, with other prominent California financiers, decided to gain control of the diamond field from Arnold and Slack.

First they had to make sure of the field's authenticity. So they convinced the prospectors to take one of their representatives to the site (blindfolded so he could not determine the field's location). When he confirmed the presence of diamonds and rubies, the syndicate of financiers sent samples to jewelers in San Francisco and New York who vouched for the gems' high quality. At that point, the investors organized the San Francisco and New York Mining and Commercial Company, capitalized at $10 million, and made plans to move Amsterdam's diamond-cutting industry to San Francisco. Slack and Arnold were paid about $600,000 and cut loose from the venture.

Although the syndicate kept the site of the field a closely held secret, word of a major diamond strike inevitably got out. No fewer than twenty-five companies were incorporated with a total authorized capital of $200 million to search for and develop diamond mines in the West.

Then the bubble burst. Geologist Clarence King, who had been surveying the 40th parallel with a team of scientists, discovered the site of the diamond field and declared it a fraud. Besides finding diamonds and rubies, King's team found emeralds, garnets, sapphires, and amethysts—a suspicious mix of gems. More important, many of the gems had been poked into anthills and mounds of earth and some bore the mark of a jeweler's tool. King forced Ralston's syndicate to announce they had been deceived and to make restitution to investors.

The stones were real and there were plenty of them, but Slack and Arnold had bought them in London for thirty-five thousand dollars. They scattered them over the mesa (just south of the Wyoming line and several miles west of today's State Route 430) in the hope of attracting some California sharps. Arnold moved back to Kentucky, paid off the syndicate with $150,000, and enjoyed the rest of his money. Slack moved to White Oaks, New Mexico.

ROCK SPRINGS

The town draws its name from a spring of fresh water that runs from a rock northwest of town. Sources of good water being scarce in this corner of the Intermountain West, a stage station was built here in the early 1860s. But after the Union Pacific arrived in 1868, interest in Rock Springs shifted to another of its natural resources: coal.

Those who drummed up support for a transcontinental railroad in the early 1860s often touted the great payoff potential of western mineral resources. The glamour metals—gold, silver, copper—captured much of the attention. Common minerals like coal tended to get overlooked, but not by the railroad. It knew that the coal on its huge land-grant holdings would not only fire its locomotives but also help fill its coffers. There was a strong eastern market for coal that had already drawn an estimated $100 million worth of the mineral from the West two full years before the railroad was completed. With the rails in place, coal-mining could be accelerated.

Near Rock Springs, vast deposits of bituminous coal were discovered, and miners began digging it up shortly after the Union Pacific track crews built past this point. Through the years miners of many different nationalities and ethnic backgrounds came to Rock Springs. At one time, forty-seven different groups were represented, including Italians, Greeks, Russians, Finns, Irish, Africans, and Chinese.

Like all the other nationalities in Rock Springs, the Chinese celebrated their heritage with colorful festivals, such as on Chinese New Year, when they paraded a hundred-foot dragon down the streets and set off strings of firecrackers. Unlike most of the other workers, the Chinese came to Rock Springs not to settle and perhaps raise families but generally to earn a chunk of money to take back home.

They began arriving in large numbers in 1875, when the railroad hired them to break a strike. They were willing to work for eighty percent of what the miners had been making before they went on strike. Within two weeks the mines were reopened with 150 Chinese and 50 white miners. The bitter ending of the strike, combined with racism and the Chinese miners' unwillingness to organize with the other workers, led to smoldering resentment against the Chinese that flared ten years later.

On September 2, 1885, a white mob descended on Chinatown. The whites killed twenty-eight Chinese, wounded fifteen, ran hundreds out of town, and burned down many of the buildings. One witness said that some of the Chinese had taken refuge in passageways they had dug between their houses, and that men were offered twenty dollars for every dead Oriental they could dig out.

Governor Warren called for federal troops to restore order, but they didn't arrive for a week. By then, Chinatown was devastated. The troops escorted the Chinese back to Rock Springs, and the Union Pacific put them up in boxcars until they could rebuild their homes. The Sweetwater County sheriff arrested sixteen white men, including a member-elect of the Wyoming legislature, but a local grand jury returned no indictments. The territory offered the Chinese no recourse to sue for the estimated $147,000 in property damage, and Wyoming public opinion strongly supported the white miners. Congress finally appropriated the money for the damage. Federal troops remained in Rock Springs until 1898.

Chinatown was rebuilt, but the number of Chinese dwindled in Rock Springs and elsewhere because Congress had suspended Chinese immigration in 1882. The railroad's coal-mining division could find few Chinese replacements for those who retired or moved back to their homeland.

Oliver Ames, president of the Union Pacific and a principal in the Credit Mobilier scandal, used the coal mines as a way to bilk the railroad. He and five other Union Pacific directors owned ninety percent of the stock of the coal company that ran the early mining operations and sold coal to the railroad at artificially high prices.

Demand for coal slid as railroads converted from steam locomotives to diesel engines and other fuels, such as fuel oil and natural gas, were used to heat houses. In the 1950s, the mines at Rock Springs closed. But the energy crisis of the 1970s spurred renewed interest in Wyoming coal and the mines reopened. Trona, a mineral used to make many basic materials such as glass and steel, is mined nearby. Oil fields near town also helped the Rock Springs economy boom during the late 1980s.

JUNCTION WITH 191

Highway 191 runs north through the east side of the Green River valley to Jackson Hole and Grand Teton and Yellowstone national parks (see page 192).

GREEN RIVER

The town, of course, took its name from the river, which runs as a persistent theme through many of Wyoming's most colorful periods of history (see pages 181–182).

In 1862, Ben Holladay's stagecoaches pulled through on the Overland Trail south of town, where he maintained a station and repair shops until the Union Pacific put it out of business.

In anticipation of the railroad's arrival, speculators laid out a town and attracted two thousand people to the site. Many who came found work as tie hacks. These men cut timber in the mountains, floated it down the river, and shaped it into railroad ties. As many as 300,000 ties jammed the river during the spring tie drives.

In spite of this activity, the railroad temporarily dashed residents' hopes for their fledgling town. The track crews paused to build a

The Union Pacific Railroad bridge at Green River in about 1868. *(University of Wyoming American Heritage Center)*

temporary bridge over the river and then swept on by, laying track faster than any crew had ever done before. Just west of Green River, workers set a world's record by laying seven and three-quarter miles of track in a single day. The record would hold only until the next spring, when a Central Pacific crew beat it with a ten-mile day.

Not all the work went so smoothly. The grading crews struck for higher pay at Green River in 1868. The strike didn't last long. Backed by federal troops, the railroad's construction engineer, Samuel Reed, threatened to starve out the workers. That broke the strike and the work continued.

Meanwhile, the town of Green River worried it might share the fate of other flash-in-the-pan towns, such as Benton, that had thrived for a couple of months as the tracks pushed through and then withered. By November, Green River was nearly abandoned. The railroad had gone on to lay out a town at Bryan, twelve miles to the west. However, the railroad did eventually come back and establish a division point at Green River. The town was saved.

Today, Green River owes much of its prosperity to large deposits of trona ore. Five plants in Green River derive soda ash from the ore. Manufacturers use soda ash to produce glass,

ceramics, soap, detergents, textiles, paper, iron, and steel. Two-thirds of the world's supply of soda ash comes from the Green River plants.

JUNCTION WITH 530

State Route 530 runs south to the Colorado line, where it joins State Route 414 and loops back up to the interstate (see page 194).

JUNCTION WITH 372

State Route 372 runs north along the banks of the Green River and connects with U.S. 189 (see page 183).

LITTLE AMERICA

This maze of gas pumps, shops, restaurants, and motels began with a promise a sheepherder made to himself while lost during a brutal Wyoming blizzard in 1890. While the snow blew, S. M. Covey pledged that if he survived, he would build a shelter in the middle of the desert. Forty-two years later he built a store here and called it Little America, after Admiral Byrd's station in Antarctica. The interstate pours a million people a year through Covey's haven here, and many more at Little Americas in Cheyenne and Salt Lake.

JUNCTION WITH 30

Highway 30 runs northwest through Granger and Opal and then heads west into Utah, passing the site of a major mountain man rendezvous (see page 198).

JUNCTION WITH 374

Beginning at the interstate's junction with State Route 374, the road picks up the route of the emigrant trails leading to Utah, California, and Oregon. Although most of the traffic for the Northwest was diverted to one of a number of cutoffs farther east during the height of the migration, the earliest emigrants came this way.

CHURCH BUTTE

On the south side of the interstate stands Church Butte, also called Pulpit Rock, where the Mormon leader Brigham Young preached on a July Sunday in 1847 as he and the first wagon train of Mormon emigrants made their way toward the Salt Lake valley.

JUNCTION WITH 414

At the little town of Urie, named for homesteader Nicholas Urie, State Route 414 heads southwest toward Flaming Gorge and the site of the first mountain man rendezvous in 1825 (see page 195).

FORT BRIDGER

By the early 1840s, the fur trade along Green River had all but dried up, and trappers had to find new ways to make a living. Jim Bridger, one of the legends of the business, built a trading post near here in 1842 with his partner, Louis Vasquez, another old trapper. Their initial idea probably was to trade mainly with the Indians and what few mountain men remained in the area. But as the tide of emigrants rose, Fort Bridger soon became the most important way station in Wyoming west of Fort Laramie. Later, it was the site of violent confrontations with Mormon colonists.

Bridger and Vasquez actually built two forts close to the present town of Fort Bridger. The first was built just south of the present Wall Reservoir, about a mile north of the town of Fort Bridger. It was probably abandoned in 1843, after the men built their second post at what is now Fort Bridger State Park.

That same year, a wagon train of one thousand emigrants pulled up to the fort, looking for supplies. Thousands more followed. Here they could buy food, repair their wagons, exchange worn-out livestock for fresher animals, and rest for a few days. They found plenty of grass and water for their animals and caught plenty of trout for themselves. James Reed, who traveled this way in late July 1846, described Bridger and Vasquez as "excellent and very accommodating gentlemen . . . They now have about 200 head of oxen, cows and young cattle, with a great many horses and mules; and they can be relied on for doing business honorably and fairly."

Still, when compared with Fort Laramie, Bridger's post wasn't much of a place to do business. Those heading for Utah were loath to spend money so close to their destination, and the bulk of travelers bound for the Pacific Coast soon bypassed Fort Bridger by following a route roughly forty miles to the north.

Most of the emigrants who came through Fort Bridger were Mormons on the last leg of their journey to the Promised Land. At first, Bridger's relations with the Mormons were cordial. He met Brigham Young in the summer of 1847 and told Young that the Salt Lake valley looked like a good place for a settlement. Young also liked the look of the Green River valley and thought it would make an excellent spot for a colony to aid the streams of Mormon emigrants who were to follow.

Three years after the Young-Bridger conversation, Utah became a territory with Young as governor and superintendent of Indian affairs. The territory included Bridger's fort and the sites of several lucrative ferries along the Green River that were operated by former trappers who refused to pay Utah taxes. Young brushed off

Bridger's friendly approaches and accused the mountain men of rousing the local Indians against Mormons.

Tensions climbed until 1853, when Young revoked Bridger's license to trade with the Indians and ordered his arrest. A 150-man Mormon posse rode into the fort in August and, when they didn't find Bridger, descended on the ferrymen. They killed two of the mountain men and robbed the rest of much of their property. Young later sent about forty men to occupy Fort Bridger and start a colony, but Vasquez and a force of mountain men held them off. The Mormons built Fort Supply instead, twelve miles to the southwest.

That's how things stood for two years, until Young decided that buying out Bridger and Vasquez made more sense than burning them out. The partners sold the fort to a Mormon Church representative in June 1855. At about the same time, Mormons gained control of the Green River ferries.

The Mormons enlarged Bridger's fort and used it and Fort Supply to provision their emigrants until 1857, when President James Buchanan sacked Brigham Young as governor of Utah. Buchanan had been convinced by federal appointees in Utah that Young and the Mormons were routinely flouting federal law and were in fact in a state of rebellion. In Young's place Buchanan appointed the former mayor of Augusta, Georgia, and sent army troops to Utah to enforce the new governor's decrees. Convinced that the government meant to annihilate them, the Mormons burned down their outposts, including Forts Bridger and Supply. They planned to burn Salt Lake City and retreat south if the army was not stopped. However, by burning the forage in front of the advancing troops and by attacking army supply trains in southwestern Wyoming, the Mormons slowed the

troops long enough for a settlement to be arranged. By the spring of 1858, the Utah War had ended.

The army occupied Fort Bridger, and it was used during the 1860s by the stagecoach lines and the Pony Express. The site was abandoned in 1890, but restoration of the fort's buildings began in 1964. Today there is a museum on the site, and a big rendezvous is held there each year on Labor Day weekend.

PIEDMONT

On May 8, 1869, the Union Pacific's vice president, Thomas C. Durant, was jollying along this section of his brand-new railroad. Finally, after four years of feverish work, the Union Pacific tracks were to be joined with those of the Central Pacific at Promontory, Utah. Driving the ceremonial last spike was to be a historic event. Durant knew it, and as the ranking Union Pacific VIP to be on hand, he was looking forward to the party. However, at Piedmont a bit of unfinished business suddenly presented itself in the form of an angry mob of tie hacks who had not been paid for five months. They surrounded his lavish private car, with its inlaid woodwork and crystal chandeliers, and refused to let it move forward until Durant paid up. He wired for the necessary $500,000, and the crowd dispersed. This incident, combined with a storm that washed out the tracks in Utah's Weber Canyon, delayed the festivities at Promontory for two days.

JUNCTION WITH 189

Highway 189 runs north along the banks of the Green River and plunges through Hoback Canyon before picking up the Snake River and following it to Jackson (see page 183).

EVANSTON

Ambitious Harvey Booth pitched a tent at the site of present-day Evanston on November 23, 1868 and opened a restaurant, saloon, and hotel. The population mushroomed in December when the railroad arrived and then nearly vanished when the road moved its division headquarters to Wasatch, Utah. Fortunately for Evanston, the railroad built a roundhouse and machine shop here the following spring.

When coal mining began in the hills three miles west of town at Almy, Evanston drew the usual cosmopolitan mix of nationalities, including many Chinese. As in most of the coal-mining towns along the Union Pacific, there was racial tension in Evanston between white and Chinese miners. Whites complained bitterly about Chinese taking their jobs and undermining the prevailing wage scale. But hard feelings here never erupted into the kind of tragic violence that marred the early days of Rock Springs. In Evanston, the Chinese not only worked the mines but also set up shop as merchants, launderers, and gardeners. While whites ignored what looked like unproductive land, the Chinese built an irrigation system, grew vegetables, and fed the town. They also built a temple that drew Chinese worshippers from great distances because it was one of only three such temples (called "joss houses" by western whites) in the United States at the time.

Although Evanston avoided racial tragedy, it wasn't immune from death in the nearby mines. Explosions in 1886 and 1895 killed seventy-four men. The mines around Almy were shut down in 1900, and most of the miners drifted north to the coal mines at Kemmerer and Diamondville. Disaster struck there in 1923, when one hundred miners died in an explosion. Between 1886 and 1938, a total of 567 miners died throughout Wyoming in accidents that involved five or more men. Most of the accidents were in mines owned by the Union Pacific.

BEAR RIVER

At Evanston, the interstate crosses Bear River, the longest river in the world that does not empty into an ocean. It meanders through three states before flowing into Salt Lake. Along its banks in 1857, J. W. Myers branded cattle with an open nine character, or Yoke 9. Some say Myers's mark is the oldest brand in Wyoming.

JUNCTION WITH 89

Running north through the Bear River valley and on to Jackson, Highway 89 passes some of the most beautiful and most interesting country in Wyoming (see page 201).

From the outskirts of Cheyenne to its junction with U.S. 26, Interstate 25 passes through country where some of the most colorful events in Wyoming's history took place. The road traces the route of the Cheyenne and Black Hills stage line as far north as Wheatland and passes through ranch land where the gunman Tom Horn committed the murder that would get him hanged in 1903. Absentee cattle owners passed along this route on their semiannual excursions from the gilded surroundings of The Cheyenne Club to the rugged grasslands where their ranch managers made their money for them. And drunk cowboys tried, and failed, to ingratiate themselves at roadhouses by shooting up the barrooms.

STAGECOACH ROUTE

For much of the trip between Cheyenne and the North Platte River, I-25 follows the route of the old Cheyenne to Deadwood stagecoach route. After gold was discovered in the Black Hills of modern South Dakota in the mid-1870s, prospectors, land speculators, saloon-keepers, merchants, gamblers, and anyone else who thought he could make a quick buck flocked to Cheyenne via the Union Pacific railroad. Then they headed north to the Black Hills by whatever means of conveyance they could find or afford. Many traveled as passengers on the Cheyenne and Black Hills Stage, Mail and Express Line.

The 1876 gold rush opened not only a major road north but also marked the beginning of the last major conflict between whites and Indians in Wyoming (see page 81). Stagecoach travel began even before the army began its seizure of the Black Hills. The first coaches left Cheyenne in January 1876, following the modern route of I-25 as far as Wheatland, then veering off to the northeast toward Fort Laramie.

By 1877, Luke Voorhees, the stage line's superintendent, was running six hundred horses and thirty specially built coaches between Cheyenne and Deadwood, the boomtown heart of the Black Hills gold rush. First-class tickets to Custer, roughly 250 miles from Cheyenne, cost twenty dollars. Third-class tickets cost ten dollars but required passengers to walk, if need be, when the coach went uphill. Average speed was eight miles an hour, and the stage ran night and day, with one driver and one man riding shotgun.

JUNCTION WITH STATE 211

State 211 swerves off to the west and follows the tracks of an important railroad line along the foothills of the Laramie mountains. The tracks were laid in the mid-1880s, when the state's first cattle boom reached its height and Cheyenne's position on the Union Pacific tracks garnered it the lion's share of livestock freight. However, a competing railroad known then as the Wyoming Central (now the Chicago and Northwestern) made a bid to siphon off much of the cattle-shipping business by laying track west to Orin on the North Platte River. Cheyenne businessmen got nervous, so Laramie County floated a bond issue of $400,000 to build a spur line (called the Cheyenne and Northern) from Cheyenne to Wendover. Later, the Union Pacific extended the line to Orin.

LODGEPOLE CREEK

One of the first stops on the Cheyenne and Black Hills stage line was the Fred Schwartze ranch, eighteen miles north of Cheyenne. While stage hands changed the horses, passengers could join local cowboys for a meal, a drink, or a few dozen drinks.

Drunken cowboys frequently annoyed the Schwartzes, as one of the Schwartze children,

Minna, recalled in later years. On one memorable day an impending thunderstorm prompted her father to call out all of the hired men, including the bartender, to help bring in a crop of hay. While they were gone, a group of neighbor ladies called on Mrs. Schwartze, who was very pregnant. While she made some coffee for her friends, a band of rowdy cowboys announced their arrival and request for service by shooting up the bar and dining room. The neighbor ladies dashed out of the kitchen and sprinted across the yard to the protective embankment of Lodgepole Creek. Mrs. Schwartze, though eager to follow, was not so fleet of foot. She had only reached the door when a bullet zinged into the kitchen. As she tried to waddle out of there, a drunk Texan lurched into the kitchen demanding more whiskey. Mrs. Schwartze grabbed him by the collar, marched him back into the bar, and told him to help himself.

By the time the cowboys were through with their party they had shot all the liquor bottles off the shelves and had riddled a large barrel of whiskey with bullet holes.

BEST SHOT, DIRTIEST TRICK

On a rainy July morning in 1901, a fourteen-year-old boy named Willie Nickell breakfasted for the last time with his family at their ranch near Iron Mountain, about twenty miles west of the present interstate.

Willie's father, Kels, had made a lot of enemies in the twenty years since he staked out his homestead on the slopes of the Laramie mountains. Some suspected him of rustling, because he had managed by the 1890s to increase his herd to some one thousand head. And he had earned the hatred of a large cattleman named John C. Coble by grazing animals on land Coble considered his own. The men had had a tussle and Kels had cut up Coble with a pocket knife. Hard feelings also abounded for years between Kels and a neighboring homesteader, James Miller. In one of that feud's incidents, Willie, a sturdy kid, whupped one of the older Miller boys. But the act that truly enraged most, if not all, of the area's cattle ranchers came in 1901, when Kels Nickell committed the unforgivable sin of selling his cattle and grazing sheep in their place.

Over breakfast that July morning, as thunder rolled through the mountains, Kels gave Willie his marching orders. The boy was to head west on Kels's horse, catch up with a herder who had passed through the previous day, and offer him work. Dressed in his father's coat and hat, Willie rode west for about a mile, then dismounted to open a gate. A rifleman, concealed behind some rocks about three hundred yards away, opened fire. Two bullets caught Willie in the body. He fell on his face and died.

Locals figured the murderer had mistaken Willie for his father, and they suspected that Tom Horn had done the killing. Horn, a range detective who openly cultivated his reputation as a hired killer, had worked closely with Coble during the 1890s when Horn first established his deadly reputation. Horn was also an acquaintance of Kels Nickell's other enemy, James Miller. He often stopped at Miller's ranch to visit a young schoolteacher who roomed with the family. In fact, Horn had visited the Miller ranch the day before the murder and had taken some target practice with his .30-30.

A couple of weeks after Willie's murder, several riflemen tried to ambush Kels at the ranch. Firing from concealed positions, they wounded Kels three times as he ran for the house. Then they shot sixty-five sheep pastured on the Nickell spread. This time, Kels took the hint. After recovering from his wounds, he sold out. The family moved to Cheyenne and Kels found work with the Union Pacific railroad.

Horn eventually confessed to Willie's murder, saying, "It was the best shot I ever made, and the dirtiest trick I ever done." Later he claimed that was a drunken boast. But in 1903, after a long trial and an attempted jailbreak, Horn was executed in Cheyenne (see page 116).

CHUGWATER CREEK

John "Portugee" Phillips opened a road ranch here for travelers on the Cheyenne-Deadwood Trail. Phillips was the man who made the celebrated 236-mile ride in 1866 from Fort Phil Kearny to Fort Laramie bearing news that the Lakota and Cheyenne had ambushed and killed eighty-one soldiers (see page 87). Phillips hung out his shingle as a restaurateur in 1876 and sold out in 1879.

Chugwater was also the headquarters of the mammoth Swan Land & Cattle Company, the biggest of the big cattle outfits that dominated the early days of the Wyoming livestock industry. It was organized in 1883 by Alexander H. Swan with $3.7 million of Scottish capital. Within a few years the firm's holdings were valued at $50 million. At its height, Swan Land & Cattle ran about 125,000 head, owned about 600,000 acres stretching from Oglalla, Nebraska, almost to Rawlins, and controlled much more. The firm stayed in business for almost seventy-five years, weathering bankruptcy following the killing winter of 1886–87, falling prices, and growing competition from small ranchers. In 1904 the company switched from cattle to sheep and operated until 1947.

Chugwater supposedly got its curious name from the "chugging" sound buffalo made when they hit the water or the ground after Indians stampeded them over nearby cliffs.

Farther north and east lived John Hunton at Bordeaux Station. The station took its name from a French trader (see page 14). Hunton bought the place in 1870 and opened it as a relay station on the stage line in 1876. He built a two-story, eleven-room hotel in 1887, as the Cheyenne and Northern railroad approached Bordeaux. In 1888 he moved to Fort Laramie as the post trader, then bought the outpost two years later when the army abandoned it.

CATTLE AND COFFINS

During Wyoming's astonishing cattle boom of the 1880s, enormous herds grazed the open range largely unattended by humans and rarely seen by their owners. Absentee owners from the East Coast as well as the British Isles bought interests in the vast herds, but few owned more than a scrap of land that acted as a ranch headquarters. Virtually all of the land surrounding the ranch buildings was publicly owned and, in theory, was as open to anyone with a horse as the ocean is to anyone with a boat. One reluctant banker said that investing in a big outfit in Wyoming appeared to be as risky as buying into a school of cod that roamed the open sea.

Some of those who invested in Wyoming cattle from afar enjoyed visiting the West to see what their money had bought. They generally arrived in Cheyenne by train and put their feet up at the swank Cheyenne Club (see page 117) before setting off for their ranches.

One such absentee owner was an Englishwoman named Rose Pender. She and her husband, James, had bought a share of a cattle operation in northeastern Wyoming and came West in 1883 to inspect it. After some time in Cheyenne, they set off for Fort Laramie during the third week of May and found the going very wet and cold. Soon these Brits learned that raising cattle in Wyoming took more than driving the herd together twice a year in jolly romps of horsemanship called roundups. Their lush profits came at a higher price than the principal they had invested. Before reaching Fort Laramie, the Penders met a wagon with a coffin slung beneath it.

"It seems that during a snow storm two men were on the hunt after some horses, and lost their way," Rose later wrote. "They had only one horse between them, so the older man persuaded the younger one, a new hand at the work, to let him ride on and seek the run-aways, whilst the other was to remain stationary and fire his gun at intervals." The young man did as he was told, but when his companion did not return, he tried to walk back to camp. Two days later, other cowboys found him, feet and legs frozen up to the knees. He died after both legs were amputated, and the older man was found dead, probably killed by lightning.

After passing the coffin, the Penders stopped at a ranch to sleep. But Rose was awakened by the sound of a wagon pulling into the yard.

> Getting up I peeped through the blinds and saw four men bringing out another coffin, which was placed in a wagon, and, after some directions, driven off the way we had come. I must confess to having felt a little uncomfortable. A coffin seemed such an ordinary way of getting folks home out here.

WHEATLAND

This farming community owes its existence to an irrigation project begun in 1885 by Joseph M. Carey, a territorial judge who went on to become governor and a U.S. senator. Carey helped organize the Wyoming Development Company to irrigate fifty thousand acres of arid land. The water came from a dam built across the Laramie River on the other side of the Laramie mountains. To get the water from the Wheatland Reservoir forty miles southwest of town to the farm fields, a three-thousand-foot tunnel was cut through the mountains. The water reaches the Wheatland Flats by way of Sybille and Blue creeks.

About eleven miles east of Wheatland, State 60 leads through a narrow passage in the cliffs known as Eagles Nest Gap. Some of the emigrants following the Oregon Trail used to haul their wagons up this pass to avoid the difficult trail through North Platte Canyon. Emigrants carved their names in the cliffs at the top of the pass, and some of their inscriptions remain. During the 1870s, the Cheyenne-Deadwood stage line ran through the pass and maintained a station there.

JUNCTION WITH U.S. 26

Here, I-25 picks up the route of the Oregon Trail. To read about events along this stretch of highway, see page 23.

As it arcs across the Laramie plains and curves around the northern point of the Medicine Bow Mountains, Highway 30 follows a controversial stretch of the Union Pacific railroad. Gen. Grenville Dodge, the UP's chief engineer, had surveyed a route farther to the south, closer to the route taken today by Interstate 80. But Thomas C. Durant, the railroad's vice president, changed the route in 1868 in order to make some fast money. This wide northwest curve from Laramie added twenty miles to the Union Pacific route, earning more cash for the construction company, Credit Mobilier, and racking up more property for the Union Pacific through its land grant from the federal government. Durant's act infuriated Dodge, who tried to countermand Durant's order. But by the time Dodge learned of the change, grading crews had already prepared too much of the new route to stop work. Durant's meddling touched off a showdown between the two men at Fort Sanders (see page 123).

The railroad played a major role in the history of the land along U.S. 30. It made coal-mining possible in Hanna, where thousands of miners worked and hundreds died in a series of explosions around the turn of the century. The railroad also attracted train robbers, some of whom got away and some of whom were lynched before they could stand trial.

BOSLER

This town takes its name from Frank Bosler, owner of the Diamond Ranch, a large cattle operation where Tom Horn hung his hat, and gun, for a while during the 1890s. Horn, a Pinkerton agent turned stock detective, hired himself out as a killer of those who threatened the interests of the big ranchers. He is said to have wiped out alleged rustlers, uppity homesteaders, and sheepmen. In 1903 he was convicted of murdering fourteen-year-old Willie Nickell, whom he had mistaken for the boy's father, a sheepman. Though he recanted his confession, he was hanged (see page 116).

ROCK CREEK

Before the Union Pacific moved its tracks to their present location at Rock River in 1900, the rails ran about a dozen miles north. A thriving community sprang up where they crossed Rock Creek. By 1883 the town had a couple of hotels, three saloons, a restaurant, smithy, and large stockyards that loaded one hundred freight cars a day with beef cattle during the roundup season. A stage line also ran from here to Montana.

As the Union Pacific grading crews made their way through this area, they uncovered promising signs that the railroad's land grant would pay off handsomely. While preparing the way for tracks in the summer of 1868, graders cut through a vein of bituminous coal eight feet thick. Coal discoveries were made all along the Union Pacific tracks that summer, and miners were soon at work in Carbon (see page 142), Rock Springs, and Almy (near Evanston).

The Union Pacific owes a great deal to the coal reserves it gained through its land grant. Union Pacific President Charles Francis Adams said in 1887 that the financially strapped road owed its existence to coal. "Those mines saved it," Adams testified before Congress. "Otherwise the Union Pacific would not have been worth picking up."

The Union Pacific used coal for fuel, sold it at a large profit, and used its track monopoly to discourage competitors. In 1874 it sold its own coal in Omaha for nine dollars a ton and charged its competition ten dollars a ton just to ship their coal to Omaha.

The salvation Adams had referred to was short-lived. Not even coal could save the railroad

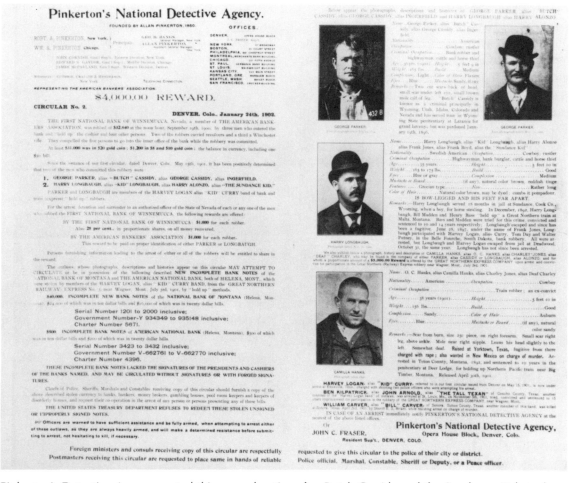

Pinkerton's Detective Agency posted this reward notice after Butch Cassidy and the Sundance Kid stuck up the First National Bank of Winnemucca, Nevada, in 1901. It offers one thousand dollars each for the arrest of the four members of the gang, plus twenty-five percent of any stolen money recovered. The Hole-in-the-Wall Gang got away with roughly thirty-two thousand dollars, mostly gold coin. (*University of Wyoming American Heritage Center*)

from declaring bankruptcy in 1893. Four years later, Edward H. Harriman and a group of investors bought the road and rebuilt it.

TRAIN ROBBERY

On June 2, 1899, an express train ground to a halt for a red lantern at isolated Wilcox Siding, about six miles west of Rock Creek.

While the engineer waited for the signal to pull forward, a gunman hopped aboard the locomotive and convinced him to stay put. Thus began another robbery for Butch Cassidy, the Sundance Kid, and the Wild Bunch.

The gunman kept the engineer occupied in the locomotive while other members of the gang tried to get the mail-car clerk, E. C. Woodcock, to open the door so they could rob the Wells

Fargo safes. They fired warning shots to scare Woodcock, but the clerk wouldn't cooperate.

In the midst of these negotiations, the robbers heard another train approaching. They ordered the engineer to pull forward across a bridge, dynamited the bridge, and separated the express and mail cars from the rest of the train. Then they got the engineer to pull forward two miles. Their patience running thin, the gang blew open Woodcock's door with dynamite, which knocked the man unconscious. They opened the safes the same way and galloped north toward Casper with a reported sixty thousand dollars in unsigned bank notes.

Several days later, a posse caught up with three of the robbers, including the Sundance Kid, in the Hole-in-the-Wall country near Kaycee. Harvey Logan killed the sheriff, and the trio escaped by jumping into the Red Fork of the Powder River (see pages 70–71).

MEDICINE BOW

This cow town provided the setting for Owen Wister's famous novel *The Virginian.* Wister traveled widely throughout the West from 1885 to 1902 and rode for the Two Bar Ranch near Medicine Bow. His book had a great influence on changing the way cowboys were viewed. Before Wister lionized them, cowboys were often thought of as rough undesirables—and no wonder. Stories abounded about them tearing through little towns on their days off. In Carbon, which stood about fourteen miles west of Medicine Bow, a group of cowboys let off a little steam in 1881 by grinding broken whiskey bottles into the faces of some of the coal miners and then riding off, guns blazing. The historian T. A. Larson quotes one cowboy of the 1890s era saying that respectable women wouldn't pay any attention to him if he arrived in town wearing his cowboy duds: "Owen Wister hadn't yet written his book *The Virginian,* so we cowhands did not know we were so strong and glamorous as we were after people read that book."

In the center of town stands the Virginian Hotel. There is a monument to Wister across the street.

The name Medicine Bow—applied to town, river, and mountain range—has its roots in Indian tradition. Indians of various tribes came to the area to harvest mountain ash, prized as a material for making fine bows.

Energy has been derived from various sources in the Medicine Bow area. Miners began digging out coal when the Union Pacific came through in 1868. The Ohio Oil Company pumped oil from fields south of town beginning in 1923. Some of the richest uranium deposits in the world are found north of Medicine Bow in the Shirley Basin, and two enormous wind tunnels south of town, built by the Interior Department, can produce enough electricity to supply the needs of twelve hundred homes.

CARBON

Now a ghost town, Carbon once boasted a population of some three thousand people supported by the Union Pacific tracks and coal mines. Carbon's mines were opened in 1868, the first on the Union Pacific line. In 1875, miners here and in Rock Springs went on strike when the railroad reduced their pay from five cents a bushel to four. Like the strikers in Rock Springs, those in Carbon were quickly replaced by Chinese. Whites in both communities resented the Chinese replacements, but it was in Rock Springs, ten years later, that tensions boiled over in a fatal riot (see page 131). When the railroad built the Carbon Cutoff to the mines at Hanna in the 1880s, production dwindled at Carbon until the mines were shut down in 1902.

In 1878, a woman named Widdowfield

The coal-mining town of Carbon as it appeared in 1875. The bandit Dutch Charlie Burris was lynched there in 1878. *(University of Wyoming American Heritage Center)*

watched her husband, Bob, ride out of town for the last time in his life. He and several other men from the area had formed a posse to hunt down "Big Nose George" Parrot and "Dutch Charlie" Burris, who had been chased off the tracks while trying to rob a train between Carbon and Rawlins. Widdowfield and Henry Vincent tracked the outlaws into the Medicine Bow Mountains but were shot dead from ambush. Mrs. Widdowfield buried and mourned her husband. Several months later, she got her chance for revenge when Dutch Charlie was captured in Montana and sent back to Rawlins for trial. When the train stopped in Carbon, citizens swarmed aboard and dragged Dutch Charlie into the depot. Apparently Dutch thought he could save himself by confessing to the shooting. After a Union Pacific telegrapher took down his words, the crowd pulled him out in the street and made him stand on a barrel. They threw a rope over a telegraph pole, put the noose around his neck, and asked if he had any last words. Before he could reply, the widow Widdowfield stepped forward, said, "No, the son-of-a-bitch has nothing to say," and kicked the barrel out from under him.

HANNA

After huge deposits of coal were discovered

here, the Union Pacific railroad ran tracks to the site in 1889. The mines soon eclipsed those opened earlier in Carbon, and their death toll eclipsed that of all other Wyoming mines.

An explosion on June 30, 1903, killed 171 miners, leaving 150 widows and about 600 fatherless children. Five years later, two explosions in the very same mine killed another fifty-eight men. The state inspector found that the first of the 1908 blasts was caused directly by the Union Pacific's haste in opening a shaft in which a fire was burning.

Production at Hanna continued until the late 1950s, when demand for coal dwindled. Natural gas had supplanted virtually all of coal's uses as a fuel except in railroad locomotives, which switched from coal to diesel. Hanna and neighboring Elmo became virtual ghost towns until the 1970s. When OPEC quadrupled the price of oil, interest in domestic sources of energy leaped, and the mines reopened.

Wyoming's reserves of coal, particularly low-sulphur coal, are estimated to be either the largest or second largest in the nation. Roughly 900 billion tons of the stuff underlie about forty percent of the state's surface area. Demand for it grew tremendously in 1990 with passage of the Clean Air Act, which forced coal-burning power plants to reduce sulphur-dioxide emissions by 1995 in one of two ways: either install expensive antipollution equipment, or buy clean-burning low-sulphur coal. This new demand boosted Wyoming's economy and vaulted it past Kentucky and West Virginia into first place among coal-producing states.

WALCOTT: JUNCTION WITH I-80

To pick up I-80 at this point, see page 125.

State 130 leads straight into the heart of the Medicine Bow Mountains, which are also called the Snowy Range because of the heavy blizzards that glaze the peaks every winter. The road climbs about thirty-seven hundred feet to Snowy Range Pass, then drops down the west slope of the mountains and loops north through one of the state's oldest cattle-ranching areas before rejoining I-80. Most of the history along the road ties in with the boom and bust of disappointing mining ventures.

LARAMIE PLAINS LINE

From Laramie across the plains to Centennial, the highway parallels a set of tracks that promoters in 1901 hoped would run clear over the Snowy Range, pausing at the various mines to pick up ore and drop off freight. Plans were made for laying track through Encampment and all the way to the area around Baggs. Originally known as the Laramie, Hahn's Peak and Pacific Railway, it was later called the Laramie Plains line. It is now owned by the Union Pacific.

Officials broke ground in 1901, but work crept along at a snail's pace. It took six years for the line to reach Centennial—painfully slow progress by any standards of the day and perhaps shamefully slow considering the easygoing terrain the rails were laid across. However, the sluggish tempo may have benefited the railroad in the long run. By the time its rails reached Centennial, the mining boom had busted. Prospects for gold, copper, platinum, rare earth, and other commercial minerals had all played out. The mining camps were pulling up stakes and the boomtowns were fast becoming ghost towns.

The railroad waited out the national economic slump of 1907 and then pushed its rails south to the coal fields of north central Colorado. By 1911 the railroad reached Coalmont and began hauling coal, livestock, timber, and a smattering of passengers. Those interested in fishing the streams and lakes of the Medicine Bow range could ask the train to stop on its morning run to drop them at their favorite fishing hole and pick them up again in the evening.

The Laramie Plains line had financial trouble from the start. But somehow—despite bankruptcies, sales, and corporate shake-ups—the line endured while many other small railroads built at about the same time died away. Some of the people who worked for the Laramie Plains line had what today would be considered an absurd loyalty to the company. W. B. Bacon, an early superintendent, walked the 111-mile length of the track from Laramie to Coalmont picking up empty whiskey bottles and tossing them into a gunnysack. He sold the bottles to a junk dealer and turned the money over to the company.

Money wasn't the only obstacle for the railroad—so were the intense winters. Temperatures often dropped far below zero, and the wind blew hard enough to rip the roofs off boxcars. Blizzards buried the tracks, stalling trains for days, even weeks, at a time. One engineer who was bogged down by snow and bitter cold kept warm in the locomotive's firebox until help arrived. During a storm in the winter of 1917 the snow fell so deep that it took twenty-one days to make the round trip between Laramie and Coalmont. The men set off for the journey stocked with boxes of canned goods, chocolate, and coffee. They cooked bacon, eggs, and hamburger on a coal shovel by holding the shovel in the firebox until the food was done.

A special locomotive with an enormous rotary attachment on the front cut through the snowbanks and freed the trains, but the chasms they sliced through the drifts occasionally trapped animals. One day, several horses trotted in front of the locomotive for seven miles. The snowbanks were too high for them to get off the track. Finally they reached a bridge, but some of the horses got stuck. The crew freed the horses and shoved them off the bridge. They fell unhurt into the soft snow below and promptly disappeared in it. The men climbed down and shoveled them out.

CENTENNIAL

Founded during the nation's centennial year, this tiny community's prospects looked very bright in 1876 when Stephen W. Downey discovered gold nearby. Downey opened a mine, refused an offer of $100,000 for his mineral rights, and then watched the vein quickly play out. In 1892, excitement flared over another supposed gold strike, but nothing came of it.

Examples of disappointing mining pursuits abound throughout the Medicine Bow Range. Two miles south of Centennial, prospectors in the late 1920s found traces of platinum in the slim pickings of gold, silver, and copper. Mining machinery was brought in, a town was platted at the foot of Centennial Ridge, and lots were offered for sale. But platinum proved as disappointing as gold. The mine lost money, and the government seized the property in 1938 for nonpayment of taxes. At auction, the $100,000 worth of machinery, camp equipment, and household articles sold for $7,000.

JUNCTION WITH STATE ROUTE 230

From here, northbound State 130 runs twenty-eight miles to I-80, passing through Saratoga along the way. To the south lie the former mining communities of Riverside, Encampment, and Battle.

RIVERSIDE

When copper was discovered in the Sierra Madre to the southwest in the 1890s, Riverside grew into a vibrant little town with a forty-room hotel. Copper mining in this area yielded more lasting prosperity than did any other mining venture in the Medicine Bow vicinity (except for coal). That's not saying much, since mining proved to be such a disappointment in this part of Wyoming. Still, copper mining employed people around here for a dozen years or so before the bust.

SARATOGA

Named for Saratoga Hot Springs in New York, the town got its start as a trading center in 1878. Like many other hot-springs areas in the state, Saratoga was popular with Indians long before whites arrived. Believing in the medicinal qualities of the waters, many Indians sought a cure here during a smallpox epidemic and died by the dozens.

The spring water is clear and odorless and feeds into swimming facilities on the banks of the North Platte River.

JUNCTION WITH I-80

To the west, I-80 continues to follow the route of the Union Pacific railroad, which was built across Wyoming during the years 1867–68. To the east, the interstate leads through Laramie and Cheyenne, hell-on-wheels towns during the railroad construction era.

The mountain range to the west of Encampment is called Sierre Madre, and State Route 70 climbs over it, becoming a good gravel road for the twenty-five-mile stretch across the Continental Divide.

Although these mountains are not those made famous by the Humphrey Bogart movie, they did draw prospectors who hoped to find treasure. A short-lived copper boom drew thousands of miners and their hangers-on to the area from 1897 to 1908. It prompted the founding of fourteen towns and camps and led to the construction of a smelter, aerial tramway, and railroad on the east side of the range. But the bubble burst in 1908, and nearly everyone bugged out.

This part of Wyoming once belonged to Mexico, hence the Spanish name of the mountains, which means "mother range."

ENCAMPMENT

When compared with the dreary results of metals mining elsewhere in this part of Wyoming, the mining of copper here at the turn of the century must have seemed like a resounding success.

Prospectors had filed claims in the Sierra Madre as early as 1868, but no one turned up anything truly promising until 1881, when George Doane found copper carbonates near Battle Lake and opened the Doane-Rambler Mine. The boom really began about fifteen years later, when Ed Haggarty uncovered a rich vein of copper ore. His discovery prompted a couple of investors to buy the town site of Encampment and begin selling lots.

People built homes and businesses and felt confident about the future. After all, officials at the Boston and Wyoming Smelter, Power and Light Company figured there was enough copper to build a smelter in 1902 and connect it to

Haggarty's mine in 1903 with a sixteen-mile aerial tramway. The tram had 304 towers and each of its buckets carried seven hundred pounds of ore. In 1905, the Penn-Wyoming company took over the properties and quickly built a railroad from Encampment to the Union Pacific's main line at Walcott.

Everything by then had fallen into place to boost Encampment into the front ranks as one of the nation's major copper production centers. But two things went wrong: the price of copper plummeted in 1907, and the copper ore around Encampment soon played out. The population in Encampment and the surrounding area soon dwindled from roughly three thousand to a few hundred. The smelter was eventually dismantled and shipped to South America. A museum in Encampment preserves relics of the copper-mining era: photographs, clothing, ghost-town buildings, a portion of the aerial tram, and horse-drawn wagons.

Encampment survived. So did the railroad line, but only after area ranchers bought it and gave it to the Union Pacific so they could continue to ship livestock to market. The other slap-together towns of the Sierra Madre copper boom perished, but their remains still scar the hillsides. One of them, Battle, stood about sixteen miles west of Encampment.

From the Continental Divide, Battle Lake is visible about one thousand feet below. There, on its banks, the inventor Thomas Edison cast for trout in 1878. Edison had come West with the Henry Draper Eclipse Expedition. A widely repeated story of doubtful veracity says Edison got his idea for a working light bulb while fiddling with a bamboo fishing rod next to Battle Lake.

SAVERY

At the western feet of the Sierra Madre lies the little town of Savery, a ranching community with a history that stretches back to the end of the fur-trapping era. Near here in 1841, a group of American Fur Company trappers was attacked by a large force of Lakota (often called Sioux) and Cheyenne Indians. Several trappers were killed, including Henry Fraeb, who had built a trading post in the vicinity with Jim Bridger in 1837.

One of the mountain men who fought in the 1841 battle near Savery eventually settled in the vicinity. His name was Jim Baker, and he had come West in 1831 at the ripe old age of thirteen. He trapped with Bridger during the height of the fur trade, watched that wild era come to an end, and then ran a ferry service across the Green River while hundreds of thousands of emigrants poured west during the 1840s and 1850s. Later, he moved to the Savery area with his two Indian wives and prospected in the Sierra Madre.

DIXON AND BAGGS

In the summer of 1897, Butch Cassidy and the Wild Bunch invaded these two towns to live it up for a while after robbing a bank in Belle Fourche, South Dakota. One witness said the gang shot up the Bull Dog Saloon in Baggs but later reimbursed the owner with a silver dollar for every bullet hole. Baggs must have seemed a hospitable municipality for such celebrations, because after a Nevada robbery in 1900 the gang returned there for another romp.

Baggs is also known for a character who walked, for the most part, on the opposite side of the law from the Wild Bunch. His name was Bob Meldrum, and he was town marshal in

1911–12. Before he arrived in Baggs, Meldrum had made a living as a strikebreaker in Colorado and a range detective and hired gun for large cattle interests on the Snake River. He had ridden with Tom Horn and was regarded as a cold-blooded killer.

Meldrum came to Baggs as town marshal in 1911. Early the following year, a popular local cowboy named Chick Bowen and a couple of friends came to town to blow off a little steam. While crossing the street from a saloon to the Elkhorn Hotel, Bowen let out a few whoops and the three cowboys ducked into the hotel for a meal.

While they ate, a waitress told them that the marshal was looking for Bowen. Apparently Meldrum was not fond of whoopers. Bowen and his friends finished their meal and then strolled over to the general store, which is where Meldrum caught up with them. Meldrum asked if Bowen had been whooping. Bowen denied it. Perhaps that annoyed Meldrum even more than the whooping, because Meldrum then knocked off Bowen's hat and started to arrest him. Bowen said he'd go quietly if he could just pick up his hat. That really seemed to get Meldrum's goat. He threatened to shoot Bowen in the legs and called him an SOB. Bowen objected to the term, then Meldrum opened fire and fatally wounded the cowboy in the stomach and groin.

Meldrum gave up his post as marshal and was charged with Bowen's death, but his lawyers kept the legal ball rolling for four years before a jury finally convicted him of voluntary manslaughter. He was sentenced to five to seven years in the state prison. After his release, he settled in Walcott as a harness-maker.

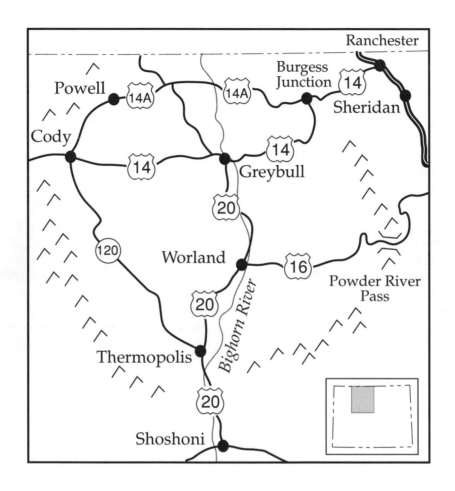

THE BIG HORN BASIN

BIG HORN BASIN: INTRODUCTION

History in the Big Horn basin covers most of the major eras in Wyoming's past, but probably the most intriguing chapter deals with the violent competition that erupted at the turn of the century between ranchers who raised cattle and those who raised sheep.

The smoldering tensions between cattlemen and sheepmen that broke murderously onto the scene were not unique to the Big Horn basin nor to Wyoming. Instead, the killing of sheepmen and the slaughter of their animals here was part of a fifty-year struggle that flared across public rangeland throughout the West. Raiders, often disguised in gunnysack masks, rode down on sheep camps about 120 times, killed more than fifty people, and butchered more than fifty thousand sheep. This sort of warring began in the 1870s in Texas and Colorado, then spread to Arizona in the 1880s, and to Wyoming, Washington, Oregon, and Idaho during the 1890s. The conflict continued through the early 1920s.

In Wyoming, trouble began in 1893 and continued until 1912. During those years, ten sheepmen, one cattleman, and sixteen thousand sheep were killed. Most of the raids took place between 1900 and 1909.

The conflict boiled down to a question of who would control the vast tracts of public land that surrounded the relatively small plots people were allowed to call their own. Due to homestead and other land laws designed for farming rather than ranching, most western ranchers could not legally gain title to more than a fraction of the acreage they needed to raise a reasonable number of animals. Once they filed on their legal allotment, they had very few ways to get more. Sharing the public land worked only until the range filled with livestock during the 1880s. Then the fatal winter of 1886–87 killed many of the cattle and left voids on the range that were quickly filled by the more resilient sheep. The cattlemen struck back violently in order to throw sheepmen off range the cattlemen had come to regard as their own.

Here, along the slopes of the mountains rimming the Big Horn basin, riders wielding clubs, poison, dynamite, and rifles struck sheep camps near Thermopolis, Meeteetse, and Ten Sleep. The range war came to a grisly climax near Ten Sleep in 1909, when two prominent sheepmen and a herder were murdered. The Ten Sleep raid marked the turning point in Wyoming. After it, cattlemen finally recognized that the sheep faction had gained sufficient clout within the state to enforce justice.

Long before whites began fighting among themselves for grazing rights on the floor of this huge oval-shaped basin, the land was controlled by the Crow Indians. It was the Crow who in 1807 greeted John Colter, probably the first Anglo to see the Big Horn basin. Colter had traveled with the explorers Lewis and Clark while the pair explored the territory of the Louisiana Purchase from 1803–1806. Rather than return to the East with the explorers, Colter chose to stay behind and trap fur in the Rockies. By 1807, he had teamed up with the St. Louis fur trader Manuel Lisa and had led Lisa's men to the confluence of the Big Horn and Yellowstone rivers, in present-day Montana. While Lisa's party of trappers built a fort, Colter set off through the Crow country, inviting the Indians to come trade at the new outpost.

He spent the fall of 1807 and perhaps the winter and spring of 1808 making a five-hundred-mile circuit through northwestern Wyoming. His walk took him through the Big Horn basin and up the Shoshone River. He saw Jackson Hole and was the first white to travel through what would become Yellowstone National Park.

Many other trappers followed Colter into the Big Horn basin. It offered plenty of streams where beaver thrived, and it also acted as a major thoroughfare to other important hunting grounds. These included the Yellowstone River to the north, the Green to the south, the Powder to the east, and tributaries of the Yellowstone and Missouri to the northwest.

After the fur trade went into a steep decline around 1840, few whites set foot in the basin until the late 1870s. Bridger's trail led through the basin, but few emigrants followed it. In 1859–60, Lt. H. E. Maynadier found gold in the basin, a discovery that should have attracted a flurry of miners but that seems to have been overlooked or undervalued until 1870, when a group of one hundred prospectors ventured as far north as modern Greybull. But they apparently had more success shooting buffalo than finding gold, because they soon broke camp and rode away.

In 1874, an army force accompanied by 136 Shoshone Indians fought a small band of Arapahos at the southern end of the basin. The battle took place on the divide between Bad Water and No Wood creeks, where the Arapahos had withdrawn after raiding the South Pass mining country. Two soldiers and two Shoshone were killed. Nine Arapaho warriors, one visiting Lakota, and eight Arapaho women were killed.

Later, as irrigation projects made farming in the basin's arid land possible, settlements began to appear along the Greybull and Shoshone rivers. Development of the Big Horn basin's oil fields also played an important part in developing its economy. Beginning in the 1880s, oil was pumped from the ground around Bonanza. In later years, refineries were built near Greybull, Cowley, Lovell, and Thermopolis. Companies literally fought for the right to drill for oil in one of the largest fields, Elk Basin. There, crews brawled with whips and clubs, and one outfit was turned back at gunpoint.

Today, the basin is one of the quietest regions of Wyoming, windswept, lonely, and beautiful.

As it plunges through Wind River Canyon and hugs the banks of the river north across the flats, U.S. 20 crosses land fought over by various Indian tribes, by whites against Indians, and by whites against whites. There are stories of outlaws riding into Thermopolis to celebrate their robberies by shooting up saloons and cafes, of citizens accelerating the judicial process by executing jail inmates, and of an elderly suitor courting and then murdering the object of his affections.

BOYSEN RESERVOIR

As the road runs north toward Wind River Canyon, it skirts the shores of Boysen Reservoir, a large body of water fed by the Wind River, which is dammed about fifteen miles north of Shoshoni. The first dam, built in 1903 by a wealthy rancher named Boysen, flooded the railroad tunnels nearby and had to be destroyed. A new dam was built in 1948.

WIND RIVER CANYON

This immense slot in the Owl Creek Mountains leads into the Big Horn basin, a flat pan of mostly arid ground almost completely surrounded by mountains. Cliffs in the canyon rise two thousand feet above the river, and the canyon runs for twenty miles. The water enters the canyon as the Wind River but leaves it as the Big Horn.

The view is spectacular from the bottom but even more impressive from the top of the cliffs. Indian legend says that a pair of young lovers once stood admiring the view from up there when the wind pulled an eagle feather from the young woman's hair. They watched the feather sail out over the river to a hot springs at the mouth of the canyon, near present Thermopolis. The lovers followed the feather, found the spring,

enjoyed themselves immensely, and told all their friends about it. Soon the hot spring was famous, and Indians came from all over to relax in its soothing waters.

Before the present highway was built along the canyon walls in 1924, drivers broke into the basin on a highway that led north from U.S. 26 at Moneta. That highway entered the mountains at about the same point that mountain man Jim Bridger marked for a wagon trail in 1864. Bridger's trail kept Montana-bound emigrants far west of the disputed Powder River country, which the Lakota, Cheyenne, and Arapaho tribes were defending from white passage. However, the terrain along Bridger's route was more difficult and did not provide enough water and forage for the emigrants' draft animals.

The canyon route has had its problems, too, even in modern times. In 1923, Badwater Creek swept away the railroad tracks from the southern entrance to the canyon. For weeks, no trains could run between the Big Horn basin and Casper.

BIG HORN BASIN

The floor of this huge oval-shaped basin measures roughly one hundred miles across and stretches between four encircling mountain ranges. The Big Horns stand to the east and include Cloud Peak, elevation 13,167 feet. The Owl Creek range forms the basin's southern boundary. The Absarokas rise to the west, and the Beartooths and Pryors hedge in the north.

THERMOPOLIS

Long a popular spot among Indians for its hot springs, the Thermopolis area began to draw white settlers in the late 1870s. However, the present town was not settled until 1897, when the Shoshone leader, Washakie, agreed to sell a sixty-thousand-acre tract of land south of Owl Creek to the U.S. government for $55,000. Until then, the land had been part of the Wind River Indian Reservation, and the whites who settled in the area tended to cluster at the mouth of Owl Creek, six miles up the road. Before Washakie agreed to the sale, he insisted that a portion of the hot springs remain open for public use. That area soon became Wyoming's first state park, Hot Springs State Park. Thermopolis developed into a resort town, drawing visitors from around the world to its soothing waters.

Sometimes, visitors who dropped into the Thermopolis area were not so welcome. Outlaws on the run from stagecoach holdups and train robberies in eastern Wyoming often headed for Hole-in-the-Wall, a notch in a red cliff west of Kaycee that leads into a wide, broken country. There, among the hills and ravines, they shook off pursuing lawmen and emerged in the Big Horn basin. Of course, after a long, hard chase there was nothing an outlaw liked better than a cold beer, a couple dozen shots of whiskey, and plenty of glassware to plink away at with his six-shooter. The little settlement at Owl Creek was just the place to raise some hell.

On election day in 1894, a group of fifty outlaws galloped in from the east and took over the town until residents regrouped and drove them out in a hail of bullets. During one especially boisterous visit by the Wild Bunch, Butch Cassidy supposedly shot up the town's cafe while the Sundance Kid pumped lead into the walls of the saloon.

Thermopolis lies in country where both sheep and cattle can thrive, and so, naturally, it is country where violence between the sheep and cattle outfits thrived. In December 1906, cattle ranchers formally declared that sheep would not be allowed to graze north of Owl Creek. The land they restricted involved some 250 square miles. When sheepmen ignored the cattlemen's declaration and drove their flocks into the forbidden zone in early 1907, the cattlemen raided their camps. In one attack, raiders burned the camp and killed four hundred sheep. In another, they drove off the herders and killed four thousand sheep.

LUCERNE

This town was named by railroad officials after the French word for alfalfa: *luzerne.* At Lucerne, State 172 heads east along the bank of Kirby Creek and parallels the route of the Bridger Road.

WORLAND

Founded in 1903, the city originally built its houses and shops on the west side of the river. However, the railroad chose to lay track on the east side, much to the regret of Worland's citizens. The following winter, when the Big Horn had frozen over, the citizens packed up and slid their goods across to the east bank and rebuilt the town.

Near Worland in 1975, archaeologists unearthed more evidence that people lived in Wyoming thousands of years before Columbus set sail for the Americas. The scientists found the remains of six immature ice-age mammoths that had been killed and butchered some 11,200 years ago. In addition to the bones, they found stone points, knives, and bone tools.

MANDERSON

If not for the prosaic imaginations of railroad bureaucrats, Wyoming might have had its own Alamo. The community's first settlers named the town after the Texas symbol of independence and defiance, but the railroad renamed the town for its top lawyer.

BASIN

In 1896, when it was still known as Basin City, the town engaged in a newspaper duel with neighboring Otto over which fledgling metropolis should become the county seat. Among the salvos fired from the copy decks of the two dreadnoughts was this broadside by the *Basin City Herald* against the editor of the *Otto Courier:* "A low-lived, brainless coward, biggest lying coward that ever breathed the breath of life, half-witted cur, brainless pup, skunk and poor fool."

Basin won the fight for the county seat and thus became the location of the most important murder trial in Big Horn basin history.

The trial, held in 1909, marked the end of the violent range war that had festered and flared between Wyoming cattle and sheep interests for nearly twenty years. Here, seven men were indicted for the murders of three sheepmen near the town of Ten Sleep (see page 156). The sheepmen had driven a herd of woollies across territory that the cattle interests had forbidden to sheep. Near Ten Sleep, raiders attacked the sheep camp at night, murdering two men in their beds and gunning down a third after he emerged from a wagon with his hands over his head. The murders outraged Wyoming citizens and turned public opinion firmly against the cattlemen's violent tactics, which, since 1893, had caused the deaths of ten Wyoming sheepmen, one cattleman, and more than sixteen thousand sheep.

The county sheriff and a U.S. marshal steadily built a case against two suspects and brought them before a grand jury. Eager to hear testimony, spectators from both the sheep and cattle sides of the conflict flocked to Basin. They jammed the hotels and staked out two campgrounds close to town—one for each faction. Testimony from witnesses placed seven men, including the two arrested, close to the scene of the crime. The grand jury returned murder indictments for the two jailed cattlemen as well as five others. Two of the latter quickly confessed and turned state's evidence.

The crowd in Basin swelled for the trial, and it looked like trouble might break out between the sheep and cattle groups. To keep the peace, and also to keep an eye on those in jail, eight members of the Wyoming National Guard were called out. Rumors flew that the large groups of armed cowboys roaming the town might swarm the jail and free the defendants. Nothing of the kind happened, but competition among spectators for seats in the courtroom grew so intense that the judge moved the trial from the courthouse to the local opera house.

For all the buildup, it wasn't much of a trial. The cattlemen hired some of the best legal talent in the state, but the high-priced lawyers put up a weak fight for the first defendant, Albert Brink. They challenged the character of one of the prosecution's witnesses, but that was about it. Other prosecution witnesses said they saw Brink shoot the sheepman who had emerged from his wagon with hands raised above his head.

The jury deliberated all night and then returned a guilty verdict for first-degree murder. Rather than fight a sure appeal, the prosecution agreed to allow Brink to plead guilty to second-degree murder at a new trial. He was sentenced to life. In the face of Brink's quick conviction, the defense saw that the cases of the other cattlemen were hopeless. So they plea-bargained: two twenty-year terms for second-degree murder; two others got three years for manslaughter; charges were dismissed against the two who turned state's evidence. Shunned by the community, these two soon left Basin.

The successful prosecution of these men for the Ten Sleep murders pretty much ended the violent confrontations between sheepmen and cattlemen in Wyoming. However, the conflict continued in other states through 1920.

Basin: Streamlined Justice

Occasionally the wheels of justice turned too slowly in Basin to satisfy the inhabitants' sense of fair play. Such was the case in July 1903, when people around town grew violently impatient with the disposition of two murder cases tediously grinding through the local court.

The first case involved an instance of unrequited love. After the death of her husband in 1900, Agnes L. Hoover took over the management of the family store in Otto. The widow soon attracted the attentions of Joseph Walters, an elderly traveling salesman who badgered her for months to return his affection. In September 1901, Hoover tried to rid herself of the suitor by taking a long vacation in Thermopolis. But Walters followed and tracked her to the state park on the east side of the river. There he opened the subject of matrimony. When she refused, he shot her dead.

Walters was convicted of first-degree murder in the spring of 1902, but more than a year later his appeal was still working its way through court. Meanwhile Walters cooled his heels in the Basin jail. With him was another man who had been convicted of manslaughter and was also waiting for a rehearing of his case.

This second man, Jim Gormon, had been convicted in 1902 of killing his brother, Tom, near Ten Sleep while the two of them were traveling with Tom's wife and infant daughter. The dead man had been found in a shallow grave, badly beaten and burned. His brother, wife, and child were found together in Red Lodge.

A year after their convictions, nothing seemed to be happening to these two killers. People in the surrounding area grew restless and decided to bring both matters to a head.

In the very early morning of July 19, a group of twenty-five to thirty armed men formed ranks and marched on the county building in Basin. They beat on the door of the jail and demanded entrance. When a deputy fired a shot over the heads in the crowd, the crowd promptly returned fire. One of the slugs struck and killed an assistant county clerk sleeping on a cot behind a counter in the lobby. The mob broke down the door and got into the jail but could not get to Walters or Gormon in their cells. Walters could see that this was the end for him, so he told the crowd to shoot him and held up a candle to make a better target. The crowd obliged, then shot Gormon five times and left. Gormon didn't die right away but was taken to a doctor's office and asked about the circumstances of his brother's death. He did not implicate his sister-in-law, who, when told of the shooting, immediately asked if Gormon had revealed anything.

A grand jury was convened to weigh the crowd's action and indicted several suspects. Only one was put on trial. Since witnesses were reluctant to testify, the case was dismissed.

Highway 16 tops the Big Horn Mountains at Powder River Pass, elevation 9,666 feet, and then winds down onto the high plains through Ten Sleep Canyon. It's a beautiful drive, and it passes the most important site in the history of the conflict between Wyoming sheepmen and cattlemen. In 1909, along the banks of Spring Creek, three sheepmen were murdered in their camp after driving a herd of sheep across territory that the cattlemen had placed off-limits to woollies. The murders turned the tide of public opinion against the cattle industry's brutal tactics, and the incident marks the end of the state's range wars.

TEN SLEEP CANYON

Gilbert Leigh, an Englishman who was fond of riding off into the Big Horn Mountains, fell off a cliff in Ten Sleep Canyon in 1884. When Leigh's horse marked his demise by returning to his ranch without him, friends tracked Leigh's course to the bottom of a six-hundred-foot cliff. They named the cliff after him and put up a monument.

TEN SLEEP

In April 1909, the range war between Wyoming cattle and sheep interests came to a grisly climax south of Ten Sleep on the banks of Spring Creek. There, night raiders attacked a sheep camp and murdered three men, including two prominent sheep ranchers. This bloody act marked a significant turning point in the conflict because it aroused public contempt for the cattlemen's outlaw tactics at a time when the state's sheep ranchers had finally gained significant clout in the courts and in government. For years, cattlemen had gone virtually unpunished for their violent raids. This time, they would pay.

Although the climax came in 1909, trouble

between Wyoming sheepmen and cattlemen had broken out nearly twenty years before. Starting in the early 1890s, scattered incidents of slaughtered sheep and wounded or murdered sheepmen were recorded across the state. Typically, masked men rode into sheep camps at night and slaughtered the animals by running them off cliffs or by killing them with clubs, dynamite, or guns. Serious violence in the Big Horn basin began in 1903, when a sheepman was shot to death between Meeteetse and Thermopolis (see page 164). The following year, a prominent sheep rancher was killed on Kirby Creek, northeast of Thermopolis.

At stake was control of Wyoming's rich grazing land. Cattlemen tried to forbid sheep from vast sections of it by openly declaring boundaries, called "deadlines," beyond which sheep would not be allowed to graze. Sheepmen complained that the cattlemen had no right to restrict them from public lands. Sometimes the sheepmen respected the boundaries because they lacked the power to challenge them. In isolated regions, sheep and cattle interests occasionally agreed on an equitable division of the public domain. But where sheepmen grazed their flocks in open defiance of the deadlines, violence often followed. Such was the case near Ten Sleep in 1909.

Area cattlemen had forbidden sheep in the badlands region between Worland and Ten Sleep. However, in late March Joe Emge decided to drive a flock of twenty-five hundred sheep from Worland across the disputed territory to his ranch east of Nowood Creek.

Emge was an interesting character. For years, he had lived as a cattle rancher and made no secret of his passionate hatred for sheep. He had erected an illegal fence to keep the woollies out of public lands on the western slopes of the Big Horns, and some say he participated in a few of the cattlemen's raids on the basin's sheep camps. However, the profits available in sheep ranching prompted Emge to sell his cattle and enter a partnership with a well-regarded sheepman, Joe Allemand. This act earned him the contempt of area cattlemen.

In March 1909, the two men picked up their sheep from winter pastures near Worland and, with the help of three hired hands, began driving them across the prohibited land. They knew the dangers of crossing the cattlemen's deadline. They had received many threats while in Worland staging their sheep drive, and they proceeded with a caution underlined by three rifles and an automatic pistol. Six days later, the party emerged from the prohibited territory unscathed. Relieved, and feeling they were safe, they made camp several miles south of Ten Sleep on the banks of Spring Creek. Three of the men, including Emge and Allemand, slept in one wagon north of the creek. Two others slept in a wagon on the south bank.

Shortly after 10:00 P.M., five raiders wearing gunnysack masks stole into the north-bank camp and opened fire on the wagon, killing Emge and one of the hired hands. Allemand, also wounded, lurched from the wagon. One of the raiders told him to put his hands over his head. When he complied, the raider shot and wounded him again. Then another raider stepped forward and, with a downward stroke from a shovel, cut Allemand's throat. Mean-

while, raiders at the south-bank camp rousted the two men from the wagon, frisked them for weapons, and told them to walk off down the road without looking back. This they did, unmolested, while the raiders doused the wagons with coal oil and set them ablaze.

News of the raid spread through the Big Horn basin and across the state the next day. The public was incensed. A reward of $5,500 was pledged by various wool growers' associations, the county commission, and an Allemand relative. The West's finest detectives converged on the Ten Sleep area and within ten days had arrested two men. By the end of the month a grand jury had convened in Basin and soon indicted them, along with five other cattlemen. After a colorful, well-attended trial in Basin (see page 154), the man who had shot Allemand pleaded guilty to second-degree murder and received a life sentence. Two others also pleaded guilty to second-degree murder but were given twenty-year terms. Two more pleaded guilty to manslaughter and got three years. Charges against the final pair were dismissed in exchange for their testimony about the murders.

After the Ten Sleep raid, violence against sheep camps in Wyoming faded from the scene. Thereafter, conflicts between the two factions were settled by private agreement or in court. The Wyoming range war was over.

This road, which leads over the Big Horn Mountains from the Sheridan area, crosses the Big Horn basin and eventually passes through Shoshone National Forest to Yellowstone National Park. After dropping down from a spectacular tour of the Big Horns, the road empties out onto the plains and passes through several communities founded at the turn of the century. Across the basin, U.S. 14 strikes Cody, an attractive resort town named after the Wild West showman Buffalo Bill Cody. From there, the road climbs over the Absaroka Mountains to Yellowstone.

BURGESS JUNCTION

Here U.S. 14 splits. For information about alternate U.S. 14, see page 160.

GREYBULL

Local legend says the town and river were named for a large gray bull buffalo that wandered the region and frustrated all hunters' attempts to kill it. Pictographs in cliffs over the river show a buffalo bull with an arrow in its body.

The town was founded in 1909 as the center of a farming area. Soon afterward, the discovery of oil and gas in nearby fields led to the construction of two refineries. It also became a center for producing bentonite.

EMBLEM

Water diverted from the Greybull River to the Germania Bench in 1902 by S. L. Wiley's Big Horn Basin Development Company prompted about six hundred people, mostly Germans, to move into the area. Their common ethnic heritage led them to name the town and the bench of land they farmed "Germania." However, intense anti-German propaganda and hostility during World War I goaded residents into renaming both the town and the bench Emblem.

BURLINGTON AND OTTO

Before S. L. Wiley's irrigation company brought water to the area, a colony of Mormons painstakingly irrigated a section of the Germania Bench and began farming. They came in 1893 and built up the towns of Burlington and Otto as centers of supply and worship. Because they had very little money, they had to dig the necessary irrigation ditches by hand. They harvested their first crop in 1895 from the first areas irrigated along the river's bottomland.

CODY

Homesteaders began settling the area in the mid-1880s, but the town of Cody was not platted until 1895, when boosters invited Buffalo Bill Cody to become president of the company developing the surrounding area. They then accepted the showman's suggestion that the town be named after him.

Thanks to its proximity to Yellowstone National Park and the celebrity status of its namesake, Cody quickly became a vacation center. Prior to the naming of the town, very little connected Bill Cody to the community or the area. He did his Pony Express riding, Indian fighting, and buffalo hunting mostly in other sections of Wyoming or outside the state entirely. However, the town now houses much of the Buffalo Bill memorabilia and continues to mythologize the man. His legend still attracts people to Cody, where the Iowa house he was born in has been moved and where the hotel he built and named

William "Buffalo Bill" Cody, Pony Express rider, army scout, hunter, and entertainer. The Iowa native took his Wild West Show throughout the United States and Europe. The Wyoming town of Cody is named for Buffalo Bill. *(University of Wyoming American Heritage Center)*

for his daughter, Irma, still opens its doors to guests.

Cody is much more than a showman's museum, though. The Buffalo Bill Historical Center, on the west end of town, shelters the Whitney Collection of Western Art—one of the finest collections of western painting and sculp-

ture in the country. In addition, the historical center boasts a fine Plains Indian museum and a collection of antique firearms. Naturally, the center also displays artifacts and mementos of Bill Cody's rich and varied career. Old Trail Town, with its long row of old buildings and artifacts, is another good stop on which to pick up the flavor of days gone by.

SHOSHONE RIVER

As U.S. 14 climbs out of Cody, it runs along the banks of the Shoshone River, which for many years went by the much more colorful name of Stinking Water River. John Colter, a fur trapper who made a five-hundred-mile circuit of northwestern Wyoming on foot in the winter of 1807–08, gave the river that name after he came across some malodorous hot springs (Colter's Hell) on the western edge of modern Cody. Trappers and settlers knew it by that name, but the area's boosters, believing that such a name might put off the tourist trade, changed the name to Shoshone in 1902.

The large body of water west of town is the Buffalo Bill Reservoir. The project to build the dam began in 1899 as a semiprivate venture backed by Buffalo Bill and a partner. However, their work stalled due to lack of funds, and in 1904 the federal government stepped in to complete the work. The dam, originally known as the Shoshone, was the first federal dam built in Wyoming. Completed in 1910, it eventually helped to irrigate some 94,000 acres and to supply hydroelectric power.

This road, which breaks away from U.S. 14 at Burgess Junction, takes a more northerly route across the Big Horn basin than does the main branch of the highway. Along this spectacular high-mountain road, travelers pass an ancient stone formation in the shape of a large wheel, several farming communities made possible by irrigation from the Shoshone River, and the site of a relocation camp that confined Japanese Americans during World War II.

MEDICINE WHEEL

Very little is known about this assembly of stones, which some have called Wyoming's Stonehenge. Most believe that it is a site of worship for early Indians. Many don't realize that it is still a sacred object for traditional people of some Plains tribes.

Located a few miles north of the highway on a small marked road, the Medicine Wheel is seventy feet across with twenty-nine spokes radiating from a central cairn. Six outer cairns face the rising sun and stand along the spokes at varying distances from the center.

The carbon-dating of wood found within the cairns indicates that portions might have been built as early as 1200 A.D. Some claim it might date back thousands of years. Hypotheses abound over the wheel's purpose, but many guess that it acted as an observatory, helping prehistoric people locate stars and planets.

Whatever its purpose, the wheel seems to correspond with another old monument that stands clear across the Big Horn basin, deep in the mountains above Meeteetse. That monument, called the Great Arrow, is fifty-eight feet long, five and a half feet wide, and points toward the Medicine Wheel.

M.L. RANCH

This restored ranch fourteen miles east of Lovell belonged to Henry Clay Lovell and Anthony Mason, who were among the first to run cattle into the Big Horn basin in 1879. Mason, who never visited the ranch, supplied the money. Lovell, a frontier veteran with three bullet wounds, supplied the know-how. Their operation, which ran about twenty thousand head of cattle, was probably the largest in the basin before the turn of the century. In 1883, Lovell was the first to ship basin cattle to market on the Northern Pacific railroad. He shipped thirty-two hundred steers and got forty-five dollars a head, more than enough to pay for the original herd he trailed into the basin just a few years before.

LOVELL

Lovell, Byron, and Cowley were laid out in 1900 by a large group of Mormon colonists who came to the Big Horn basin under the banner of the Big Horn Colonization Company. They intended to build a large canal that would divert water from the Shoshone River and irrigate twenty thousand acres of cropland. They were confident they would prosper because another group of Mormons had succeeded in a similar endeavor farther south, along the Greybull River near Burlington and Otto (see page 158). The canal here, called the Sidon Canal, was thirty-seven miles long and took just two years to build.

Lovell was named for Henry Clay Lovell, the working partner of the M.L. Ranch. Cowley was named for Mathias F. Cowley, a Mormon leader. Byron was named for Byron Sessions, another Mormon leader and the man in charge of building the canal, which made the whole scheme of farming (sugar beets) in the area possible.

Two neighboring farmers accidentally discovered a large natural-gas field near Byron in 1905 while one of them was building a fence. Noticing gas venting from a posthole, the two decided to see if the gas would burn. It did. It came from a mammoth gas field that eventually provided heat and light for neighboring towns, as well as for sugar factories, oil refineries, and other plants that needed intense heat. Today, oil pumps bob in the ranch fields beside the highway.

POWELL

During the 1890s, the Interior Department set up a camp here for workers involved in the Shoshone reclamation project (see page 159). The camp later grew into a town, which was incorporated in 1910 and named for John Wesley Powell, the famous explorer of the Grand Canyon and a reclamation advocate.

HEART MOUNTAIN RELOCATION CENTER

Several miles beyond Ralston, a small brown sign marks a road leading to the site of Heart Mountain Relocation Center, one of ten camps where the U.S. government confined Japanese Americans during World War II.

After Pearl Harbor, the War Department decided that the security of the West Coast required forcing American Japanese from their homes in California, Washington, and Oregon and moving them inland. Hastily constructed, the Heart Mountain Relocation Center began receiving the first of roughly eleven thousand internees in August 1942. Soon, the camp became the third-largest city in the state.

Most of those who arrived on the arid slopes of Heart Mountain were loyal Americans. Two-thirds had been born in the United States and were therefore citizens. The rest were foreign-born and were barred from citizenship by the nation's naturalization laws.

Conditions at Heart Mountain came as an abrupt and unwelcome change. The "evacuees" had been forced to sell their homes and businesses at bargain-basement prices, to store most of their personal belongings, and to move from the mild West Coast climate to a dusty mountainside where the temperature dropped well below zero during the winter. They lived within a barbed-wire perimeter guarded by watchtowers. There were no sidewalks, no lawns, no trees. They slept on cots in tar-paper barracks. The rooms had no running water and were illuminated by a single light bulb dangling from the ceiling. They shared bath, laundry, and mess-hall facilities.

Gradually, conditions improved. The residents made their own furniture from scrap lumber left behind by the workers who had built the compound. Each room got a coal-burning stove to beat back the cold. Trees and shrubs were planted. A 150-bed hospital was built. Three general stores opened and plowed their profits back into the Heart Mountain community. Children attended the center's elementary school and high school (and even won the Big Horn basin football championship in 1944). Adults worked in the center's mess halls, stores, police and fire departments, and farmland. A small newspaper staffed by residents kept track of community events and acted as its collective voice. Group activities ranged from harmonica classes to sumo wrestling competitions.

Spartan though life was for Heart Mountain's residents, one of Wyoming's U.S. senators accused administrators of pampering the Japanese. Senator E. V. Robertson, himself foreign-born, cited a series of inflammatory articles published by the *Denver Post* about coddling, high living, and the alleged hoarding of rationed food. The residents of Heart Mountain "are the same kind of Japs that American boys are fighting in the Pacific," the *Post* wrote. "They are the same breed of rats as those over in Japan who have murdered American prisoners." Though completely off base, the articles pandered to the prejudices of many Wyoming citizens, especially those who lived near Heart Mountain.

The Japanese had been unwelcome from the start. The state legislature passed laws denying the American citizens of Heart Mountain the right to vote, own property, or obtain hunting and fishing licenses. Heart Mountain residents could obtain temporary passes to leave the camp, but some in the neighboring communities of Cody and Powell shut them out by hanging "No Japs" signs in the windows of private businesses. Powell's city council even passed a resolution largely barring Heart Mountain residents from town—except as much-needed laborers during the harvest season. In retaliation, the camp's administrators refused to issue passes of any kind, even for harvest work. The ensuing labor shortage, combined with pressure from merchants who counted on the patronage of Heart Mountain residents, prompted the city councils of Powell and Cody to ask the camp's director to resume issuing passes.

Among those allowed to leave the camp were nine hundred young men inducted into the U.S. Army. They joined highly decorated Japanese-American units that fought in Europe. Twenty were killed in action.

CODY: JUNCTION WITH 14

This pleasant resort town stands as a monument of sorts to the memory of Buffalo Bill Cody, the Pony Express Rider and army scout who became famous as an entertainer and took his Wild West show all over the world (see page 158).

Like many of the roads through the Big Horn basin, State 120 leads through valuable grazing land where the interests of cattle ranchers and wool growers collided violently around the turn of the century. Between Thermopolis and Meeteetse, sheep were slaughtered, wagons were burned, herders were beaten up, and one sheepman was killed. The road leads across the southwestern perimeter of the basin and ends at the resort town of Cody.

THERMOPOLIS

Built on land bought from the Shoshone tribe in 1897, Thermopolis was frequently disrupted by cheerfully violent outlaws who galloped in after robberies to celebrate. Today, most strangers who ride into Thermopolis come to enjoy the fine hot springs (see page 152).

MEETEETSE

Built at the foot of a steep hill on the Greybull River, Meeteetse got its official start in 1896, when the town site was platted. However, civilization actually came to the area in 1884, when a Frenchman named Victor Arland and his partner opened a saloon and store nearby. Arland's letters to a friend back in Illinois provide a striking description of life in the basin during the boom-and-bust years of Wyoming's nineteenth-century cattle industry:

> The cowboys are singular characters, very violent and without their equals in their spirit of independence. But they know how to appreciate a man of courage and energy. In the towns of the Far West they are getting a most deplorable reputation through their audacity and lack of restraint. But at our place, I can assure you, they behave very well, which astonished very much those who don't know cowboys thoroughly. In the early days, when I first kept a saloon, they

thought that I would permit them all liberty at our place. But after having thrown into the river several of these desperate characters, they showed lots of respect for us and our place.

Indians still frequented the Big Horn basin in the 1880s, especially the Crow tribe, which came south from their reservation in Montana to hunt.

"Lately a band of Crow Indians came to camp close to our place," Arland wrote in 1885. He added a comment typical of the time for its intercultural misunderstanding and dash of Anglo arrogance: "They thought that they were giving me a great gift in giving me two scalps of Indians killed by them . . . I must tell you that I am far from putting the same value on these scalps as those Indians do."

During his years as a bartender, Arland had to do more than throw a few drunk yahoos in the river to keep the peace at his place. In 1888, he wrote his friend:

> I was obliged to kill a man in order to avoid being killed myself. If he had not been killed himself, he would have killed one or several persons. There were close to 50 people here, as I was giving a dance that day in honor of Washington's birthday. This incident didn't in the least prevent the dance from taking place. Far from it. Everybody, feeling safe from being attacked by that "bad man," began to have a good time in the best of spirits.

Soon Arland's luck in gunplay ran out. He was shot dead while playing poker in Red Lodge, Montana.

Meeteetse: Range War

The sometimes violent struggle between cattlemen and sheepmen over control of Wyoming's rangeland surfaced near Meeteetse in

1902. Southwest of town, in the Wood River drainage, raiders struck three times trying to keep sheep off public land they claimed the exclusive domain of cattle. At one camp they stampeded two bands of sheep over a cliff. At another they pushed a herder's wagon off a cliff. At the third they killed more than thirty sheep. Unfortunately these incidents were just a warmup.

During the winter, sheepman William Minick angered area cattlemen by grazing his sheep on land between Meeteetse and Thermopolis that had been recognized as cattle country for many years. The reprisal came on a cold February morning at the sheep camp where Minick's brother Ben and another man tended the flock. They were sitting inside a herder's wagon, keeping warm, when they heard a knock at the door. Ben opened up, greeted a man wearing a bandana (not unusual considering the weather), and invited him inside. When Ben turned his back, the man shot him. The gunman apparently understood quickly that he had shot the wrong man, because he apologized, claimed it was an accident, and helped Ben's companion lift him onto the bed in the herder's wagon. The gunman then joined two accomplices in killing two hundred of Minick's sheep. Ben Minick, his spinal cord severed, died that night.

A few months later, "Driftwood Jim" McCloud was arrested for the murder and jailed in Thermopolis. McCloud was wanted for other crimes as well, including the robbery of the Buffalo post office. The authorities wanted to move McCloud to Basin for the trial, but they were worried that he might be killed before the judge could rap his gavel and bring the court to order. (A Basin mob had just broken into the jail and killed two men accused of murder. See page 155.) So the governor called out the state militia to keep the peace while McCloud was tried. He beat the murder rap, but that wasn't the end of

McCloud's adventures. He still had the robbery to answer for. Transferred to Cheyenne, he shared a jail cell with Tom Horn, recently convicted of killing Willie Nickell, a sheepman's son. The two men broke out of the Cheyenne jail but were quickly recaptured. McCloud was sentenced to a term in Leavenworth. Horn was executed. (For more about Horn and the jailbreak, see page 116.)

PITCHFORK

The Pitchfork Ranch, home to a German count turned cattleman (originally) and to a famous Western photographer (later), lies sixteen miles west of Meeteetse on State 260. Count Otto Franc von Lichtenstein came to the basin in 1878 and established the Pitchfork with twelve to sixteen hundred cattle he trailed to the site from western Montana. By 1886, Franc had increased his herd to about six thousand head. Small but energetic, he was a progressive rancher. Unlike most stockmen of the day, he bought a large tract of farm land where he grew alfalfa to protect his cattle against lean winters. Also, Franc often toured his spread on a bicycle, but that particular innovation never caught on with the other cowpokes. Franc died in 1903.

Charlie Belden was the next proprietor of the Pitchfork. His photos of working cowboys in the 1920s and 1930s made him famous, and prints of his work hang in museums all over the state. Belden kept a herd of antelope on the ranch and delivered them by airplane to zoos. One shipment crossed the Atlantic by zeppelin in the 1930s. His descendants still own the place.

CODY

For information about this pleasant resort town, or to pick up the east-west U.S. 14 route at this point, see page 158.

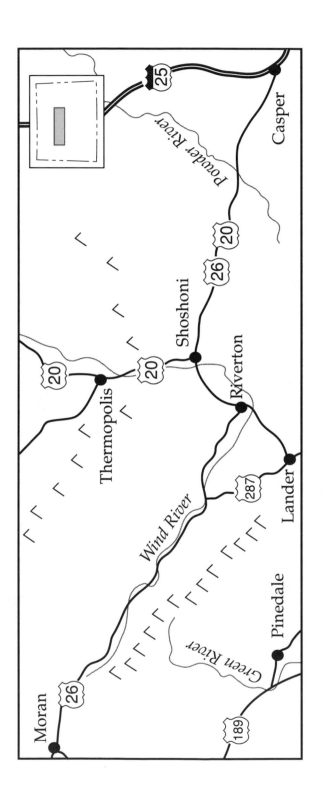

THE WIND RIVER VALLEY

THE WIND RIVER VALLEY: INTRODUCTION

This beautiful valley, which runs along the feet of some of Wyoming's highest peaks, acted as a highway for Indians and Anglos long before steamrollers pressed hot asphalt onto the banks of the Wind River. Crows and Shoshones, who had an ancient enmity, lived and hunted in this valley, and Crows often wintered near Dubois, where the ground stays free of snow most of the winter. If John Colter came to that area on his grand walking tour in the autumn of 1807 (see page 150), he was the first white man to visit the valley of the Wind River.

The first whites known to have been here passed through in 1811 on their way to Oregon. The party was financed by John Jacob Astor and led by Wilson Price Hunt. The men intended to build a trading post at the mouth of the Columbia River in order to control the Northwest fur trade. Their passage through Wyoming was pleasant and uneventful, but problems on the Columbia prompted Hunt to send a small party back to New York the following year. These returning Astorians, led by Robert Stuart, never did find the Wind River Valley again. They got lost in western Wyoming and nearly starved. But then, with directions from a friendly Indian, they walked over South Pass and down the Sweetwater River, thus "discovering" what would be called the Oregon Trail.

Later, the trappers who followed the Astorians into the Wind River Valley found plenty of beaver and had encounters with Indians that were both dangerous and sublime. In the summer of 1829, Jim Bridger and Jim Beckwourth separated in the valley in order to trap two forks of a stream. While poking along his fork, Beckwourth suddenly found himself surrounded by Crow Indians. He might have been a goner, but Beckwourth was lucky. Another trapper, while living with the Crow, had told them a preposterous fib. Beckwourth, according to the man's story, was

Wilson Price Hunt, who led a party of fur trappers through a portion of Wyoming in 1811. Hunt established a trading post on the Oregon coast for the American Fur Company. Problems there prompted him to send a small overland party back East the following year. These men, led by Robert Stuart and assisted by friendly Shoshone Indians, were probably the first whites to cross South Pass. *(University of Wyoming American Heritage Center)*

Chief Washakie, *center,* allied his tribe, the Shoshone, with white civilization in order to fend off traditional enemies—the Lakota, Cheyenne, and Arapaho. Today Washakie's descendants live on the Wind River Indian Reservation in central Wyoming, sharing the land with the Arapaho. *(University of Wyoming American Heritage Center)*

the son of a great Crow chief. The Cheyenne had kidnapped him as a boy and raised him to be a great warrior. Then the whites got hold of him for a while and he came back to the mountains as a trapper. Well, once Beckwourth's credentials had been established by the Crows, he was treated better than the New Testament's Prodigal Son. He was given twenty horses and four wives. Beckwourth later wrote, in *The Life and Adventures of James P. Beckwourth:* "I could not find it in my heart to undeceive these unsuspecting people and tear myself away from their untutored caresses."

Trappers traveled, camped, rendezvoused, and wintered in the Wind River Valley because both the Crows and Shoshones were generally friendly to whites.

From Shoshoni through the Wind River Valley, the road crosses the Wind River Indian Reservation. When the Shoshone leader Washakie signed a treaty with the government in 1863, his tribe was promised an area twenty times the size of today's reservation. Through the years, white ambitions for the Popo Agie (pronounced poh-POH-zhuh) and Wind River valleys chipped off large chunks of the reserved lands. And, in 1878, the federal government moved the Arapaho tribe onto the reservation – a bitterly ironic move because the army had just defeated the Arapaho tribe with much help from Shoshone warriors. (For more about the reservation's history, see page 175).

After beaver trapping, the next substantial white enterprise was the livestock industry. By the 1890s, and for twenty years thereafter, cattlemen and sheepmen fought over the valley's grazing lands, often violently.

Tie hacks came to the valley about the time of World War I to cut conifers, shape them into railroad ties, and float them down the river to Riverton. Later, the timber industry did lots of clear-cutting, a controversial technique, on the vast forests of the upper valley.

In the 1950s the Riverton area experienced a uranium boom.

Now the Wind River Valley is mostly a heaven of a place to live and a hell of a place to make a living. The entire region suffered from a loss of jobs in the 1980s because of the closing of a steel mine and a lumber mill. Now people guide dudes, wrangle cows, work for the government, cut timber in a small way, and live on hope.

RIVERTON

The highways run northwest through this valley like a divining rod; one of the handles is at Lander, the other at Riverton.

Riverton was built on land that the Shoshone and Arapaho tribes gave up under the 1904 agreement that made way for homesteading. Here as in Shoshoni, disputes between potential homesteaders in the summer of 1906 led authorities to call in troops to keep the peace. The settlers who flocked to the area counted on an extensive irrigation project proposed by the Wyoming Central Irrigation Company. Progress stalled, however, and after four years many gave up and left. In 1920, the federal government rescued the project by spending $26 million to irrigate about 53,000 acres under the Riverton Reclamation Project. Except for land included in the project, most of the territory ceded by the tribes in 1904 was restored to the reservation in 1939.

Riverton did not prosper in a big way until discovery of the uranium in the Gas Hills east of town kicked off a mining boom. During the early years of the cold war, the government guaranteed the price for all uranium of a certain grade discovered in the United States. Prospectors with geiger counters combed likely areas throughout Wyoming, discovering paying quantities as early as 1949. Wyoming eventually proved to contain a significant proportion of all the usable uranium deposits in the nation. The boom hit Riverton in 1953 when a local mechanic discovered deposits in the Gas Hills.

The radioactive ore brought prosperity to the town, but it also brought some problems. The Environmental Protection Agency reported in 1973 that tailings from an abandoned uranium mill near Riverton were contaminating the area. There were similar troubles with uranimum

mining elsewhere in the state.

Riverton: Trappers

Long before Chief Washakie moved his people here, the site of modern Riverton was a major landmark for Indians and mountain men. The confluence of the Popo Agie and Wind rivers acted as a crossroads. From here the traveler could follow the Wind River northwest to Union Pass and over to the head of the Green River valley or into Jackson's Hole. Those bound due north for the Big Horn basin simply followed the river downstream, and those headed for South Pass could mark their way along the banks of the Popo Agie.

The tradition of an annual rendezvous of Rocky Mountain trappers began in 1825, when William Ashley packed supplies into a site near modern McKinnon in the extreme southwest corner of the state. His idea was to bring a mobile trading post to a large gathering of trappers and collect all their *plews* (beaver pelts) in one big swap (see page 186). The rendezvous caught on in a big way, and much of the mountain man's lore revolves around the annual blow-out.

Though most of the Wyoming rendezvous were held in the Green River valley, two were held near Riverton. The first was in 1830, at the height of the fur trade, when beaver were plentiful and prices high. The 1838 rendezvous was a more somber affair. By then, demand for the skins had plummeted, and there was depressing talk that a way of life was coming to an end.

BULL LAKE

In winters gone by, an odd groaning sound was occasionally heard along the shores of Bull Lake, located about two miles south of Highway 26. The Shoshone named it The Lake That Roars,

Alfred Jacob Miller's painting of a trappers' rendezvous on Green River with the Wind River Mountains as a backdrop. *(University of Wyoming American Heritage Center)*

and legend says hunters chased a white buffalo into its waters, where it drowned. The odd groaning, the legend says, is the angry spirit of the white buffalo.

A less colorful explanation is that the sounds were produced when wind blew through ice faults that heaved up from the surface.

CROWHEART BUTTE

This prominent butte, which stands just a few miles southeast of the town with the same name, is supposed to be where the Shoshone leader Washakie killed a Crow chief in single combat and then ate his heart. Although Washakie did lead a force of Shoshone and Bannock warriors to victory against a Crow raiding party near here in 1866, the battle was not fought on the butte. When pressed later about whether he actually ate a human heart, Washakie answered that sometimes young men do foolish things.

DUBOIS

Early settlers knew the area as "Never Sweat." It was christened as such by a pioneer woman ribbing local men about their apparent attitude toward work. When settlers applied for a post office in 1886, they asked that the town officially adopt the name. Instead, the post office named the place Dubois. Some say the name was intended to flatter U.S. Senator Dubois of Idaho, who happened to be sitting on the committee governing the postal service. Others say a local suggested the name to honor a family he knew in Colorado.

However it got its name, Dubois could easily qualify as the post office that proved the famous saying about the mailman: Neither rain nor sleet nor dark of night shall keep him from his appointed rounds. That's because during the winter, mail had to be delivered by snowshoe from Fort Washakie, a sixty-mile walk.

In its early days, Dubois was a supply point for neighboring ranches. Some say Butch Cassidy, of Wild Bunch fame, bought one of the ranches with proceeds from the robbery of the San Miguel Valley Bank in Telluride, Colorado.

In later years, Dubois became a center for producing railroad ties. A monument about ten miles northwest of town commemorates the tie hacks, the men who cut the timber, hewed and sawed it to size (eight feet long, seven inches thick), and floated the ties downriver. The forest hacks were paid ten cents a tie, and they could fashion about thirty of them every day. For this intense labor they required an astonishing nine thousand calories a day to keep the axes swinging.

Between 1914 and 1946, some 400,000 to 700,000 ties were cut every year in the forests above town and floated downstream to the railhead at Riverton. In the 1930s, the tie-production headquarters on Warm Creek west of town had a population of 350. The hacks are gone now, victims of the general decline of railroads and a more efficient (some say destructive) timber industry.

The lumber mill of Louisiana-Pacific, in fact, was a major employer in Dubois until it closed in the 1980s. The surrounding national forests were not cutting enough timber to keep the mill operating, a policy both praised and damned locally.

UNION PASS

This important route across the Rockies lies

A tie hack. These hardy men, who operated in the forests around Dubois until the late 1930s, began felling trees in Wyoming in 1868 for the Union Pacific. They went through an astonishing number of calories each day. *(Jackson Hole Museum and Teton County Historical Society, Jackson, Wyoming)*

astride the Continental Divide northwest of Dubois at an elevation of 9,210 feet. It was used in the earliest of times by Indians, and later by the mountain men, in order to cross between the Wind River and Green River valleys, or into Jackson Hole. It was a fine pass for those on horseback, but far too rugged for most emigrants, who preferred to cross the Divide over South Pass.

In 1811, Wilson Price Hunt and the Astorians used the pass to get to Oregon. Many other trappers, explorers, and dignitaries followed, including Jim Bridger, Ferdinand Hayden, Gen.

Phil Sheridan, and even a president, Chester Arthur, in 1883. The pass is one of the few places in the United States where the waters divide into three major watersheds. Fish Creek is a source of the Columbia River. Jakey's Fork empties into the Mississippi. Roaring Fork runs into the Green and thence to the Colorado and the Gulf of Cortez. A primitive road nine miles northwest of Dubois travels fifteen miles to the pass.

DU NOIR RIVER

In mid-August 1835, Osborne Russell and a group of trappers camped along the Du Noir River, northwest of modern Dubois. They wanted to get to the headwaters of the Shoshone River, which they knew as the Stinking River, but of course the Absaroka Mountains stood in their way.

To get to the other side of the range today, one has two choices: drive through the national parks or take the long loop through the Big Horn basin. The mountaineers' route was more direct, and much more difficult. Russell described their passage in his journal:

> We followed the glen east as far as we could ride, and then all dismounted and walked except for the wounded man who rode until the mountain became so steep his horse could carry him no longer. We then assisted him from his horse and carried or pushed him to the top of the divide over the snow . . . In the meantime it commenced snowing very hard. After gaining the summit we unloaded our animals and rushed them on to the snow on the other side which

being hard they went helter skelter down to a warmer climate and were arrested by a smooth grassy spot. We then lowered the wounded man down by cords and put our saddles and baggage together on the snow, jumped on top and started slowly at first. But the velocity soon increased until we brought up tumbling heels over head on a grassy bench in a more moderate climate.

Russell didn't say whether the wounded man enjoyed the descent.

TOGWOTEE PASS

Pronounced TOW-guh-dee by local people, the Shoshone word means "lance thrower." The pass climbs to 9,658 feet through dense conifer forests and broad, open meadows. It's the highest point along U.S. 26 and, like Teton Pass and Union Pass, Togwotee is one of the ancient routes used by Indians to reach hunting grounds in Jackson Hole and the Yellowstone country.

Pinnacle Butte, a prominent rock formation on Togwotee Pass. *(University of Wyoming American Heritage Center)*

Thirty-six miles northwest of Riverton, U.S. 26 is joined by U.S. 287, which travels back along the other handle of the highway divining rod toward the principal population centers of the Wind River Reservation and Lander.

WIND RIVER INDIAN RESERVATION

Though the Wind River Reservation occupies most of the far reaches of the Wind River Valley, most of its five thousand members, Shoshones and Arapahos, live in the small towns of this region. Today's reservation of some 2.2 million acres represents just five percent of the land recognized by an 1863 treaty as a reservation for the Shoshone tribe alone. Through the years, white interests in mining, railroads, resort development, farming, and irrigation whacked off large hunks of the 44.6 million acres originally set aside for the tribe. In addition, the Shoshone were forced to split the reservation with the Arapaho in 1878. This was a bitter irony, because the tribes had been traditional enemies and the Shoshones had helped the U.S. Army defeat the Arapaho.

Yellow Calf, the last Arapaho chief recognized by the U.S. government. *(University of Wyoming American Heritage Center)*

Long before the 1863 treaty was signed, the Shoshone territory stretched from the Cascade Mountains east to the northern plains and south almost to Mexico. In the late seventeenth century, a portion of the tribe consolidated east of the Rockies, where it acquired the horse and gun and became one of the most powerful tribes on the Wyoming and Montana plains. It fought for control of the buffalo country against the Lakota, Cheyenne, Arapaho, and Crow tribes but was steadily beaten west, especially after the Lakota arrived. Understandably, the Shoshone allied themselves with the whites in wars against their traditional enemies.

The Arapaho had migrated west from Minnesota across the Great Plains to the slopes of

the Rockies, where they became part of a vast confederacy of such powerful tribes as the Lakota and Cheyenne. In the Fort Laramie Treaty of 1851, the U.S. government recognized them as a powerful tribe when it ceded them part of an enormous territory covering the southeastern quarter of Wyoming and much of Colorado. However, the Colorado gold rush pushed these tribes off those lands, beginning a violent struggle that did not end for the Arapahos until 1878, when they joined their reluctant hosts, the Shoshones, on the Wind River Reservation.

By then, the reservation boundaries already had been rolled back roughly to what they are today. However, in 1897, the tribes sold the

An early twentieth century photograph of the Saint Stephens Mission on the Wind River Indian Reservation. *(University of Wyoming American Heritage Center)*

Thermopolis area to the government for fifty thousand dollars. Then, in 1904, they sold more than half of the present reservation (lands north of the Wind River) to the U.S. government, which opened the area for homesteading. Later, most of this land was restored to the tribes and $1 million was paid for the land covered by the Riverton Reclamation Project (see page 171). Also, the Shoshone tribe won a $4.4 million settlement against the U.S. government in 1938 for being forced to split their reservation with the Arapaho.

Today's reservation, a combination of broken plains and high mountains, supports large herds of cattle and horses owned by the tribes. About seventy thousand irrigated acres produce hay and grain, but revenue from oil and gas production accounts for most of the tribal income.

FORT WASHAKIE

The town takes its name from Chief Washakie, who led the Shoshone tribe during the turbulent period when whites arrived in the West and destroyed forever the hunting and gathering societies of the region's various Indian tribes. A military post until 1909, Fort Washakie is today the administrative center of the reservation.

Washakie was born early in the nineteenth century, at about the same time Lewis and Clark set out on their 1804–06 expedition of the Mountain West. He rose to power around 1840, at the end of the fur trade era and shortly before large numbers of settlers began moving through Wyoming along the Oregon Trail. He led the tribe through the most intense years of white migration, through the building of the transcontinental railroad, through the Indian wars of the 1860s and 1870s, through the fledgling years of the Wyoming cattle industry, and even into the era when Wyoming began selling its charms as a vacation spot.

Although his policy was to maintain peace with the whites, Washakie was a capable war leader. In his sixties he is said to have taken seven scalps during a solo raid against the Lakota. Through the years, he and Shoshone warriors repelled several raids in the Wind River Valley by other tribes and joined the U.S. Army for various campaigns against the Lakota, Cheyenne, and Arapaho.

Washakie died in 1900 and is buried in the town cemetery.

Another famous Shoshone, Sacajawea, may be buried south of town (turn west on Trout Creek Road, north on Cemetery Lane). She interpreted for Lewis and Clark as they crossed the plains and Rockies in 1805–06. As a child she had been abducted from her tribe by raiders and later sold as wife to Jean Baptiste Charbonneau. Charbonneau was a French Canadian trader based at the Mandan villages along the Missouri. When Lewis and Clark wintered there in 1804–05 and learned of Sacajawea's familiarity with the country ahead of them, they hired her and Charbonneau as guides and interpreters. Some say Sacajawea died on the North Dakota border in 1812. However, historian Grace Raymond Hebard and Lakota scholar Charles Eastman concluded that Sacajawea actually died on the Wind River Reservation in 1884.

LANDER

Settlement began in the Lander area in the late 1850s, after surveyors of what would become known as the Lander Road built some cabins nearby in 1857–58. The road, con-structed under the supervision of Gen. Frederick W. Lander, broke away from the route of the Oregon Trail just before reaching South Pass, then skirted the foothills of the Wind River Mountains and crossed the Green River near Big Piney. After climbing over the mountains into Idaho, the road rejoined the Oregon Trail. Lander's route was more rugged than the Oregon Trail route, but it shortened the trip considerably and kept the emigrant trains close to water, wood, and forage for their animals. It also detoured around Mormon strongholds at a time when the United States had just barely avoided a war with the followers of Brigham Young and when an emigrant train of some 120 settlers had been wiped out by Mormon zealots and Indians at Mountain Meadows.

The road ran straight through territory recognized as Shoshone land, but Gen. Lander negotiated the right of way for the U.S. government from the Shoshone leader, Washakie. However, by treaties in 1863 and 1868, the Shoshone tribe's reservation included the ground where the town of Lander had sprouted. The white settlers were, in effect, squatters until 1874, when Washakie agreed to sell reservation lands south of the Popo Agie for twenty-five thousand dollars.

Originally the town was called Push Root because grass grew so quickly here in the spring, but a local renamed the town after Gen. Lander in 1869. The town thrived as a center of supply for the surrounding ranches and, as the seat of Fremont County, it played host to many criminal trials.

During one such trial in 1893, a young Butch Cassidy was convicted for possessing stolen horses and sentenced to two years in prison. This was about ten years before Butch rose to fame as a leader of the Wild Bunch. Some say Butch passed through Lander many times in the years after his 1893 trial to visit a certain lady friend and perhaps father her child. It is also said that Butch survived the big 1909 shootout in Bolivia that was supposed to have killed him and that he returned to Lander in the 1930s to look for loot he and the Wild Bunch had buried during their heyday.

As in so many other Wyoming regions suitable for raising livestock, the Lander area experienced some of the turmoil associated with the guerrilla warfare waged by Wyoming cattlemen against sheepmen from 1893 to 1912. In the hopes of keeping his sheep safe from raiders, a Lander sheep rancher named J. W. Blake leased some pasture land in 1908 on the Wind River Indian Reservation. However, Blake's maneuver failed to keep his sheep from harm's way. During a heavy rainstorm one night in early April, Blake's camp manager and a couple of herders woke to the sound of gunfire. The raiders rousted the sheepmen and tried to burn their wagons. Since the wagons were too wet to burn, the raiders chopped up the spokes on one wagon and turned the wagons over. Then they chased the sheepmen from camp and started killing the animals. When they had finished, 350 sheep lay dead.

Lander is also the hometown of Wyoming's best-known anonymous cowboy, Albert "Stub" Farlow. In the 1930s, someone took a photo of Stub hanging tough on the back of a bucking bronco named Deadman. Today, a silhouette version of the photo appears on Wyoming's license plates.

For decades the town has lived as a supply center for outlying ranchers, miners, and other workers. When the U.S. Steel mine closed on South Pass in the 1980s, Lander suffered from high unemployment. Wyoming is a boom-and-bust state.

KILLINGS

A few miles south of Lander, a boulder commemorates the 1870 deaths of three miners who were killed by Indians as they returned to Lander from the South Pass goldfields. Barr and Mason were killed almost right away, but Harvey Morgan holed up in a wolf's den and held off the Indians until he ran out of ammunition. When they finally got to Morgan, the Indians drove a miner's hammer through his head. The skull was recovered later, and today it occupies a prominent place at the Pioneer Museum in Lander, hammer protruding.

OIL STRUCK

A dozen miles south of Lander and east of the junction with State 28, Wyoming's first oil well was drilled in 1884. Long before that particular steel bit whirled into the ground, mountain men knew there was oil in the area. In the early 1830s, the trapper Osborne Russell and his chums entertained themselves by setting fire to an oil spring in the area.

Trappers held the medicinal qualities of the oily substance oozing from the ground in high regard. They used the stuff to salve their horses' saddle sores and to alleviate the rheumatism endemic to a trade that required men to spend much of their time wading ice-cold mountain streams.

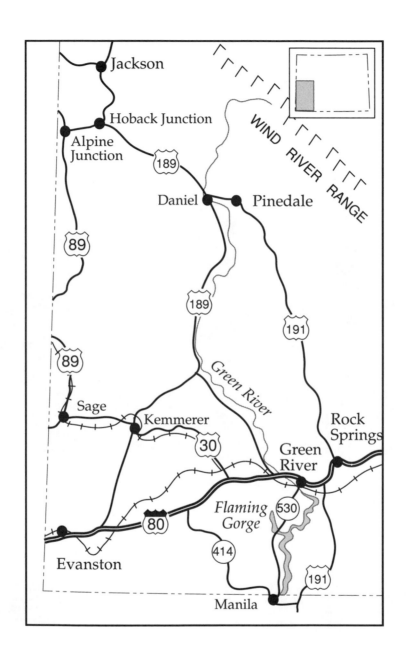

MOUNTAIN MAN COUNTRY

MOUNTAIN MAN COUNTRY: INTRODUCTION

Although stories from the western valleys of Wyoming include the experiences of such varied characters as missionaries, settlers, and oil-field roughnecks, the history really centers around one group: that hard-bitten fraternity of souls known as the mountain men. They began trapping for beaver fur in the Rockies during the early nineteenth century; the mountain men's heaven and haven was the Green River valley. Here they first found beaver so thick one could (metaphorically) kill them with a stick. Here they found friendly Indians, the Shoshone, who liked to trade, and who often provided hearth and home and even wife and children and language and religion, to beaver men.

These mountain men were a singular breed of westerner—independent, tough, ruthless, adventurous to a fault. They were an odd blend of two previous kinds of frontiersman—the French *coureur de bois* and the Kentucky backwoodsman, with a touch of the Spaniard of New Mexico thrown in for spice.

Ironically, their economic success depended less on their ability to trap beaver and to fight and survive in an unforgiving environment than on the clothing tastes of fashionable easterners. Felt hats were all the rage in the East, and no fur felted up better than beaver.

Trapping in the Rockies of the United States began in the first two decades of the nineteenth century but did not thrive until the 1820s, when William Ashley led one hundred men into the mountains to scour the streams for beaver. The rendezvous system was Ashley's great innovation for the Rocky Mountain fur trade. Rather than build a network of fixed trading posts that he would have to stock and defend all year long, Ashley decided to outfit the trappers and pick up their furs at one big gathering every summer. His idea caught on in a big way with the trappers, who saw the business meeting as a chance for serious recreational pursuits such as drinking, brawling, and renting the affections of young Indian maidens. The mountain men held more than half of their rendezvous in the Green River valley.

The mountain fur-trade era continued until 1840. By then, felt hats were no longer so popular in the East and the beaver were no longer so plentiful in the mountains. And the Green River valley once more was the realm of the Shoshone.

Two roads in the Green River region, U.S. 189 and U.S. 191, form a five-hundred-mile loop that circles through the richest lode of fur-trade history in the United States. But there's more. Along these roads, as well as along U.S. 89 — which runs beside the border of Wyoming and Idaho — travelers will turn up history about the Oregon Trail, mining disasters, and early exploration of the Green and Colorado rivers.

Of the two roads that run north through the Green River valley, U.S. 189 follows a path richer in history than does U.S. 191. Several miles north of Evanston, U.S. 189 picks up the original route of the Oregon Trail and, farther north, passes sites where emigrants forded and ferried their wagons across the Green River and carved their names into cliffs. The highway also passes through areas where the presence of coal and oil brought prosperity—often short-lived—and occasional death. As the road reaches into the headwaters of the Green, it picks up the colorful history of the annual mountain man rendezvous. The fur trapper's story continues all the way to Jackson Hole and beyond, into Teton and Yellowstone national parks. In addition to mountain men, emigrants, and miners, the characters who surface along U.S. 189 include rustlers, robbers, and murderers, as well as the early and latter-day settlers of Jackson Hole.

OREGON TRAIL

As it makes its way north along Albert Creek, the highway parallels the original route of the Oregon Trail. In the early years of emigration, most of the wagon trains bound for Oregon and California stopped at Fort Bridger, about twenty-five miles east of here, to repair wagons and re-stock their provisions, if need be. Then they headed northwest, crossing Albert Creek a bit shy of the present junction with State Route 412. From there, they made their way across the Bear River divide to the Bear River, which they followed northwest into Idaho.

In later years, most of the West Coast traffic bypassed Fort Bridger on one of two major short-cuts—the Sublette (or Greenwood) Cutoff and the Lander Road, both of which more or less struck due west from the vicinity of South Pass.

KEMMERER

Kemmerer lies at the center of a large coal-mining district that includes the towns of Dia-mondville, Elkol, and Frontier. Coal was first discovered near Diamondville in 1868 but was not developed until 1894. Three years later, a state coal inspector got the backing of a rich Pennsylvania man named M. S. Kemmerer to start a coal company and lay out the town.

The only Wyoming woman ever convicted of cattle-rustling, Anne Richey, stood trial in Kemmerer. Richey, the self-reliant daughter of a wealthy rancher and railroad contractor, ran her own ranch near what is now Fossil Butte National Monument, about ten miles west of town. Eight of thirty-two cattle she shipped to Omaha in 1919 bore altered brands. She was arrested for rustling and shot while riding into Kemmerer for her trial. The bullet didn't kill her, though, and after she recovered she was convicted and sentenced to six years in prison. However, the judge released her on bond long enough to wrap up her business affairs at the ranch. Before she could do that, she died. Many say she was poisoned.

Kemmerer is also remembered as the site of a saloon run by a bartender with a social conscience. The man, called Preaching Lime Huggins, hung signs over the bar extolling thirsty customers to make sure their kids were well fed and clothed before they spent any of their money on liquor. One customer is reported to have said that he preferred Preaching Lime's place to other saloons because he could repent while sinning and get the whole thing over at once.

HAM'S FORK

At the northern edge of Kemmerer, the high-way crosses Ham's Fork of the Green River. The stream was probably named for one of the trappers in William Ashley's company of mountain men who began hunting beaver in the Rockies during the early 1820s. One of the mountain men's infamous rendezvous was held on Ham's Fork in 1834, farther downstream near Granger (see page 198).

FONTENELLE CREEK AND RESERVOIR

Several miles beyond its junction with State Route 372, the highway parallels the Fontenelle Reservoir and passes Fontenelle Creek, which flows in from the west. Both are named for Lucien Fontenelle, a man who fled an aristocratic background in New Orleans to become a leader of the mountain men. Fontenelle was born in New Orleans around 1807 to parents who had moved there when Louisiana still belonged to France. Fontenelle ran away as a teenager and joined the fur trade in St. Louis. During the early 1830s he led brigades of American Fur Company trappers who learned where the beaver were by tailing groups of trappers working for "the competition"—the Rocky Mountain Fur Company. In 1834 Fontenelle helped to merge the rival companies by going into partnership with the leaders of the Rocky Mountain Fur Company and buying Fort Laramie.

NAMES HILL

Another well-known landmark on a branch of the Oregon Trail, Names Hill is a long sandstone cliff on the west bank of the Green River where travelers stopped to carve their names and leave notes behind for friends and relatives farther back on the trail. Most of the signatures visible today date from the 1970s, 1980s, and 1990s, making sections of this historic cliff seem as common as a railroad overpass where high school kids scrawl their names and years. Fortunately, few have tried spray paint.

Here and there, names from the 1840s and 1850s remain vividly legible despite the best efforts of modern-day vandals. Signatures supposedly include Jim Bridger's, but it is doubtful he carved his name here or anywhere else, because he was illiterate and signed important documents with an X. Obviously, someone else carved it for him, but whether they did it in 1844 or later—or even in his presence—is anybody's guess.

Emigrants weren't the only ones to carve relics of their passing. J. Goldsborough Bruff, who came this way in August 1849, described an "engraving" presumably made by Indians: "On the face . . . was engraved with a fine-pointed instrument, an Indian diagram, representing 43 rifles, nearly vertical, and a chief and horse, apparently separated from four other Indians and a horse laying down, by a stream with a small fork to it." No trace of this pictograph remains.

Roughly two and a half miles upstream from Names Hill, emigrants traveling on Sublette's Cutoff could ford Green River near the mouth of Steed Canyon as long as the water was not running too high. The ford was used heavily until commercial ferries opened for business during the late 1840s.

One ferry, run by mountain men, crossed the Green just north of Names Hill, where a bridge now spans the river. The mountain men built their ferry from four dugout cottonwood logs lashed together like pontoons, which they planked over. They rolled the wagons up onto the planks, secured the wheels, and pushed off from shore. James Pritchard, who crossed during the gold rush summer of 1849 recorded this glimpse of the men who ran the ferry: "The ferry is kept by some Frenchmen who live in lodges made of skins and propped up with poles," he wrote. "They have Indian squaws for wives."

During the heaviest years of emigration, several outfits ferried wagons across the Green. Some were run by mountain men, others by Mormons. Relations between the two factions grew bitter and violent during the early 1850s, when the Mormons tried to monopolize the business (see page 133).

Once emigrants crossed the Green, those following the Sublette Cutoff headed southwest to Ham's Fork (several miles above modern Kemmerer), then northwest to join the main branch of the Oregon Trail near modern Cokeville.

LABARGE

This little town boomed during the 1920s after oil was discovered nearby. As the drilling rigs moved in, boosters confidently named the town Tulsa, after Oklahoma's oil mecca. The rigs soon milked the pools dry and the boom collapsed in 1935. Residents then picked up the present name from nearby LaBarge Creek, which was named in 1824 for a friend of the fur-trading entrepreneur William Ashley.

BIG PINEY AND MARBLETON

Both of these towns were founded by members of the Budd family, which began running cattle in the valley as early as 1878 — and still does. D. B. Budd established Big Piney in 1888. His son, Charles, moved up the hill in 1912 and built Marbleton. In the 1920s, gas and oil wells pumped up a small boom here that quickly fizzled. In the early 1990s, however, the accoutrements of natural-gas wells dotted the landscape once more and drilling equipment crowded makeshift parking areas on the outskirts of town. In spite of the latest boom, the towns remain what they have always been — centers of supply and recreation for the cattle and sheep ranchers.

Here, as elsewhere in Wyoming, these two livestock factions clashed violently at the turn of the century over grazing rights on public lands. When tensions rose during the spring of 1895, the two factions tried to head off trouble by agreeing to a division of the range. However, several sheep owners violated the pact by combining their flocks, hiring armed guards, and venturing onto forbidden land. Within a few days, raiders struck their camp, tied up the herders and guards, and clubbed two thousand sheep to death. The next morning, the raiders drove the herders and the rest of the sheep from the cattlemen's domain.

LANDER ROAD

A sign at the Sublette County Fairgrounds north of Marbleton marks the approximate area traversed by the route of the Lander Road. Built in the late 1850s by Frederick Lander, the road ran northwest from the vicinity of South Pass and stuck more closely to sources of wood, water, and forage than either the main branch of the Oregon Trail or the Sublette Cutoff (see pages 49–50).

FIRST MASS

A few miles north of Muddy Creek, Father Pierre DeSmet offered the first Catholic Mass in Wyoming back in 1840. DeSmet was a Jesuit who traveled widely in the West, converting Indians to Christianity and representing the tribes at important treaty conferences.

DANIEL AND THE TRAPPERS

Most of the history surrounding Daniel and the upper Green River valley concerns the lives of the mountain men, who came to the mountains in pursuit of beaver fur.

William H. Jackson's watercolor of the 1837 rendezvous on Green River *(Jackson Hole Museum and Teton County Historical Society, Jackson, Wyoming)*

Osborne Russell, a trapper in the 1830s and one of the trade's best diarists, left this description of a typical mountain man:

> A trapper's equipment . . . is generally one animal, upon which is placed one or two epishemores [saddle pads], a riding saddle and bridle, a sack containing six beaver traps, a blanket with an extra pair of moccasins, his powder horn and bullet pouch with a belt to which is attached a butcher knife, a small wooden box containing bait for beaver, a tobacco sack with a pipe and implements for making fire with sometimes a hatchet fastened to the pommel of his saddle. His personal dress is a flannel or cotton shirt (if he is fortunate enough to obtain one, if not antelope skin answers the purpose of over and undershirt), a pair of leather breeches with blanket or smoked buffalo skin, leggings, a coat made of blanket or buffalo robe, a hat or cap of wool, buffalo or otter skin. His hose are pieces of blanket lapped round his feet which are covered with a pair of moccasins made of dressed deer, elk or buffalo skins with his long hair falling loosely over his shoulders completes his uniform.

The Rendezvous

The mountain men wandered all over the Rockies, wading ice-cold streams to trap beaver, roasting up buffalo ribs and hunks of elk for dinner, living with and learning from friendly Indians, fighting off the hostiles, and surviving some of the most conspicuous hardships men have ever had the misfortune of stumbling into. For most of the year, the trappers traveled in small bands to collect their beaver pelts, or "plews," as they often called them. Come summer, when their packs were full, they converged at a prearranged site for the annual rendezvous, an event so drunk and disorderly as to make a convention of today's motorcycle gangs seem like a church picnic. These gatherings were held from 1825 to 1840 in a variety of Rocky Mountain locations. Many were held in the Green River valley, and six took place on the grassy plains northwest of Daniel.

Technically, the rendezvous was a business meeting where the trappers traded their furs for goods brought to the site by caravan. In actual fact, it was much more. It was the social event of the year.

"Joy now beamed on every countenance," wrote the trapper Osborne Russell after Rendezvous 1836 got underway. "Some received letters from their friends and relations. Some received the public papers and news of the day. Others consoled themselves with the idea of getting a blanket, a cotton shirt or a few pints of coffee and sugar to sweeten it, just by way of a treat."

Mostly Americans and French Canadians, the trappers counted among their number a few Dutch, Scotch, Irish, Mexicans, and English. The Indians who came to trade represented nearly every tribe in the Rockies.

"Some were gambling at cards, some playing the Indian game of hand, and others horse racing," Russell wrote. "Here and there could be seen small groups collected under shady trees relating the events of the past year all in good spirits and health."

At rendezvous, trappers got a taste of the good life and indulged appetites sharpened by the long, lonely winter. From the packs strapped to the caravan's animals came plenty of whiskey — raw alcohol watered down to about 50 proof, with a handful of tobacco tossed in for color and flavor and maybe some ginger and chiles for kick. From the mouths of companions they had not seen sometimes for years, they heard brags, ribald stories, and news of others rubbed out in

fights or eaten by bears or starved and frozen to death by endless blizzards. And from the tipis of Indians camped nearby came the daughters, sisters, and wives of braves who knew what else the trappers craved.

"Today I was told that Indian women are a lawful commerce among the men," wrote the missionary William Gray, who attended Rendezvous 1836:

> They named to me a man by the name of Dr. Newell, as he is called, who won a woman on a wager. On hearing his old Flathead wife was coming with McLeod's party, he said he must get rid of the woman. Accordingly, he went and sold her to her previous owner for $100. A second individual, they tell me, lost his wife on a wager. A few days after, he won a horse and bought his wife back again. The buying and selling of Indian women is a common occurance [sic] at this rendezvous.

The landscape painter Alfred Miller observed the buying of brides the following summer on the Green. He sketched a scene from one trapper's "wedding" and wrote:

> The price of acquisition in this case was $600, paid for in the legal tender of this region: Vis: guns, $100 each, blankets, $40 each, red flannel, $20 per yard, alcohol, $64 a gallon, tobacco, beads etc. . . . A free trapper . . . is a most desirable match, but it is conceded that he is a ruined man after such an investment, the lady running into unheard of extravagances. She wants a dress, horse, gorgeous saddle, trappings, and the deuce knows what beside. For this the poor devil trapper sells himself body and soul to the fur company for a number of years.

The rendezvous were bawdy and raucous celebrations greatly enjoyed by the insiders and often deplored by those who hitched a ride West

with the supply caravan. Drunk trappers sere-
naded missionaries' wives and sometimes
shocked them with their tales of gleefully slaugh-
tering the very souls the missionaries had come
to the wilderness to save. Usually, though, it was
just the high spirits and unabashed sinfulness of
the mountain men that grated on churchly
nerves.

The Rev. Samuel Parker at least appreciated
the creativity of the trappers' cussing:

> They disdain commonplace profanities
> which prevail among the impious vulgar in
> civilized countries, and have many set
> phrases, which they appear to have manu-
> factured among themselves, and which, in
> their imprecations, they bring into almost
> every sentence and on all occasions.

Dust-Up with the Bannocks

Besides the duels and brawls that broke out
among the trappers themselves, a rendezvous
would have seemed incomplete without some
kind of trouble with one of the many bands of
Indians. At Rendezvous 1836, a group of French
trappers recognized a band of Bannocks who
had robbed them of some horses and traps on
the Bear River several months earlier. The
French, along with a couple of Nez Perce
chums, stole back the horses. It didn't take long
for the Bannocks to discover the repossession.

"The same day 30 Bannocks came riding at
full gallop up to the camp, armed with their war
weapons," wrote Osborne Russell. "They rode
into the midst and demanded the horses which
the Nez Percey had taken, saying they did not
wish to fight with the whites. But the Nez Percey,
who were only six in number, gave the horses
to the whites for protection."

On seeing this, some of the Bannocks started
to leave the camp. After all, one of the pluckiest
of mountain men, Jim Bridger, was holding one
of the horses by the bridle. However, one of the

Jim Bridger, legendary mountain man, spinner of
tall tales, and survivor of many a scrape. *(University
of Wyoming American Heritage Center)*

Bannocks shamed the rest by reminding them
they had come for horses or blood and he, for
one, wasn't going to leave empty-handed.
Russell continued:

> One of the Bannocks rushed through
> the crowd, siezed [*sic*] the bridle and at-
> tempted to drag it from Mr. Bridger by force
> without heeding the cocked rifles that sur-
> rounded him any more than if they had been
> so many reeds in the hands of children. He
> was a brave Indian but his bravery proved
> fatal to himself, for the moment he seized
> the bridle two rifle balls whistled through his
> body. The others wheeled to run but 12 of
> them were shot from their horses before they
> were out of the reach of rifles. We then
> mounted horses and pursued them, de-
> stroyed and plundered their village and fol-
> lowed and fought them three days.

Only Wimps Need Anesthetic

The mountain men were nothing if not tough. At Rendezvous 1835, the Reverend Parker got a close look at one of the toughest, Jim Bridger, undergoing back surgery with nothing to control the pain but his own will-power.

> Dr. Whitman was called to perform some very important surgical operations . . . He extracted an iron arrow, three inches long, from the back of Capt. Bridger, which was received in a skirmish, three years before, with the Blackfeet Indians. It was a difficult operation, because the arrow was hooked at the point by striking a large bone, and a cartilaginous substance had grown around it. The doctor pursued the operation with great self-possession and perseverance; and his patient manifested equal firmness.

A Tragic Figure?

Parker seems to have respected the mountain men but also to have found their lives tinged with a bit of sadness, maybe even tragedy. "Few of these men ever return to their country and friends," he wrote. "Most of them are constantly in debt to the company, and are unwilling to return without a fortune; and year after year passes away, while they are hoping in vain for better success."

Still, Parker appears to have understood that many of them kept at it not just because they hoped to make some money, but because the trapper's life, in spite of its hardships and dangers, suited them. They liked it. "They appear to have sought for a place where, as they would say, human nature is not oppressed by the tyranny of religion, and pleasure is not awed by the frown of virtue," Parker wrote.

Osborne Russell described some of the pleasures:

> A large fire was soon blazing encircled with sides of elk ribs and meat cut in slices supported on sticks down which the grease ran in torrents . . . The repast being over, the jovial tale goes round the circle. The peals of loud laughter break upon the stillness of the night which, after being mimicked in the echo from rock to rock, it dies away in the solitary gloom. Every tale puts an auditor in mind of something similar to it but under different circumstances which, being told, the "laughing part" gives rise to increasing merriment and furnishes more subjects for good jokes and witty sayings such as Swift never dreamed of. Thus the evening passed with eating, drinking and stories enlivened with witty humor until near midnight all being wrapped in their blankets lying around the fire, gradually falling to sleep one by one until the last tale is "encored" by the snoring of the drowsy audience.

The Decline

Parker rode with the mountain men in 1835, when the fur trade was still going strong. Just four years later, when the German physician Frederick Wislizenus attended a Green River rendezvous, the trappers' way of life seemed to be breathing its last. Wislizenus wrote in 1839 that constant hunting had reduced the beaver population and that the mountain men seemed strangely quiet at the rendezvous. "There was little drinking of spirits, and almost no gambling," he wrote. "Another decade perhaps and the original trapper will have disappeared from the mountains."

It happened sooner than that. The trappers gathered on the Green the following year for the last rendezvous, not because they had trouble finding beaver, but because no one wanted the plews. Beaver hats were out. Fashion had shifted to the tall, silk top hat.

The trappers melted from the scene. They found work as trail guides for the burgeoning number of emigrants headed for the Far West, as hunting guides for wealthy Europeans, as scouts for the army, as Indian agents, as ferryboat operators, and as farmers in the settlements of the U.S. or the Oregon country. Or they lived with the Indians, vulnerable to another sort of death a generation later.

JUNCTION WITH U.S. 191

From here, U.S. 191 runs south through arid land to Rock Springs on I-80, and then on to the Utah border. The road crosses three major routes followed by emigrants headed for the Far West (see page 192).

JUNCTION WITH STATE 354

State 354 runs west a couple of miles to the site of Fort Bonneville, built in 1832 by a military expedition led by Capt. B. L. E. Bonneville. Working under the pretense of trapping beaver, Bonneville may have been in the area to keep an eye on the British. His edifice was mocked by the mountain men with the name Fort Nonsense.

BONDURANT

After watching the mountain men whoop it up at the 1835 rendezvous, the Reverend Samuel Parker got down to the serious business he had traveled West to pursue: converting the Indians to Christianity. He traveled north from the rendezvous through the upper Green River valley with a mixed caravan of Indians and trappers. On August 23, a Sunday, the group stopped a few miles north of the present town of Bondurant and listened to Parker deliver the first sermon preached in Wyoming. A sign on the west side of the road marks the approximate site. Parker wrote in his journal:

In the afternoon we had a public worship with those of the company who understood English. The men conducted with great propriety, and listened with attention. I did not feel any disposition to upbraid them for their sins, but endeavored to show them that they are unfit for heaven, and that they could not be happy in the employments of that holy place, unless they should first experience a great moral change of heart.

But Parker told only half the story. He did not describe how his solemn oration came to an end and what sort of change of heart suddenly manifested itself within the congregation. That was left to others. Biographer Frances Fuller Victor, in *River of the West,* attributes the following account of the sermon to mountain man Joe Meek:

The men were as politely attentive as it was in their reckless natures to be, until, in the midst of the discourse, a band of buffalo appeared in the valley, when the congregation incontinently broke up, without staying for a benediction, and every man made haste after his horse, gun and rope, leaving Mr. Parker to discourse to vacant ground.

BATTLE MOUNTAIN

A red sandstone mountain visible straight up the road from Kozy Campground, Battle Mountain got its name from a tragic skirmish in 1895 between a small band of Bannock Indians and a foolish posse of Jackson Hole residents.

Under the Fort Bridger Treaty of 1868, the Shoshone and Bannock tribes were given the right to hunt at any time on unoccupied public land. Early in the summer of 1895, a hunting party of nine men, thirteen women, and several children were hunting in the Hoback Canyon area when a posse of twenty-six Jackson residents surprised, disarmed, and arrested them. They were charged with violating state game laws by hunting out of season and escorted back toward Jackson Hole for trial. Along the way, the group paused on the slopes of Battle Mountain. There, a deputy fired his rifle, which naturally alarmed the unarmed Indians. Believing they were going to be killed, the Indians made a run for it. All managed to escape into the dense forest except for an old man who was shot and killed by the posse.

This sorry incident kicked off an Indian scare among settlers in Jackson Hole and a wave of inaccurate newspaper reports about a murderous uprising among the Bannocks. Jackson's residents barricaded themselves at several of the ranches and waited for a reprisal that never came.

HOBACK CANYON

Today, cars glide through Hoback Canyon with ease, but the narrower spots could intimidate those who came this way by horseback.

"This stream runs through a tremendous mountain in a deep narrow canyon of rock," wrote the trapper Osborne Russell during the 1830s. "The trail runs along the cliffs from 50 to 200 feet above its bed and is so narrow in many places that only one horse can pass at a time for

several hundred yards and one false step would precipitate him into the chasm."

A remnant of the old trail is still visible about three and a half miles north of Kozy Campground at Red Ledges, a large crescent-shaped outcropping of reddish stone. The trail crossed the cliffs on a series of ledges two hundred feet over the river. It was a dangerous spot, and many of the travelers watched one or more of their pack horses or mules tumble down the escarpment into the river or onto the rocks below. One sad party of trappers watched a packhorse carrying one hundred pounds of precious tobacco plummet into the river.

Wilson Price Hunt named the river for John Hoback, an early trapper who guided Hunt's party of Astorians through the area in 1811.

HOBACK JUNCTION

This little crossroads community marks the spot where the Hoback River flows into the Snake. It is also where U.S. 191 and U.S. 189 join U.S. 26 and U.S. 89. South of this point, the latter highways skirt the edge of the South Canyon of the Snake. Then U.S. 26 breaks away toward Idaho and U.S. 89 runs south along the Wyoming border through some of the most sublime scenery in the state.

U.S. 191 cuts across the main branch of the Oregon Trail at Farson. It also intersects with two important shortcuts on the emigrant trail: the Sublette Cutoff and the Lander Road. South of Interstate 80, it runs toward the Flaming Gorge National Recreational Area, the beginning of the spectacular canyon country created by the Green and Colorado rivers.

FLAMING GORGE AREA

The gorge was dammed in 1964 and the reservoir that fills it provides hydroelectric power and irrigation. Perhaps the best view of the gorge, a thousand-foot half-dome of salmon red sandstone, is from the Antelope Flats campground south of the border. (For more about the history of Flaming Gorge, see page 194.)

ROCK SPRINGS

Although Rock Springs got its start as a railroad construction camp, rich deposits of coal soon established it as a mining center. The work drew miners of many nationalities, including Chinese, who became the target of an 1885 race riot that killed twenty-eight (see page 130).

BLAIR'S STOCKADE

North of Rock Springs and just west of Killpecker Creek is the site of an old stone trading post built in 1866 by Archie and Duncan Blair. They built their place close to a freshwater spring that flowed out of some rocks. The town of Rock Springs takes its name from these springs. At the Blair roadhouse, travelers could get venison steaks and coffee. Water being scarce, they paid ten cents a head to quench their horses' thirsts.

Life could get pretty dull out on the desert, and people had to make their own entertainment. In July 1891, a couple of men got more excitement than they bargained for two hundred yards south of the old station. There, in a small building, some twelve hundred kegs of blasting powder and seven hundred pounds of dynamite had been stored for use in the coal mines around Rock Springs. When the simple pleasure of being drunk had worn thin, the men decided it might be kind of fun to fire their guns at the powder house. So they started plinking away and pretty soon the whole place blew up. They went with it, and took two others with them.

EDEN

Eden may strike some as an odd name for a town out in the middle of a desert, but the Mennonites who settled here had high hopes of turning this plateau of arid dirt into a paradise of irrigated cropland. They succeeded by storing water in the Eden Reservoir northeast of Farson.

Evidence abounds among the immense sand dunes east of Eden that people lived here as long as six thousand years ago. Ancient arrowheads and other stone tools have been found throughout the valley, as have bison-kill sites, a meat-processing camp, and petroglyphs on the walls of rock outcroppings.

JUNCTION WITH 28

The Farson area is rich with history of the Oregon Trail, which more or less parallels State 28 (see page 52).

SUBLETTE CUTOFF

About eight miles north of Farson, Highway 191 crosses one of the most heavily used shortcuts on the Oregon Trail. Called the Sublette (or Greenwood) Cutoff, the route veered away from the main branch of the Oregon Trail about fifteen miles northeast of Farson. It forded Big Sandy Creek, east of the present highway, and then ran clear across the Little Colorado Desert to the Green River.

Opened in 1844, the route saved emigrants about forty-five miles of hauling. But after they crossed the Big Sandy, they did not strike water again for about fifty miles. Such a long arid stretch scared off many of the early emigrants. But during the California gold rush summer of 1849 and thereafter, most of the West Coast traffic headed this way instead of dipping down to Fort Bridger. The usual practice was to rest the livestock at the Big Sandy all day, then journey across the desert at night hoping to strike Green River by morning. Emigrants filled every available water container for the trek and sometimes left piles of gear behind to lighten their loads. In 1849, J. Goldsborough Bruff came across one such dump. "Potts had been camped on the opposite side of us, in the bottom, just above the road, and had broken up a wagon, leaving the sides etc. for the benefit of our cooks," Bruff wrote. "We also found on their campground several hundred weight of fat bacon, beans, lead, iron, tools, a cast-iron stove."

Another cutoff, called the Lander Road, crossed the Green River valley farther north in order to keep closer to sources of wood, water, and forage. The Lander Road emerged in the vicinity of Big Piney, crossed the mountains, and rejoined the Oregon Trail's main branch in Idaho.

PINEDALE

Settled in the late 1870s by ranchers drawn to the rich pastureland, Pinedale is still a center for ranchers, and also for hunters, fishermen, climbers, backpackers, and those who enjoy re-enacting the gatherings of mountain men. Many of the annual rendezvous of the fur-trade era were held in the Green River valley, and six of them were held about eleven miles west of here, near Daniel (see page 185). Pinedale sponsors a pageant of the mountain-man era on the second weekend of each July, and has a museum, the Museum of the Mountain Man, devoted to the beaver trade.

North of Pinedale, both cattle and sheep thrived on the lush grassland of the New Fork region of the Green River valley. Here as elsewhere, cattlemen and sheepmen clashed violently over who had the right to graze which animal on land that technically belonged to everybody. In July 1902, a large flock of sheep nibbled its way onto land that area cattlemen had claimed as their own. To enforce their restrictions, a group of 150 masked men raided the sheep camps. They killed a herder, clubbed two thousand sheep to death, and ran the remaining animals and herders off the land.

JUNCTION WITH U.S. 189

To the south, Highway 189 runs through the Green River valley, abundant with history about mountain men and the emigrant era. To the north, it picks up more exploits of the fur trappers and the settlement of Jackson Hole.

From the town of Green River, State Route 530 leads south along Flaming Gorge Reservoir and traces a small portion of the route of John Wesley Powell's journey of exploration through the canyon country of the Green and Colorado rivers in 1869. At Manila, State Route 414 heads back toward I-80, passes the site of the first mountain man rendezvous (1825), and crosses through country where sheepmen and cattlemen feuded violently around the turn of the century.

GREEN RIVER

This town started out as a stage station, railroad camp, and lumbering center. When the Union Pacific moved its traveling headquarters twelve miles west, Green River nearly died. Fortunately, the railroad came back and established a division point here (see page 131).

FLAMING GORGE RESERVOIR

This reservoir was created in 1964 when the federal government built Flaming Gorge Dam across the Green River farther south in Utah to provide hydroelectric power and irrigation. Though still spectacular, Flaming Gorge is a much-altered landscape.

John Wesley Powell, one of the first whites to explore Flaming Gorge, pushed off from the town of Green River in 1869 and began a thousand-mile journey down the Green and Colorado rivers, venturing into a great unknown. During the 1869 expedition and on other trips, Powell floated and mapped the canyon country of modern Wyoming, Utah, Colorado, and Arizona—including the Grand Canyon.

Today, the placid waters of Flaming Gorge reservoir, which reach a depth of 435 feet in some places, submerge a portion of the stunning landscape and turbulent waterway Powell navigated with ten men in four small boats.

Even in Powell's time, the stretch of the Green that remains in Wyoming was relatively mild. This was fortunate, because the men needed a chance to learn the rudiments of river travel. Powell wrote:

> In trying to avoid a rock an oar is broken on one of the boats, and, thus crippled, she strikes. The current is swift and she is sent reeling and rocking into the eddy. In the confusion two other oars are lost overboard, and the men seem quite discomfited, much to the amusement of the other members of the party.

Though the current remained swift, the river offered Powell's boatmen no great challenges for sixty miles. The real adventure began below the mouth of Henry's Fork, where the cliffs rose twelve hundred feet above the river and the water slipped through a narrow gateway into a deeper canyon. Powell described what it looked like in 1869:

> The river is running to the south. The mountains have an easterly and westerly trend directly athwart its course, yet it glides on in a quiet way as if it thought a mountain range no formidable obstruction. It enters the range by a flaring, brilliant red gorge, that may be seen from the north a score of miles away. The great mass of the mountain ridge through which the gorge is cut is composed of bright vermillion rocks, but they are surmounted by broad bands of mottled buff and gray, and these bands come down with a gentle curve to the water's edge on the nearer slope of the mountain. This is the head of the first of the canyons we are about to explore—an introductory one to a series made by the river through this range. We name it Flaming Gorge.

This view of Flaming Gorge no longer exists. Gone too is the first serious length of white water that Powell's group encountered shortly after entering the canyon. "I stand up on the deck of my boat to seek a way among the wave-beaten rocks," Powell wrote in his journal:

> All untried as we are with such waters, the moments are filled with intense anxiety. Soon our boats reach the swift current. A stroke or two, now on this side, now on that, and we thread the narrow passage with exhilarating velocity, mounting the high waves, whose foaming crests dash over us, and plunging into the troughs, until we reach the quiet water below. Then comes a feeling of great relief. Our first rapids run.

By the time the current swept Powell and his men into Red Canyon, the blazing red walls had climbed about a half-mile over their heads. When Wallace Stegner published *Beyond the Hundredth Meridian,* his 1953 account of Powell's expedition, Red Canyon still looked like it had during Powell's day. Instead of the broad, quiet waters that lap at the red walls today, travelers who gazed over the rim saw the Green River as a tiny ribbon — green at low water, reddish at high.

From such a remote vantage point, Stegner wrote, the visitor

> will not see the rapids that for the first time gave Powell and his men a touch of danger and exhausting work, and he will not hear what is perhaps the most nerve-wearing accompaniment of any voyage in these canyons: the incessant, thundering, express-engine roar of the water. In many parts of the canyons it never ceases, day or night. It speeds the heartbeat and deafens the ears and shakes the ground underfoot. It comes from every side, echoed and multiplied by the walls. A man's voice is lost, shouting in it.

MCKINNON

Just north of present-day McKinnon, about 120 fur trappers gathered on July 1, 1825, on the banks of Henry's Fork of Green River for the first of the great mountain man rendezvous. Here, William Ashley, who had been struggling for three years to establish a viable fur trade in the Rocky Mountains, finally hit upon a dependable system of resupplying trappers and collecting their furs. It would make him a fortune.

Previously, the approach had been to build a network of trading posts, stock each one with provisions and equipment, leave enough men behind to defend the goods, and then wait for the trappers and Indians to bring in furs. In 1825, Ashley brought the trading post to the trappers. When he arrived at the rendezvous his packs were filled with tobacco, gunpowder, lead, knives, traps, brass wire, kettles, coffee, sugar, and trinkets. When he left, the packs were full of furs. From Ashley's perspective, the new system dramatically reduced overhead and accomplished the season's trade in one fell swoop. To the trappers, a rendezvous in the midst of productive fur country was more convenient and a whole lot more fun. At trading posts, trappers arrived in dribs and drabs, conducted business, maybe got drunk for a few days, and then took off for another season. At a rendezvous, everybody showed up pretty much at the same time, and with that many hell-raisers in one place at one time there was bound to be a tremendous celebration.

Compared with the brawling bacchanalias the mountain men were to enjoy at the zenith of the fur trade, Rendezvous 1825 was a sedate, businesslike affair. Ashley had brought only the basics of the mountain trade with him in 1825 and omitted the one great staple of future get-togethers: whiskey.

Ashley collected roughly 9,700 pounds of beaver furs at the rendezvous, paying the trappers in merchandise at the rate of three dollars a pound for independent trappers and two dollars a pound for trappers on Ashley's payroll. At St. Louis prices, this represented between forty and fifty thousand dollars worth of fur. Ashley was making roughly two dollars a pound—not a bad profit until you begin to consider what he had to do to earn it. A major overland expedition from St. Louis did not come cheap, even when it got through without Indians attacking it or without pack horses drowning in the rivers with the goods. In later years, transportation costs on the return trip alone amounted to a little over one dollar a pound.

Ashley made money on fur, but he and the suppliers who followed him probably made a lot more money by jacking up the prices charged for supplies.

The rendezvous system continued until 1840. By then, the beaver population had thinned considerably and eastern fashions had shifted from beaver-felt hats to hats of silk.

Though the summer of 1825 was good to Ashley, he started off by nearly dying on the Green River. Before the rendezvous, Ashley had decided to take some of his men and explore new territory by floating down the Green.

On Ashley's trip, the men did not have the benefit of riding in fine oak rowboats with watertight compartments such as those Powell shipped west on the Union Pacific nearly half a century later. Ashley and his men stretched animal skins over a light wooden frame to make a bullboat sixteen feet long and seven feet wide. In this and a companion craft built forty miles downriver, they bobbed along safely until they reached the rapids in Flaming Gorge, south of the present Wyoming border.

"The channel of the river is here contracted to a width of 60 or 70 yards, and the current, much increased in velocity as it rolled along in angry submission to the surpentine [sic] walls that direct it, seemed constantly to threaten us with danger as we advanced," Ashley later wrote.

The group managed to line their boats through Red Canyon, where Ashley carved his name and the year in the rocks over the river. The inscription is now submerged. Below Red Canyon, at the mouth of what is now called Ashley River, Ashley's boat washed over a falls, filled with water, and began to sink. Ashley couldn't swim. Lucky for him, others could. They managed to drag a couple of ropes to shore and pull the boat, and Ashley, to safety. So much for river-running. The men clambered out of the canyon, caught up with the rest of their party, and headed for the rendezvous on horseback.

LONETREE

This former stage stop took its name in 1872 from an isolated pine tree that became a landmark for area pioneers. Lonetree also serves as a minor landmark of sorts in the range war between cattlemen and sheepmen. Here, as in most areas of Wyoming where prime grazing land could support both cattle and sheep, competition between the two interests sometimes grew violent.

During January 1894, about one hundred cattlemen rode through the Henry's Fork Valley, forcing bands of sheep from the region. The cattlemen later held a meeting at Fort Bridger to establish a division of the range between sheep and cattle interests. Only one sheepman turned up at the meeting, and he cast the only vote against the cattlemen's plan to exclude sheep from a region the size of Rhode Island. The sheepmen seem to have agreed to keep their flocks out of the restricted area, because there was little trouble for a while. The only violent encounter between the two factions seems to have broken out at a dance in Lonetree a couple of months after the cattlemen drove out the sheep. There, a cattle rancher and a sheepman swung at each other for about a half-hour while scuffles broke out among their friends. This knuckle-to-knuckle dispute was mild compared with the shootings of sheepherders and clubbing of sheep that characterized the range war elsewhere in Wyoming.

Between the years 1893 and 1912, a total of ten sheepmen, one cattleman, and sixteen thousand sheep were killed across the Wyoming range (see page 149).

JUNCTION WITH 412

Interstate 80 lies about six miles north of Mountain View. The restored site of a trading post and fort established by the legendary mountain man Jim Bridger stands four miles west, on State Route 411 (see page 133).

In little more than seventy-five miles, this section of Highway 30 plunges through some of the most important eras of Wyoming's history: fur trade, emigration, railroad-building, and coal-mining.

GRANGER

Granger got its official start as a railroad construction camp in the autumn of 1868, but emigrants had passed this way since the early 1840s, and a stagecoach station appeared nearby. Known as the South Bend Stage Station, the stone outpost was built in 1850 and lay along the first transcontinental stage line. Sir Richard Burton, the nineteenth-century English adventurer, rarely had a kind word for any of the stations his coach stopped at during his tour of the West in 1860. The South Bend Stage Station was no exception:

> It was a disgrace. The squalor and filth were worse almost than the two . . . we called our horrors . . . The shanty was made of dry-stone piled up against a dwarf cliff to save backwall, and ignored doors and windows. The flies darkened the table and covered everything put upon it. The furniture, which mainly consisted of the different parts of wagons, was broken, and all in disorder. The walls were impure, the floor filthy.

Although Granger is the approximate site of the South Bend Stage Station, historian Aubrey Haines says the buildings marked by the monument in town are probably not the remains of the 1850 stage station. Instead, they probably date back no further than 1895.

WET YOUR WHISTLE?

Southwestern Wyoming can be awfully thirsty country, especially if you travel on horseback or by covered wagon. The emigrants had to stick close to the sources of water they knew about: rivers and streams. But mountain men, resourceful and a whole lot less squeamish, could roam more freely because they were skilled at finding water in unlikely places. While accompanying a group of them to the 1834 rendezvous near Granger, Jason Lee, the Oregon missionary, learned of one such place: dead bison.

> With his knife [the hunter] opened the body so as to expose to view the great stomach, and still crawling and twisting entrails . . . We saw our hunter plunge his knife into the distended paunch, from which gushed the green and gelatinous juices, and then insinuate his pan into the opening, and by depressing its edge, strain off the water which was mingled with its contents.

Lee declined the opportunity to drink to the trappers' health.

THE 1834 RENDEZVOUS

When the Rocky Mountain fur trappers got together on Ham's Fork in 1834 for a week of drinking, brawling, gambling, and trading, the tradition of an annual rendezvous was nine years old. William Ashley, founder of the Rocky Mountain Fur Company, had kicked off the practice in 1825 by leading a supply caravan into southwestern Wyoming (see page 195). Like most rendezvous, the affair of 1834 was an excuse for a good party. The naturalist Kirk Townsend complained:

> These people, with their obstreperous mirth, their whooping, and howling, and quarreling, added to the mounted Indians, who are constantly dashing into and through our camp, yelling like fiends, the barking and baying of savage wolf-dogs, and the incessant cracking of rifles and carbines,

render our camp a perfect bedlam . . . I am confined closely to the tent with illness, and am compelled all day to listen to the hiccoughing jargon of drunken traders, the sacre and foutre of Frenchmen run wild, and the swearing and screaming of our own men, who are scarcely less savage than the rest, being heated by the detestable liquor which circulates freely among them.

Except to wet blankets like Townsend—and perhaps those who were knifed, shot, raped, or badly beaten—the rendezvous was a glorious outrage. William Anderson, another outsider, seemed to enjoy every minute of it. A Louisville, Kentucky, lawyer, Anderson had come west with the trapper's supply caravan in order to recover from a spell of yellow fever.

"Whilst dining in our tent today, I heard the simultaneous cry from English, French and Indian mouths, of 'a bull, un caiac, tsodlum' and 'oh, Spirit of Nimrod, what a spectacle!'" he wrote in his journal:

A huge buffalo bull, booming through the camp like a steamboat, followed by an Indian yelling and shaking his robe. Loud shouts of "hurrah for Kentuck," "Oka-hey tsodlum," "go ahead bull," and whiz, whiz, went a dozen arrows, bang, bang, as many guns and poor John Baptiste leaped from the bank and floated, broad side up, down the rapid current of Green River.

The joy was apparent among trappers greeting one another for perhaps the first time in years or perhaps after they had heard exaggerated accounts of others' deaths.

"Vasquez and Sublette are shaking hands with their right and smacking and pushing each other with the left. They both ask questions and neither answer," Anderson wrote. He caught on quickly to the jocular spirit of rivalry between the trappers of competing fur companies. "This evening both camps are nearly deserted from

vanity," he wrote. "Mr. Fitzpatrick and Mr. Sublette [both associated with the Rocky Mountain Fur Company] have gone, attended by the greater part of both parties . . . to return a visit made us yesterday by the American Fur Company and to outbrag them, if practicable."

Next day, Anderson reported on the party's success: "The horse from this camp beat the horse from their camp, and our bully beat their bully. Ergo, say we, ours are the best horses and best men."

Besides offering the mountain men a chance to load up on firewater and rooster about, the rendezvous was the place to catch up on the news.

"This evening we were visited by six trappers from Dripps and Fontenelle's camp," Anderson wrote. "They were exceedingly glad to see us. We gave them the news in broken doses, beginning with matters three years old. This was delightful, fresher by several years than any they had heard."

The news would get fresher: The Rocky Mountain Fur Company was about to collapse. Operating under various names since Ashley formed its first band of trappers in 1822, it had offered the trade's only serious opposition to the monolithic American Fur Company. By 1834, Ashley had sold out his interest in the company and was a member of Congress. His role as supplier at the annual rendezvous—the role that really made the money in the fur business—had been supplanted by William Sublette and Robert Campbell. The fur-trapping end of the business, controlled by five partners, was in disarray. Two of the partners sold out at the 1834 rendezvous, and a year later those who remained sold out to the American Fur Company.

In twelve short years, Ashley and the trappers who carried on in his stead had opened up one of the wealthiest fur regions in the West, shipping about $500,000 worth of beaver to

St. Louis. Their adventures and the hardships they endured while doing their jobs were to become the stuff of legend. And their vast knowledge of the new territory and of the Indians who lived there would be of great service to those who followed them to the West. (For more about the mountain men, see page 185.)

JUNCTION WITH 189

From this point, Highway 189 runs north through the coal-mining towns of Kemmerer and Diamondville to the banks of the Green River, where tales of mountain men and emigrants abound (see page 183).

Skirting the state's border with Idaho, U.S. 89 runs north through some of the most beautiful country in Wyoming. The idyllic alpine scenery along the Salt River yields northeast of Alpine to the rugged spectacle of the Snake River Canyon. The history along this lovely drive concerns itself mainly with the doings of the earliest fur trappers, the procession of emigrants who followed in covered wagons, and the establishment of Mormon communities in Star Valley during the last quarter of the nineteenth century.

BEAR RIVER

From Sage to Salt River Pass, U.S. 89 parallels the Bear River, said to be the longest river in the world that does not empty into an ocean. It is another of the West's many important water routes that provided passing Indians, trappers, and emigrants with water and forage for their animals.

Robert Stuart and his party of eastbound Astorians followed the river into Wyoming in 1812. As part of a larger expedition the previous year, they had traveled west through northern Wyoming to Oregon's coast. There they had helped to build a trading post for the American Fur Company at the mouth of the Columbia River. When problems developed at the fort, Stuart's party was sent back to New York to tell John Jacob Astor that all was not well on the Columbia. The route they stumbled and starved over on their way back to civilization became known as the Oregon Trail.

Before Stuart and his men found that grand highway, they took some major detours. They learned of South Pass from a Shoshone Indian in Idaho and followed his directions up the Bear River into modern Wyoming. There, in mid-September, they ran into a large band of Crow Indians and tried to avoid them by turning north, crossing Salt River Pass, and traveling through

Star Valley to the Snake River. A week later the Crows caught up and stole all their horses.

At that point, the returning Astorians were only twenty-five miles from the route they had followed west the previous year. But instead of traveling upriver and regaining that route, they built a raft and floated about 110 miles the wrong way. Finally, they abandoned the Snake in modern Idaho and walked back into Wyoming over Teton Pass, near what would become Wilson. Eventually, they walked down into the Green River valley, where intense hunger led one of the men to suggest they draw lots to see which of them should be killed to provide meat for the others. Stuart squelched such talk, and the next day they killed a buffalo. Soon they were able to trade for a horse with some Shoshone Indians, who probably pointed them again toward South Pass, the Sweetwater River, and hence to the North Platte. There they spent the winter and then traveled down to St. Louis, where they reported that the South Pass route could be negotiated by wagons.

For about twenty-five years after Stuart's party came through, the Bear River area would remain virtually untraveled by anyone but neighboring Indian tribes and the trappers who plied its streams for beaver pelts.

In the late 1830s, however, the first trickle of emigrant wagons began rolling down the Bear River valley toward Oregon. The rush came in the late 1840s and early 1850s, when tens of thousands of emigrants poured through the valley every summer. Some followed the old trail that crossed into the valley at modern Sage. Others, who took various shortcuts across the Green River valley, struck the valley farther north. The main branch of the trail then followed Bear River out of modern Wyoming to Soda Springs. Then the trail picked up the Snake River and followed it to modern Boise, where people heading to California turned southwest and

Tin lizzies line up in front of the State Bank of Cokeville early in this century. *(University of Wyoming American Heritage Center)*

those bound for Oregon continued along the Snake.

COKEVILLE

Tilford Kutz built a trading post and ferry here in 1873 to serve the diminishing stream of emigrants on the Oregon Trail. Although trade with the emigrants proved disappointing, Kutz's business thrived with Bannock and Shoshone Indians living nearby. Sheep and cattle ranches spread across the area and, when tracks for the Oregon Short Line were laid through the valley around 1890, Cokeville became a major shipping point for livestock.

Emigrants on the Oregon Trail crossed Smith's Fork of the Bear River at Cokeville. Smith's Fork was named for the mountain man Jedediah Smith, who mapped the area in the 1820s.

One of the emigrants who drove a wagon along Smith's Fork was named Albert Dickson, just thirteen years old when he went west in 1864 with a family named Ridgely. It had been a long, arduous pull to Smith's Fork, but things got better when they camped near some Missourians.

Dickson caught a half-dozen trout, the first he'd ever seen, and Mrs. Ridgely cooked one of the best meals the group had enjoyed on the trail. She pulled out chokecherry "butter" and plum jelly she had made along the Sweetwater River, tomatoes she had canned before they left Wisconsin, hominy, a loaf of fresh-baked bread, and fresh coffee.

After dinner, a delegation from the Missouri camp arrived to say they were traveling with a troupe of actors headed for the Montana mining camps. Would anyone like to watch a show? What a question. In no time, the whole camp had pitched in to build a little theater in the wilderness.

"Equipment in our corral was put in the wagons or shoved underneath so as to leave the enclosed space clear," Dickson wrote. "Logs were cut in convenient lengths and placed in the 'pit' forward of the entrance for the audience to sit upon. Meanwhile a stage was in process of construction out of materials at hand . . . Sheets salvaged from somebody's store of linen and strung on wires served for curtains."

When dusk fell, the show began. The actors presented a melodrama about how a young girl forced into "a marriage that was hateful to her, succeeded with the help of her sweetheart in disclosing some embarrassing situations in the elderly suitor's past," Dickson wrote. In addition to the melodrama, there were acrobats and a ventriloquist who "convulsed his audience by mimicking cat and dog fights, Irish and Negro dialect, familiar sounds from the farm, etc., besides making various persons say things they hadn't intended."

BORDER

As its name implies, this town stands astride the Wyoming-Idaho border. During Prohibition, whiskey made and shipped from here enjoyed a favorable reputation throughout the West. One vendor shipped his cargo in a fleet of yellow Packards outfitted with secret compartments.

STAR VALLEY

This beautiful valley acted as a thoroughfare during the emigrant era for travelers following the Lander Cutoff. The valley is about fifty miles long, about a dozen wide, and some of the peaks that surround it stand some six thousand feet above the valley floor.

Mormons came here in the late 1870s when the swelling population of the Salt Lake valley prompted church leaders to look to neighboring states and territories for farmland. Church leader Moses Thatcher came to Star Valley in the late 1870s and approved it for Mormon colonization.

The Mormon population throughout Star Valley grew after 1882, when Congress passed the Edmunds Anti-Polygamy Act. Here, polygamous families were welcomed and protected by Wyoming authorities, who were interested in increasing the territory's population so it would have a better chance of becoming a state.

Through the years, the Mormons turned the valley into a center for production of milk as well as children. In 1927, three eight-hundred-pound tubs of cheese were hauled out of the valley to a railroad station in Idaho during subzero weather. The farmers kept the enormous cheeses from freezing by packing them in straw and warming them by a fire at night.

SIGNAL HILL

With many of the valley's families living as fugitives from the anti-polygamy law, residents were understandably nervous. When tensions with the federal government were high, a lookout stood on Signal Hill. If the lookout spotted strangers approaching, he sent up a column of smoke and some of the valley's men took cover while their wives rehearsed the children on answers to questions about their fathers. If the strangers proved harmless, another signal was given and the patriarchs emerged.

AFTON

Afton became the predominant town in Star Valley because the Mormon church leader Moses Thatcher picked it as the site for the valley's temple. Built of sandstone in the Middle English style, the tabernacle, and thus Afton, became the religious and social center of the valley.

The Mormons surveyed Afton's streets in 1896 with a carpenter's square, a rope, and the celestial guidance of the North Star and the noonday sun.

Outlaws sometimes lived in the valley while they waited for trouble to blow over. The robbers Matt Warner and Tom McCarthy wintered here in 1889 after sticking up a series of banks and stagecoaches. They posed as wealthy Montana cattle ranchers, opened the valley's first saloon, and, it is said, papered its walls with bank notes. With them, and just learning the ropes as an outlaw, was Butch Cassidy, who was arrested on a ranch west, near Auburn, for horse theft (see below).

The novelist Vladimir Nabokov stayed in Star Valley and wrote his best-known novel, *Lolita,* here.

AUBURN

The purity of salt deposits lying along the tributaries of Stump Creek west of Auburn drew Indians to the Star Valley area long before the first wagons creaked across the valley floor. The Indians used the salt for medicine, tanning leather, jerking meats, and flavoring foods. During the Idaho and Montana mining booms of the late 1860s, entrepreneurs from the area hauled the salt to the mining camps, where it sold for as much as sixty cents a pound.

Settled in 1879, Auburn was the second Mormon town in Star Valley.

From the earliest stages of his criminal career, Butch Cassidy, who grew up in a Mormon family, often dodged the law in various Star Valley communities. Three years after he wintered in Afton with the McCarthy gang in 1889, he was living on a ranch near Auburn when

deputy Bob Calverly came to arrest him for horse theft. The deputy later reported that when he told Cassidy why he had come, the outlaw said, "Well, get to shooting," and pulled his pistol. Calverly tried to start shooting, but his gun misfired. In the meantime, a third man got between the two. The next time Calverly got a clear shot, his pistol fired. The bullet grazed Cassidy on the head and knocked him down. With Cassidy offering no further resistance, Calverly took him to Lander, where he was convicted and sentenced to two years in prison. Cassidy's years as leader of the notorious Wild Bunch came later, around the turn of the century.

FREEDOM

Freedom, which conveniently straddles the Idaho-Wyoming border, is the oldest town in Star Valley. When federal authorities began prosecuting polygamists in Idaho, Freedom's position on the border proved to be a great advantage to citizens who had several wives. During a raid, all they had to do to avoid arrest was step across the street.

ALPINE

Robert Stuart, on his way overland from the Oregon coast to St. Louis, camped near here in the autumn of 1812 with his band of not-so-merry men (see page 201). The previous year, Stuart and his men had come west with a larger expedition of fur trappers. Two men from this first party of Astorians explored the South Canyon of the Snake River, which U.S. 89 follows north of Alpine, hoping they could float the Snake all the way to the Columbia. However, after taking a gander at the canyon, which is as narrow as forty feet in some places and as deep as three hundred feet, they decided it might be better to stick with the horses. They climbed out of Wyoming over Teton Pass.

HOBACK JUNCTION

Here, three major north-south routes through Wyoming come together to form one road stretching between this point and the West Thumb of Yellowstone Lake in Yellowstone National Park. Nearby, the Hoback River curls into the Snake. The river was named for a trapper who guided the westbound Astorians through the area, John Hoback.

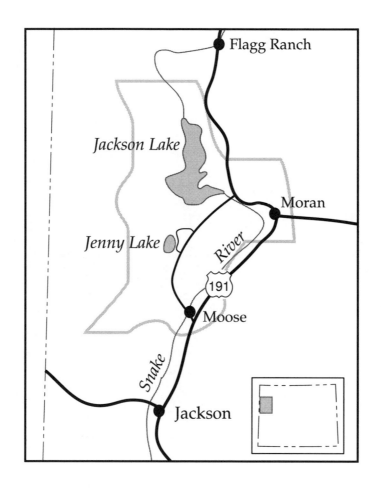

Flagg Ranch

Jackson Lake

Moran

Jenny Lake

River

191

Snake

Moose

Jackson

JACKSON HOLE AND
GRAND TETON NATIONAL PARK

JACKSON HOLE AND GRAND TETON NATIONAL PARK: INTRODUCTION

Stretching from the town of Jackson nearly to Yellowstone is an extra-ordinary valley, or "hole," as the trappers called mountain-circled valleys. It's Jackson Hole, and it includes the town of Jackson, several other small towns, the Teton Range, Grand Teton National Park, and some of the most spectacular lakes and mountains on the continent.

Thousands of years ago, prehistoric people and wandering tribes hunted in Jackson Hole during the summer, but the harsh winters that today draw thousands of downhill skiers to the valley discouraged anyone from settling here until the 1880s.

John Colter, a trapper who accompanied Lewis and Clark during their exploration of the Louisiana Purchase territories from 1804–06, probably first came to the valley in the fall of 1807. Colter was working for a St. Louis fur entrepreneur who had built a fort on the Yellowstone River and had asked Colter to travel through the land of the Crow Indians and invite them to come trade at the fort. Few of the details of Colter's trek are known, but it is thought that he entered the valley through Togwotee Pass and got the first Anglo look at the Hole and much of what is today Yellowstone National Park.

A few years later, an expedition of trappers bound for the Oregon country passed through the valley. Known as the Astorians, they were on their way to the mouth of the Columbia River to build and operate a trading post for the New York entrepreneur John Jacob Astor. Although this group of trappers merely passed through the valley, many other trappers followed and stayed during the season to hunt and skin beaver. Some of those who worked the streams and rivers became legends of the trade: Jim Bridger, William Sublette, and Jedediah Smith, to name a few.

David Jackson, the mountain man from whom the valley takes its name, partnered with Sublette and Smith, acting more or less as the field manager while Smith explored promising new territories and Sublette handled the tasks of shipping out the furs and resupplying the trappers. Sublette named the valley after Jackson, according to tradition, because the trapper loved the hole.

Jackson favored the valley for good reason. It lies among the head-waters of three important river systems, which can be thought of as the interstate highway system of the trapper's day. To the west, water from the Snake River flows through the Pacific Northwest and empties into the ocean along the Oregon Coast. To the north, the Yellowstone River flows into the Missouri, the Mississippi, and finally into the Gulf of Mexico. To the south, the Green River runs down to the Colorado and eventually to the Sea of Cortez.

After the decline of the fur trade, few whites visited the area until the 1860s. Then, a series of scientific expeditions rolled through the Teton and Yellowstone country, mapping it, photographing it, cataloging its flora and fauna. The most famous of these expeditions arrived in 1872, led by Ferdinand Hayden and immortalized by the photographs of William Henry Jackson.

After the scientists came prospectors, hunters, and, in the mid-1880s, settlers.

The Town of Jackson and Environs

SNAKE RIVER

White-water rafters who have blasted through rapids on the Snake River will appreciate the trouble that even the most accomplished western travelers – the mountain men – got into when floating the Snake. In those days, the portion of the river that ran through Jackson Hole was known as the Lewis Fork, and it was much wider and much wilder than it is today in the spring and early summer because there were no upstream dams to control its flow.

The Indians who guided Father Pierre DeSmet through the area in 1840 made the crossing look easy – even to a very nervous DeSmet. He wrote:

Its roaring waters rushed furiously down and whitened with their foam the great blocks of granite which vainly disputed the passage with them. The sight intimidated neither our Indians nor our Canadians. Accustomed to perils of this sort, they rushed into the torrent on horseback and swam it. I dared not venture to do likewise. To get me over, they made a kind of sack of my skin tent, then they put all my things in and set me on top of it. The three Flatheads who had jumped in to guide my frail bark by swimming told me, laughing, not to be afraid, that I was on an excellent boat. And in fact this machine floated on the water like a majestic swan, and in less than ten minutes I found myself on the other bank.

JACKSON: THE TOWN

Although settlers had lived in the valley since the mid-1880s, the town of Jackson was not laid out until 1901. For several years the town had only four buildings worth noting. One was the general store owned by Charles Deloney, who so trusted his neighbors that when he got the urge to go fishing he left the door open so people could walk in and help themselves. Another building, called the Clubhouse, served as a combination dance hall and courthouse.

Although primitive in many ways, Jackson was progressive in others. For instance, Jackson was the first town in the United States to be governed entirely by women. Grace Miller, the mayor, and four other women made up the town council of 1920–24.

At first, most residents of Jackson Hole made their livings on ranches, raising cattle and other livestock. Early on, though, Jackson gained a reputation among visitors for its outstanding scenery, fishing, hunting, and general frontier atmosphere. Some residents soon found that they could make a more dependable living catering to the needs of these visitors, or "dudes," as they came to be known.

One of the earliest dudes, John K. Mitchell, visited Jackson around the turn of the century and, though he was drawn to its scenery, the people repelled him. "All Jackson's Hole [is] a community of scalawags, renegades, discharged soldiers and predestined stinkers," Mitchell wrote in his diary. "We stayed and ate elk meat in the house of the game protector and justice of the peace two days before the season opened."

Mitchell was a cousin of the novelist Owen Wister, who published *The Virginian* in 1902. Wister often visited and for a time lived in Jackson. He was one of the first of many writers to make a home here. By the late 1940s, writers were so thick in Jackson that Donald Hough, one of the best, said that if you shot an arrow into the sky and traced its downward flight you were very likely to find it protruding from the back of some poor wretch hunched over a typewriter. Today, the same applies equally to writers, painters, sculptors, and photographers. In fact, those who make their livings on a working ranch are a tiny minority in modern Jackson. Most people pay the rent with money earned in

Yee-ha! A bull rider catches some air at a dude ranch rodeo near Jackson in the 1920s. *(Jackson Hole Museum and Teton County Historical Society, Jackson, Wyoming)*

one way or another through the area's reputation as a vacation spot. They serve meals. They pour drinks. They run motels. They teach people to ski, ride horses, and climb mountains. They sell fly rods, sleeping bags, silver belt buckles, and bronze sculptures of bucking horses. They paddle rafts through white water, build vacation homes, and pretend to shoot and lynch one another in the town square. All services for the visitors.

Although Jackson's general attitude toward visitors is welcoming today, it wasn't always so. When Hough arrived in the late 1940s, he worked in a bar that wasn't about to go out of its way to please visitors.

"We serve only beer, gin, straight whiskey, and whiskey and soda," Hough wrote in *Snow*

Above Town. "Some of the dudes want fancy drinks. If it is a drink that is made with a whiskey base we give them straight whiskey, and if it is one made with gin, we pour them a shot of gin. If they complain, we tell them we're sorry, this is all we serve . . . Most of them drink their drinks and shut up."

Today, Jackson's bartenders think nothing of tossing together Singapore Slings, Fuzzy Navels, huckleberry margaritas, or other such alcoholic exotica.

WILSON AND TETON PASS

From the south end of town, State 22 veers off to the northwest and leads about five miles to Wilson. This small town was named for Elijah "Uncle Nick" Wilson, who spent part of his boyhood as an adopted son of the great Shoshone leader Washakie. He later rode for the Pony Express, served in the army, and drove stagecoaches before helping to bring the first wagons into the valley over Teton Pass. Wilson first settled in South Park but later moved to the present site of Wilson, where he built a cabin, store, and saloon.

Just beyond the Stagecoach Bar, State 22 begins its long ascent to the summit of Teton Pass. To get over this slight droop between the Teton and Snake mountain ranges, travelers must climb roughly twenty-two hundred vertical feet. Heavily used by Indians before Wilson Price Hunt and his band of westbound Astorians clopped over it in 1811, Teton Pass became one of the most famous trails through the mountains during the fur-trading era.

Though it was a major thoroughfare for anyone on horseback, Teton Pass was no place for wagons. The great waves of emigrants in their prairie schooners traveled through the Rockies far to the south. Settlers avoided the valley until the mid-1880s, and then nobody brought a wagon over the pass until 1889. In that year, the Sylvester Wilson clan (including Uncle Nick) struggled for eleven days to haul their six wagons over the pass. They cut trees, built ramps, pulled, pushed, and swore at their animals. On the downslope they braked their wagons by dragging trees behind them.

In 1901 the county made the trip marginally easier by building a wagon road over the pass, but it remained a trial for all who hauled because it included grades nearly twice as steep as those that force today's motorist to shift to a lower gear.

For many years, the pass was the only way in or out of Jackson Hole. On the other side of the mountains you could catch a train in Victor that ran once a day, once a week, or once a month depending on the season.

JACKSON OUTLAWS

Never as famous a hideout as the Hole-in-the-Wall country in Wyoming's Big Horn Mountains, Jackson Hole still has the right to brag that it was at one time a popular spot among outlaws on the run. Butch Cassidy spent some of his time off from bad behavior in the Jackson area. So did many of the lesser lights in the galaxy of western outlaws. Generally, though, the outlaws kept a low profile in Jackson. They committed their crimes elsewhere and passed quietly through the valley.

One outlaw who spent time in Jackson Hole never did seem to get the hang of crime. Ed Harrington, alias Ed Trafton, started out as a small-time horse thief on the Idaho flats just over Teton Pass. He and his partners were still learning the ropes when a posse caught up with two members of the gang, shot one, and arrested the other. Trafton heard about the arrest and killing and decided to skedaddle, but first he robbed a store in Rexburg. He failed, and was arrested and thrown in jail with his partner.

But fate smiled on them. They found an opportunity to escape, grabbed a couple of horses, and ran for it. Then fate frowned. The Snake River was too wild to ford and they were recaptured along its banks. After prison, Trafton carried mail back and forth over Teton Pass. On his rounds he met the author Owen Wister, who was also living in Jackson Hole during the 1890s. Trafton later claimed that Wister regarded him as the model for the hero of his novel, *The Virginian,* but a close reading indicates that if Wister modeled any character after Trafton, it was Trampas, the villain.

Trafton did not stay in Jackson long. He drifted away and was not heard from until 1914, when he made history by robbing, in less than an hour, fifteen stagecoaches bearing tourists through Yellowstone Park. Still a bit hazy on the outlaw methodology, Trafton blew his chance to make off safely with the loot by allowing tourists to snap his photo (see page 236).

ELK REFUGE

During winter, between seven and ten thousand elk graze and eat hay on the wide pan of flat land beside U.S. 89 just north of Jackson. The refuge got its start around the turn of the century when sympathetic ranchers began feeding the herd during severe winters. In later years, the state and federal governments bought hay for the elk. Eventually, the federal government and the Izaak Walton League managed to set aside 23,754 acres of land and create the National Elk Refuge.

Every autumn, the elk gather in the refuge and stay throughout the winter months, when visitors can ride among them on horse-drawn sleds. As the snow melts in the spring, the elk move off into the mountains. Before they leave, many drop their antlers, which local Boy Scouts retrieve and auction off. Considered an aphrodisiac in some parts of the world and prized as ornaments in others, the antlers sell for high prices.

GROS VENTRE RIVER

The river and the mountain range to the east take their names from the Gros Ventre Indians, an Arapaho band that allied itself with the powerful Blackfeet tribe in the early 1800s. Pronounced "grow-VAHNT," the words mean "big belly." The tribe now lives on the Fort Belknap Reservation in Montana.

THE VIEW

As U.S. 89 runs north of Jackson, it skirts a high brown hill and then breaks out onto the broader valley floor and a tremendous view of the Tetons. In 1835, the Reverend Samuel Parker climbed one of the smaller mountains at the south end of Jackson Hole and recorded the astonishing view:

> About 60 miles to the east, the Rocky Mountains lay stretched through the whole extent of vision, spread out like luminous clouds in the horizon; their summits so elevated, that no soil ever rises to sully the pure whiteness of their everlasting snows and tinged and mellowed with a golden hue by the rays of the sun. Not very far to the north, the Trois Tetons, a cluster of high pointed mountains, covered with perpetual snow, rising ten thousand feet almost perpendicularly, were distinctly visible, with two others of the same form but of less magnitude.

Parker exaggerated the perpendicular rise of the Tetons from the valley floor by nearly three thousand feet. The valley's elevation is 6,200 to 6,400 feet, and the peak of the Grand Teton is 13,770 feet.

KELLY

Shortly after the turn of the century, William and Sophie Kelly settled beside the Gros Ventre River. They built up their ranch, opened a sawmill, and established a post office. Eventually, eighty other people joined them on the river to form the community of Kelly. The town thrived until the mid-1920s, when two natural disasters combined to wipe it out.

The first, a massive landslide, came in the summer of 1925. A local rancher named Huff happened to be plowing a field four miles above Kelly when the entire end of Sheep Mountain broke away and slumped toward him. Huff jumped on a horse and fled. Glancing back, he could see waves of soil surging across the fields he had just been working in. Some 50 million tons of debris slid from Sheep Mountain that day and formed a dam across the Gros Ventre River. Huff's house was behind the dam, and within several hours of the slide, water had flooded it up to the eaves.

Residents called the new lake Slide Lake and lived beneath the dam for two years. Then, in the spring of 1927, the dam gave way and an eight-foot wall of water thundered murderously through town. Six people were killed and all of the buildings were swept away except for the church and the school. Downstream, the flood knocked out bridges, swamped the town of Wilson, and temporarily boosted the water level in the Snake River Canyon by fifty feet.

After the flood, the Kellys packed up what was left of their belongings and moved to Idaho.

GRAND TETON NATIONAL PARK

Few places in the world rival Grand Teton National Park for its mountain scenery. Here, rugged mountains burst more than seven thousand feet above the flat valley floor, and the

Horsepacking in Grand Teton National Park. The Grand Teton is a spectacular backdrop. *(Jackson Hole Museum and Teton County Historical Society, Jackson, Wyoming)*

meandering curves and turns of the Snake River flow down from a series of beautiful mountain lakes.

Established in 1929, the early park encompassed only the major peaks and the lakes at their feet. By then, however, a plan was afoot that eventually enlarged the park to its present size.

In 1923, a group of local residents had proposed to Horace Albright, superintendent of Yellowstone National Park, that a portion of the Jackson valley be set aside as a national recreation area. Three years later, Albright brought John D. Rockefeller, Jr. and his family to Jackson Hole. While touring the area, Albright described his notion of making the whole valley a national park. Rockefeller said nothing then, but soon

formed the Snake River Land Company, which began buying up ranches and other private land at the northern end of the valley. He eventually put together some thirty-two thousand acres and offered to give them to the government if it would include them in an enlarged version of Grand Teton National Park.

However, many local ranchers opposed the plan because they believed it would deprive them of grazing privileges they had enjoyed for years on national forest land. The park extension became mired in political battles for nearly twenty years. Finally, after Rockefeller threatened to sell his holdings on the open market, President Roosevelt declared much of the valley floor a national monument in 1943. Rockefeller deeded his lands to the government in 1949, and Congress extended the original park boundaries the following year. They include the monument lands as well as Rockefeller's donation and protect about 485 square miles of mountains, lakes, streams, forests, and open valley.

"There are many peaks in the Rockies as lofty as the Teton, but beyond this point all parallelism ceases," wrote William Owen, after an unsuccessful attempt at climbing the Grand Teton in 1891. "The country surrounding the peaks is rugged and wild beyond the power of words to convey, and when the region becomes more accessible, by means of railroads already projected, it will doubtless rival, as a pleasuring ground, the famous National Park [Yellowstone] itself."

Indeed it has.

Moose, Wyoming, nestled in the firs and aspen trees at the feet of the Teton Range, is park headquarters for Grand Teton National Park. *(University of Wyoming American Heritage Center)*

Teton Park Road: Moose to Jackson Lake Junction

THE TETONS

From this perspective of the range, visitors and residents alike are often puzzled by how these sharp, angular peaks could have earned the name "Teton," a French word for breast. Some wonder if the French trappers who named them had been out on the trail too long. Others, who have more confidence in the discerning eye of the French male, marvel at how foundation garments must have changed through the years. Still others explain that the French trappers named the range from the west side and that from that perspective the peaks bear a closer resemblance to the body part in question. However, even from the west one needs to squint pretty hard to see the resemblance. Perhaps the best explanation is that the French trappers did not apply the name *Les Trois Tetons* to these peaks at all but rather to three smoothly curved, fulsome hills on the Idaho side of the range, and that the term was later transposed to the more obvious landmarks.

The first notable claim to have ascended the Grand was made by N. P. Langford and James Stevenson, members of the Hayden expedition, in 1872. However, William Owen, who reached the summit in 1898, disputed Langford's claim and eventually got the Wyoming legislature to give him official credit for the first ascent.

Both parties came across evidence that Indians had been climbing at least most of the way up the peak many years before them. About five hundred feet below the summit and eleven hundred feet west, they found a stone enclosure that Indians had used for either religious rites or as a lookout.

MOOSE

Named for the moose that frequent the area, this small village acts as headquarters for Grand Teton National Park.

The Ed Chambers family with their winter transport system out in front of their cabin in Moose in the early 1930s. *(Jackson Hole Museum and Teton County Historical Society, Jackson, Wyoming)*

MENOR'S FERRY

Bill Menor came to the valley in 1894 and homesteaded on the west bank of the Snake, right under the most spectacular peaks in the Teton Range. He built a log cabin among the cottonwoods, plowed up a small field for a garden, and raised a few chickens and some cows. He also built a cable ferry across the Snake, a welcome improvement in the valley because many of the settlers cut timber on the west side of the river and needed a way across it. Often, the ferry provided the only crossing within forty miles. Menor's Ferry was a simple platform on pontoons connected to an overhead cable and pulled across the river by the current. Menor charged twenty-five cents for a horse and rider, fifty cents for a wagon and team. Sometimes Menor decided the river was too dangerous to cross. On those days he often provided room and board free of charge to those waiting for the river to calm down.

CHAPEL OF THE TRANSFIGURATION

Built in 1925, this pleasant chapel traces its history to a 1920 campfire chat at the outlet of

Passengers crossing the Snake River at Menor's Ferry in the winter, after the ferry had been dismantled for the season. *(Jackson Hole Museum and Teton County Historical Society, Jackson, Wyoming)*

Leigh Lake. There, a group of weary summer visitors complained among themselves about the long trip to Jackson required for those who wanted to attend church services. They wished that a chapel could be built near Menor's Ferry, the heart of dude country. Five years later, Maude Noble, successor to Bill Menor as owner of the ferry, donated the necessary land and the churchly dudes got their wish. A lovely little building, the chapel has a picture window behind the altar that frames the Tetons.

WINDY POINT

On the mountains on the east side of the valley floor, the reddish scar of a 1925 landslide is clearly visible on the flanks of Sheep Mountain (often called Sleeping Indian). The landslide dammed the Gros Ventre River, creating a steadily growing lake. Two years later the natural dam suddenly burst, and an eight-foot wall of water washed through the town of Kelly, killing six people and destroying nearly every building (see page 212).

GLACIER GULCH TURNOUT

This turnout provides a fine view of most of the major peaks at the southern end of the park. At 13,770 feet, the Grand Teton is the tallest of the group. Officially, William O. Owen made the first ascent in 1898. Although the Wyoming legislature gave its seal of approval to Owen's claim, others have contested it.

To the right of the Grand is Mount Owen, named after the climber. At 12,928 feet, it is only about 850 feet lower than the summit of the Grand. It was first climbed in 1930.

To the right of Mount Owen is Teewinot, 12,325 feet. The name is a Shoshone word meaning "many pinnacles." It was first climbed in 1929.

The Middle Teton, 12,804 feet, and Nez Perce, 11,901 feet, stand to the left of the Grand. Nez Perce hides the South Teton at 12,514 feet.

NORTH JENNY LAKE JUNCTION

Here, a beautiful one-way scenic road winds into String and Jenny lakes before rejoining the park road at South Jenny Lake Junction.

Jenny Lake was named for Jenny Leigh, the wife of Richard "Beaver Dick" Leigh, a trapper who lived on the Idaho side of the Teton Range. Beaver Dick guided the Hayden scientific expeditions through the Teton and Yellowstone areas in 1871 and 1872. He enjoyed the job and even brought along the wife and kids. Everybody got along so well that the expedition's cartographers named three lakes after the Leigh family: Jenny Lake, Leigh Lake (which is not visible from the road), and Beaver Dick Lake. The latter connects Jenny and Leigh lakes and has been renamed String Lake.

Leigh was born in England but came to America as a boy and to the Rocky Mountains

Jenny Lake Overlook, circa 1920. *(Jackson Hole Museum and Teton County Historical Society, Jackson, Wyoming)*

in the late 1850s as a twenty-eight-year-old veteran of the Mexican-American War. By then the fur-trade era had long since passed, but Beaver Dick trapped the streams that run along the western slopes of the Tetons and made a good-enough living.

He and Jenny, a Shoshone, had five children together, but Beaver Dick never saw his kids grow up. In 1876, the whole family came down with smallpox. Only Beaver Dick survived. In a letter to a friend, he described Jenny's tragic death:

She was laying very quiet now for about

two hours when she asked for a drink of water. I was laying down with one of my daughters on each arm keeping them down with the fever. I told Aynes [a neighbor who had come to help] what she wanted and he gave her a drink and 10 minutes later she was dead . . .

Dick [his son] turned over in bed and said, "God bless my poor mother!" He then said to me, "Father, maybe we will all die."

Three years later, Beaver Dick married Susan Tadpole, a Bannock. He had assisted at Susan's birth sixteen years before. Together they

Beaver Dick Leigh and his first family, who died of smallpox. *(Jackson Hole Museum and Teton County Historical Society, Jackson, Wyoming)*

had three children, including Emma, who broke horses for settlers at five dollars a head and so impressed Theodore Roosevelt with her marksmanship that he gave her one of his rifles.

Beaver Dick turns up in the diaries of many who visited Jackson Hole to hunt, fish, or explore. John K. Mitchell, a close friend of the novelist Owen Wister, visited Jackson Hole in the 1890s and described Beaver Dick as a round-shouldered, long-bearded man who "drops his H's like a hansom cabby in the Strand." He hated the encroachment of the settlements, Mitchell said, and kept away from them. "Now he is getting too old and has to spend his winters in a house." But every spring he packed his ponies and set out with his family to spend three or four months in the Tetons.

MOUNT MORAN TURNOUT

First climbed in 1922, this 12,605-foot peak was named for the landscape painter Thomas Moran, who visited the Tetons in 1879 with his brother, Peter. The painter described the Tetons

as the "finest pictorial range in the U.S. or even in North America."

In 1950, a DC-3 airplane carrying twenty-four passengers slammed into the mountain's northeast flank in late autumn, killing all aboard. It was impossible to retrieve the bodies, so the climbing route that passed the wreckage was closed for five years to give them time to return to the soil.

SIGNAL MOUNTAIN ROAD

The 7,593-foot mountain was named for a smoke signal sent from its peak in 1891 by a search party that had just found the body of Ray Hamilton, who had disappeared while hunting. The signal let others know that Hamilton had been found.

JACKSON LAKE DAM

The dam that bars the outlet from Jackson Lake forms a reservoir for Idaho farmers and ranchers. The Wyoming legislature gave away the water rights, even though the water could have been used in Jackson Hole. That act, as well as other Idaho attempts to control water in the valley's other lakes created lasting resentment among valley residents. A sign in the men's room of the Jackson courthouse reads: "Please flush the toilet. Idaho needs the water."

The first dam was built in 1909 and raised the water level three feet. The following spring it washed out, wrecking Menor's Ferry. During the summer of 1910, an earthen barrier replaced the ruined dam. It raised the lake level ten feet and remained intact until a replacement was completed in 1916. That dam raised the water level thirty-nine feet and made for a much more sedate river downstream. It was rebuilt in 1989.

DEADMAN'S BAR

Aptly named, Deadman's Bar is the site of an 1886 triple murder. No one knows what really happened on Deadman's Bar because the only eyewitness was John Tonnar, the man who was accused of the murders.

At his trial in Evanston, Tonnar said he and three other men had come to the banks of the Snake River to prospect for gold and had set up their camp on Deadman's Bar. Although he claimed he had grubstaked the other men, Tonnar soon found himself the odd man out. The other three beat him, he said, in the hopes that he would quit the claim and abandon his share of whatever gold they might find. Rather than leave, Tonnar stuck around and tried to make friends. It was a mistake. While two of the prospectors were off working the claim, Tonnar got into an argument with the third and was compelled, he later told an Evanston jury, to shoot him in self-defense.

Although the dead man's body showed he had been shot in the back, the jury believed Tonnar and acquitted him. As for the other two prospectors, Tonnar's courtroom story does not adequately explain how they may have died. Investigators believed they were killed with an axe and concluded that Tonnar had murdered all three men while they slept.

Today a good road leads down to Deadman's Bar and is used primarily by boaters to float the Snake.

CUNNINGHAM CABIN

Built by a trapper-turned-homesteader named Pierce Cunningham in 1890, this modest cabin was the site of a shootout between alleged horse thieves and a posse composed of Jackson residents and Montana lawmen.

In the winter of 1892–93, Cunningham allowed a couple of strangers named Burnett and Spencer to winter a herd of horses on his ranch. The horses bore the brand of a Montana ranch, however, and the following spring a Montana U.S. marshal and several deputies came looking for them. The Montana posse enlisted some more men in Jackson, then they all rode out to Cunningham's cabin and surrounded the place at dawn. (Cunningham was spending the winter on Flat Creek, twenty-five miles south.)

A dog started barking, and when Spencer walked out to the corral to investigate, he was told to throw his hands up. Instead, he drew a pistol, fired, and was shot dead. Meanwhile, Burnett got up, strapped on his pistol, grabbed a rifle, and walked outside. One member of the posse took a shot at him but missed. Burnett fired back and taunted the posse to show themselves. No one did, but as he turned away and walked toward the cabin door, someone shot him in the back.

Both men were buried southeast of the cabin.

MORAN JUNCTION

Moran got its start in 1903 as headquarters for Ben Sheffield's dude ranch and hunting and fishing camp. Sheffield's place soon gained a worldwide reputation for its hospitality, food, and service. It drew many wealthy families, including some European royals, to Jackson Hole for a good dose of the old yippi-i-oh.

Beginning in 1909, the construction of dams at the outlet of Jackson Lake brought much work to the area and helped Moran grow into a busy frontier town.

Sheffield sold out to the Snake River Land Company for $100,000 in 1928, and retired. That is, Sheffield thought he had retired. Unfortunately, the stock-market crash in 1929 wiped him out and forced him to find work as a fire lookout on nearby Signal Mountain—not a bad way to make a living, considering the view.

In addition to Sheffield's place, the Snake River Land Company bought up more than thirty-two thousand acres of land at the north end of the valley to donate to the government as part of an extended Grand Teton National Park.

JACKSON LAKE JUNCTION

Here Teton Park Road reconnects with U.S. 89.

A pack string crosses Leigh Lake Flat, at the foot of Mount Moran, in Grand Teton National Park. *(Jackson Hole Museum and Teton County Historical Society, Jackson, Wyoming)*

JACKSON LAKE

Backpackers who huddle around pots of freeze-dried glop at suppertime should not read about the meals enjoyed on the shores of Jackson Lake by the trapper Osborne Russell in the 1830s. Russell loved Jackson Lake and wrote rhapsodically about it in his journal. He loved it for the scenery, but one suspects that he also loved it for the fat times he enjoyed there. Russell celebrated Independence Day 1839 in high style: "I caught about 20 very fine salmon trout which, together with fat mutton, buffalo beef and coffee and the manner in which it was served up, constituted a dinner that ought to be considered independent even by Britons."

The doings weren't always so appealing for the mountain men, especially during the cold months. While living in Jim Bridger's camp during the winter of 1835–36, Russell and his fellow trappers lived off buffalo meat so rubbery it bounced.

The drive along Jackson Lake to the north is lovely. And that way lie Jackson Lake Lodge, Colter Bay, and the south entrance to Yellowstone.

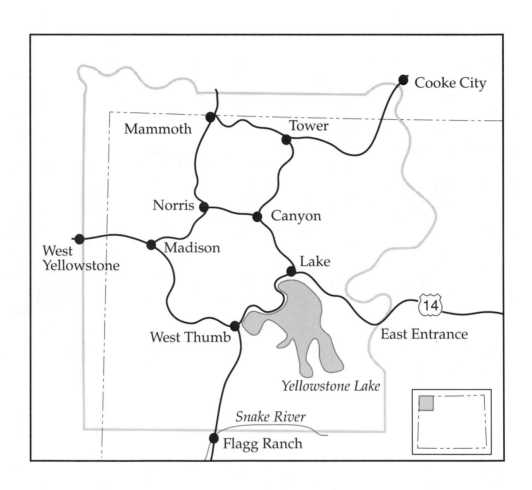

Mammoth
Cooke City
Tower
Norris
Canyon
West
Yellowstone
Madison
Lake
West Thumb
East Entrance
14
Yellowstone Lake
Snake River
Flagg Ranch

YELLOWSTONE NATIONAL PARK

YELLOWSTONE NATIONAL PARK: INTRODUCTION

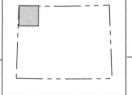

Yellowstone National Park was established by Congress as the country's first national park in 1872 "for the benefit and enjoyment of the people." Some people say it was created by Congress, but nature is the real creator.

The phrase "for the benefit and enjoyment of the people" has not prevented tumults of controversy about the uses of the park in the ensuing 120 years. In the early years the park was seldom visited and mostly unwatched, so poachers took advantage. Then roads and grand hotels were built for high-style visitors. They traveled in stagecoaches, and some even lobbied for an elevator to the base of Lower Yellowstone Falls so they could descend and ascend in comfort.

In 1916 the era of the automobile came to the park, and with it the "sagebrushers," people who didn't use the grand hotels but camped out in the sagebrush. Auto camps catered to their needs with meals and bed space under canvas covers. The bellhops and waiters in the hotels resented these folks because of the reduced tips.

The biggest change for the park came after World War II, when Americans had lots of cars, cheap gas, and an improving national road system. Yellowstone began to get huge numbers of visitors. Which meant better roads in the park, more grocery stores, gas stations, hotels, and campgrounds—more development.

The number of annual visitors has grown to about 3 million now, from all over the world. All require services, so the park is taking care of a lot of people. Better care, some critics say, than it's taking of its animals. Buffalo are shot in Montana when they leave the park. The big elk herds might not be able to survive a hard winter. The grizzly bear is on the endangered species list. The development of the park, and its commercialization, are controversial issues.

Yet the 3 million people come to see something real: Yellowstone Falls; the Grand Canyon of the Yellowstone; the geysers; the paint pots, mud volcanoes, and hot springs. Most of all the buffalo, elk, antelope, deer, and bighorn sheep. And the grizzly bear, not so common a sight anymore.

Still, it is a wonder and deserves the description given it (and surrounding country) by the Crow leader Arapooish long ago:

> The Crow country is a good country. The Great Spirit has put it in exactly the right place . . . It has snowy mountains and sunny plains, all kinds of climates and good things for every season. When the summer heats scorch the prairies, you can draw up under the mountains, where the air is sweet and cool, the grass fresh, and the bright streams come tumbling out of the snowbanks. There you can hunt the elk, the deer, and the antelope when their skins are fit for dressing; there you will find plenty of white [grizzly] bears and mountain sheep.
>
> In the autumn when your horses are fat and strong from the mountain pastures, you can go down into the plains and hunt the buffalo, or trap beaver on the streams. And when the winter comes on, you can take shelter in the woody bottoms along the rivers. There you will find buffalo meat for yourself and cottonwood bark for your horses . . .
>
> The Crow country is in exactly the right place. Everything good is to be found there.

GATEWAY ARCH: GARDINER

At the entrance of the park stands a huge stone arch. Built in 1903, it calls to mind two of the park's great champions, Hiram M. Chittenden and President Theodore Roosevelt. Chittenden, a road engineer and one of Yellowstone's historians, conceived the arch and drafted the notes from which architect Robert C. Reamer designed it. Roosevelt laid the cornerstone of the arch when he visited the park as president.

The president spoke to about three thousand people at a dedication ceremony and, perhaps uncharacteristically for a politician, he recorded nothing of what he said. Instead, he later wrote about the animals he saw as he rode toward the site:

> We put spurs to our horses and cantered rapidly toward the appointed place, and on the way we passed within forty yards of a score of blacktails, which merely moved to one side and looked at us, and within almost as short a distance of half a dozen antelope. To any lover of nature it could not help being a delightful thing to see the wild and timid creatures of the wilderness rendered so tame.

Roosevelt was a great fan of the park, and he took the opportunity of dedicating the arch to spend some time in its wilds with his pal John Burroughs, the naturalist. Burroughs wrote later that "even the secret service men and his physician and private secretaries were left at Gardiner. He craved once more to be alone with nature; he was evidently hungry for the wild and the aboriginal."

Roosevelt and Burroughs saw some bighorn sheep near Tower Fall scrambling up and down a rock face so perpendicular that "it seemed to me impossible" to climb on, Burroughs wrote.

When word of the bighorns came, Roosevelt was shaving,

> with coat off and a towel around his neck. One side of his face was half shaved, and the other side lathered.
> "By Jove," said the President, "I must see that. The shaving can wait, and the sheep won't."
> So on he came, . . . coatless, hatless, but not latherless, nor towelless.

Roosevelt also indulged in some rough humor. Burroughs recorded that the president sometimes got requests for help from former Rough Riders.

> In camp one night TR read a letter from one who had ended up in jail in Arizona: "Dear Colonel, — I am in trouble. I shot a lady in the eye, but I did not intend to hit the lady; I was shooting at my wife."
> And the presidential laughter rang out over the tree-tops.

GARDNER RIVER

Here, the road follows the steep canyon of the Gardner River, which bears the oldest place name in the park except for the Yellowstone River. (The Gardner River is not spelled the same as the town of Gardiner, Montana.) The river takes its name from the mountain man Johnson Gardner, who first trapped beaver in Gardner's Hole, a few miles south of here, in the early 1830s. An agent of the American Fur Company, Johnson was, according to park historian Aubrey Haines, an "illiterate, often brutal trapper."

MAMMOTH HOT SPRINGS AREA

Mammoth Hot Springs is park headquarters, a role it has played almost since the creation of the park. In the early days, the nearest vestiges of civilization were nearby Montana towns like Livingston and Bozeman. The Northern Pacific tracks ran up the Yellowstone valley to these towns and led most early visitors to the park.

In 1886 the army took over administration of the park. Congress had failed to provide the Department of the Interior with funds to run the park, an oversight that damaged Yellowstone. Poachers and vandals chipped away at the geyser and hot-spring formations and wantonly slaughtered the game. Unfortunately, civilian superintendents had neither the legal authority nor the enforcement personnel to protect the park. The army did.

At Mammoth Hot Springs the army built Camp Sheridan as a base for its troops. Then, in 1891, it began Fort Yellowstone. Much of the old fort is still visible. The big grassy area at town center is the former parade ground. The officers lived in the houses that stand along its southern fringe. The enlisted men lived behind these houses in barracks. Nearby, the noncommissioned officers lived on Soap Suds Row. It got its name from the laundry the noncoms' wives took in to make ends meet.

Travelers from all over the world have come to Mammoth to admire the terraces of travertine created by the hot springs here. Dr. Ferdinand V. Hayden, leader of a government exploring expedition to Yellowstone in 1871, recorded his impression of the hot springs enthusiastically:

> The steep sides of the hill were ornamented with a series of semi-circular basins, with margins varying in height and so beautifully scalloped and adorned with a sort of bead-work that the beholder stands amazed. Add to this a snow-white ground, with every variety of shade in scarlet, green and yellow as brilliant as the brightest dyes.

But Hayden did not like everything he saw. He specifically complained about the quality of the accommodations. He and the rest of the "explorers" (mountain men had known the park intimately for decades) found a hotel, of all things, at the hot springs. Variously known as the National Park Hotel, Horr and McCartney's Hotel (after the proprietors), and Mammoth Hot Springs Hotel, this establishment's accommodations were, according to Hayden, "very primitive, consisting, in lieu of a bedstead, of 12 square feet of floor-room." Guests were obliged to provide their own blankets. The food, Hayden went on, "is simple, and remarkable for quantity rather than for quality or variety." Not every visitor, though, was unappreciative. Windham Thomas Wyndham-Quin, the Earl of Dunraven, called the Mammoth Hot Springs Hotel, "the last outpost of civilization—that is, the last place where whiskey is sold."

In 1889 a young man who would one day be counted among the world's preeminent men of letters visited the park: Rudyard Kipling. On his way from India to England, Kipling visited parts of the United States, including Yellowstone. He didn't see much that impressed him. His gleeful comment about the hot-spring formations at Mammoth was that "the ground rings hollow as a kerosene-tin, and some day the Mammoth Hotel, guests and all, will sink into the caverns below and be turned into a stalactite."

MAMMOTH TO TOWER

Even before the park was created in 1872, a pack trail followed the approximate route of this road from Mammoth Hot Springs to Tower Junction and on to the northeast entrance of the park. Cooke City, Montana, just beyond the northeast gate, was already an active mining area.

BLACKTAIL PLATEAU DRIVE

Blacktail Plateau Drive, a dirt road that turns off to the south, is worth driving for a couple of historical reasons. First, it is the approximate route of the old Bannock Trail. The Bannock Indians lived on the Snake River plains in what is now Idaho. They used the trail periodically in the mid-nineteenth century to cross the Rocky Mountains to the east side for buffalo hunts.

Second, Truman C. Everts was found along this route, then called Devil's Cut, after a grim and harrowing challenge to survive.

In September of 1870, Everts got separated from his horse and his companions in rough country south of Yellowstone Lake. His horse had carried off his weapon, his food, and his means of making fire. Confident that other members of his party, the exploring expedition led by Gen. H. D. Washburn in 1870, would search for him, Everts set out on what he thought was their trail. But he got it wrong. They had gone off in another direction. Ravenous, he came to a small lake filled with waterfowl, but he could not shoot any of them. That night a mountain lion ran him up a tree and scared him half out of his wits. By now the poor man was suffering terribly from cold, hunger, and fear.

Soon he discovered three lifesavers: He could keep warm in the hot springs beside the lake; he could eat a certain thistle; and he could make fire with the lens of his opera glass.

After days of anxiety waiting for rescue, Everts reached a frightening conclusion. He wrote a letter, "I knew my escape from the wilderness must be accomplished, if at all, by my own unaided exertions. This thought was terribly afflicting."

Weeks passed, and he grew weaker and weaker. Once he lost his precious lens, went back after it, and luckily found it. But the amount of time he could travel in a day was getting shorter and shorter, and he was losing his grip on sanity.

Meanwhile, Everts's friends offered a reward of six hundred dollars for the recovery of his body. Collins Jack Baronett, known as "Yellowstone Jack," set out to find the remains. On Blacktail Plateau, his dog started growling at something dark that Baronett took for a bear. But when Baronett closed in to shoot the bear, he noticed that "it was making a low groaning noise, crawling along upon its knees and elbows, and trying to drag itself up the mountain. Then it suddenly occurred to me that it was the object of my search."

Park service historian Aubrey Haines adds that:

> At the time of his rescue, Everts was described as weighing about fifty pounds, his clothing was in shreds, and he had no shoes. The balls of his frost-bitten feet were worn to the bone, and his scalded thigh was likewise exposed. Other areas of his body were seared and blackened, while his fingers resembled bird's claws. He was both inarticulate and irrational when found, and doubtless would soon have died of exposure to the cold sleet that was then coating the ground.

He had been lost for thirty-seven days.

So thank goodness for Yellowstone Jack, who, in the end, got nothing for his trouble but satisfaction in a job well done. Everts's pals told Baronett that the money was offered for the body only. Evidently the living man was not worth a reward.

THE NORTH FORK FIRE

Here, the largest of the historic wildfires of 1988 swept through, reducing the landscape to what appeared to be a region of utter blight, a depressing vista of gray and black. However, just six weeks after the burn green grass sprang up along the edge of the pavement where the little bit of rain that had fallen that autumn had run off. Since then, the natural process of renewal has continued. (For a description of the major fires of that summer and a discussion of the park's fire policies, see page 244).

Uncle John Yancey. *(Jackson Hole Museum and Teton County Historical Society, Jackson, Wyoming)*

PLEASANT VALLEY

Between the road and the mountains to the north lies Pleasant Valley, or Yancey's Hole. Yancey was Uncle John Yancey, and he built the Pleasant Valley Hotel here between 1884 and 1887. It enjoyed the patronage of the novelist Owen Wister, the writer and illustrator Ernest Thompson Seton, and other notables, especially fishermen. The accommodations were basic. A guest described them like this in 1901:

> An inspection of the bedrooms prove them to be large enough for a single bedstead with a box in which are washbowl, pitcher and part of a crash towel. Of the four window lights at least one was broken in every room. The cracks in the wall are pasted up with strips of newspaper . . . The beds showed they were changed at least twice, once in the spring and once in the fall of the year. A little bribe on the side and a promise to keep the act of criminality a secret from Uncle John induces the maid to provide us with clean sheets.

TOWER JUNCTION AREA

The ranger's residence here is one of three remaining soldier stations in the park. The others are at Norris Junction and Bechler.

The soldier stations housed soldiers at outlying sites in the park. Their duty: prevent vandalism of thermal areas, enforce campfire rules, and control poaching. In the early decades of the park's existence, elk were killed indiscriminately. At Mammoth Hot Springs in the spring of 1875, for instance, a couple of local ranchers killed two thousand. A visiting party of the Secretary of War witnessed the slaughter that year and asked why the park superintendent allowed it. But the superintendent had neither the laws nor the manpower to stop the poachers.

After 1886, when the army began administering the park, the soldiers took up their stations at lonely billets for months at a time in remote locations such as Soda Butte, Riverside, Norris, Lower Geyser Basin, and Shoshone Station. In the winter months the only way to see anybody was to visit them on "Norwegian snowshoes." That's what they called skis—very long skis, used with a single long pole. The soldiers became expert at travel on these skis and learned techniques of winter survival.

During the 1890s, the novelist and journalist Emerson Hough (author of *The Covered Wagon,* among other tales) tried skiing on these contraptions and left us a vivid description of his experience:

> A pair of skis make about the liveliest way of locomotion, if you give them a chance, of anything on earth, and if you don't think they are alive and full of soul, you just try them and see. They've got a howling, malignant devil in every inch of their slippery

surface, and the combination will give the most blasé and motionless man on earth a thrill a minute for a good many minutes.

Ski patrolling may have had its lighter moments, but the intent was serious: Stop the poaching. The patrolling worked. Soon the poaching of elk, buffalo, deer, antelope, and bighorn sheep was mostly under control. Perhaps poaching was reduced, too, because the people of the towns near the park realized the truth of Theodore Roosevelt's comment: "A deer wild in the woods is worth to the people of the neighborhood many times the value of its carcass, because of the way it attracts sportsmen, who give employment and leave money behind them."

The park superintendents then turned their attention to what they regarded as another problem: the control of predators, primarily coyotes, wolves, wildcats, grizzlies, and mountain lions. They thought these animals, if unchecked, would destroy the prized game herds. But their policy of eradicating the predators soon created an unanticipated problem. With predators diminishing, the number of elk could increase drastically. That started a heated, and ongoing, debate about the complicated relationship of predators to game animals.

ROOSEVELT LODGE

Named for the twenty-sixth president, Roosevelt Lodge was a tent camp in the early days and then became an auto camp in the 1920s. Thus, it became a symbol of a revolution in the way people saw the park. In the early years, automobiles were forbidden because they scared the horses pulling carriages and wagons.

In 1915, though, the first cars were admitted to the park. The entry fee was five dollars for single-seaters, seven-fifty for five-seaters, and ten dollars for seven-seaters—prices similar to today's, but in more valuable dollars. The speed limit averaged twenty miles per hour, slowed to twelve when going up, to ten when coming down, and to eight when approaching sharp curves. Motorists were clocked from one soldier station to the next. If they arrived too soon, they got ticketed for speeding.

Within a decade the park filled with auto campgrounds that were patronized by an eager public. Thus did technology overturn entirely the old way of doing things.

In its first several decades, the park's visitors were either exemplars of the carriage trade, sagebrushers, or practitioners of the Wylie Way. The carriage-trade style came first in chronology and in the hearts and minds of the park's concessionaires. But the public had different ideas.

From the start, railroad magnates saw Yellowstone as a hugely successful commercial resort. They wanted thousands of visitors to travel west by rail each year, tour the park in big Concord coaches (drawn by as many as six horses and carrying up to twenty-nine passengers), and live in style at sumptuous hotels. All these facilities, naturally, would be owned by the railroads or by firms they controlled. Sounds like a formula for printing money, but this affluent trade never caught on sufficiently to turn much of a profit.

"Sagebrushers"—people who toured by foot, horseback, or even bicycle—started visiting the park early on. They cooked out and slept on the ground. They brought little profit to the concessionaires, or to the tip-hungry hotel staffs, and so met a certain amount of resentment. Presumably, they didn't care.

Then, around the turn of the century, William W. Wylie, Bozeman's school superintendent, hit on a compromise between the carriage trade and sagebrushing—permanent tent camps. The Wylie Way quickly proved popular. It was relatively cheap and refreshingly informal. Wylie's young, cheerful staff pleased the guests with sound interpretive information and provided impromptu entertainment in the evenings.

Sometimes Wylie's Way proved too popular. One guest remarked that "during the height of the season the principle upon which the beds are populated is said to be the addition of visitors so long as they may arrive, or until the occupants 'go for their guns.'" Though frowned upon and fought by railroad interests, camping in permanent tents survived to the end of the stagecoach era.

The automobile, though, turned the tourist trade on its head. After World War II even the railroads bent their knees to the car and began closing their spur lines to the towns near the park.

TOWER TO COOKE CITY

To get off the loop road and pick up information about the route to Cooke City, see page 248.

TOWER FALL

Tower Fall, southeast of Tower Junction on the loop road, seems elfin in a country of grand waterfalls. It's named after the row of black basalt gendarmes. A large rock once perched at its lip, and members of the Hayden expedition jokingly bet on how soon it would fall. The rock fell 115 years later, in 1986.

The half-mile trail down from the viewpoint offers terrific views of the falls from the bottom and of the Yellowstone River to Bannock Ford. The ford is where the Bannock Indians crossed the river on their hunting trips to the buffalo plains east of here.

John Colter, the first white to see Yellowstone, probably crossed the river here. A member of the Lewis and Clark expedition, Colter stayed in the mountains when the captains turned toward home. Probably he was enamored of the high lonesome. Sent out by the fur trader Manuel Lisa to contact Indians in 1807, Colter turned his journey into a huge ramble — from the mouth of the Big Horn River on the Yellowstone River clear to Jackson Hole, then north into what is now Yellowstone National Park, and back to the fort — over five hundred miles of wandering.

While on this trip, Colter saw boiling springs near Cody, at the forks of the Shoshone River. When he told his tale to other mountain men and around St. Louis, he got an undeserved reputation as a liar.

Not that Colter or any other mountain man would take offense at people laughing him off as a liar. Few skills better defined the mountain man than his ability to stretch the truth. An old-hand scout, once a trapper, might string along some emigrants with a persuasive yarn about a hand-to-hand fight he had with a grizzly bear, for instance, and cap it straight-faced with the information that in the end he was killed and et by the bear.

Jim Bridger in particular got himself a bad reputation for these stories among people who didn't catch on. And sometimes listeners couldn't tell what was the literal truth and what was a stretcher. The editor of a western newspaper got a full account of the wonders of Yellowstone from Bridger in the 1840s. But the editor didn't print this big scoop because he feared he'd be "laughed out of town if he printed any of old Jim Bridger's lies."

THE CHITTENDEN ROAD

The Chittenden Road, named for the park road engineer and historian Hiram M. Chittenden, breaks from the highway and heads for the summit of Mount Washburn. Gen. H. D. Washburn, head of the important Yellowstone exploring expedition of 1870, rode to this summit to get a look at the country. A year later, Dr. Ferdinand Hayden, head of that year's U.S. Geological Survey of Yellowstone, did the same: "The view from the summit is one of the finest I have ever seen . . . an area of fifty to a hundred mile radius in every direction could be seen more or less distinctly."

Thomas Ewing, who toured the park in 1877 with his father, Gen. William T. Sherman, felt differently when he saw the view from Mount Washburn: "Society in general goes to the mountains not to fast but to feast and leaves their glaciers covered with chicken bones and eggshells."

DUNRAVEN PASS

Dunraven Pass and nearby Dunraven Peak are named for Windham Thomas Wyndham-Quin, the Earl of Dunraven, who visited the park in 1874, and in 1876 published a book about his experiences here, *The Great Divide.*

GRAND CANYON OF THE YELLOWSTONE RIVER

The walls of this immense canyon, the two huge waterfalls, and the river below have drawn people to see them as have few sights in the world. Many, including the historian Hiram Chittenden, think that the ochre walls of this canyon gave the Yellowstone River its name, which the French took from one of the Indian names for the river. But it is more likely that the Indian name comes from the canyon rimrock much farther downstream—it is also yellow.

You need to take two short drives to get good views of the canyon and the upper and lower falls. First go east from Canyon Junction

along the north rim of the canyon to Inspiration Point, Grandview Point, and Lookout Point. This road leads back to the Grand Loop Road after less than two miles. Then, two and a half miles south of the junction, take the drive along the south rim to Artist Point for a spectacular view of the Lower Falls.

Artist Point got its name from the painter Thomas Moran, who toured the park with the surveying expedition led by Dr. Ferdinand V. Hayden in 1871. Little known at the time, Moran later became celebrated for his paintings of the national parks and was regarded the dean of American landscape painters.

The pioneer western photographer William Henry Jackson was also along on the Hayden expedition. His photographs (many now synonymous with certain scenes in Yellowstone in the public mind) helped Hayden influence Congress to create the first national park the next year.

The canyon, though, has not been admired so universally that it prohibits attempts at exploitation. The western novelist Owen Wister loved the park and traveled through it extensively on horseback. He recounts one group's idea of exploiting the Lower Falls:

> Boutelle [Capt. Frazier A. Boutelle, an acting park superintendent] had a hard time to stop a commercial clique from installing an elevator at the Lower Falls. Politics was behind it, as usual. To put a lot of machinery by those Falls at the head of the canon, where the sublime merges with the exquisite, and which alone is worth crossing the continent to see, would have been an outrage more abominable than the dam at Jackson Lake.

HAYDEN VALLEY

Continuing south along the loop road toward Fishing Bridge, travelers pass through Hayden Valley, the broad, open land stretching

The pioneer Yellowstone photographer William Henry Jackson and assistant prepare to shoot some film in the late nineteenth century. *(Jackson Hole Museum and Teton County Historical Society, Jackson, Wyoming)*

west toward Yellowstone's central plateau. One of the most common places to see buffalo in the park, it is named for Dr. Ferdinand V. Hayden, who led a Yellowstone expedition for the U.S. Geological Survey in 1871. Hayden, trained as a medical doctor, was an enthusiastic geologist.

Hayden Valley was a principal site of the grizzly bear research done in Yellowstone from 1959–1970 by the brothers and scientists John and Frank Craighead. Their Yellowstone fieldwork was the first intensive study of the grizzly. It pioneered techniques of tracking animals with radio collars now commonly used by researchers and game managers worldwide. From that field-

work the Craigheads produced a number of scientific papers, and Frank Craighead wrote a popular book, *The Track of the Grizzly,* which gave early warning of that creature's deteriorating status in Yellowstone.

ALUM CREEK

Alum Creek is said to have gotten its name from Old Gabe, the Blanket Chief, the greatest of the mountain men, Jim Bridger himself. It seems that one day Jim rode up the creek several miles and then back. He noticed on the way back that he didn't have to go as far as on the way up. "Seeking the cause," says historian Hiram Chittenden, "he found it to be the astringent quality of the water, which was saturated with alum to such an extent that it had the power to pucker distance itself."

Later stage drivers would tell about fording the creek with their big coaches only to find on the other side that their outfits had shrunk to Shetland ponies and a buggy.

THE MUD VOLCANO

The Mud Volcano was named (though probably not discovered) by the Washburn expedition in 1870. The journalist Charles Dudley Warner visited the Mud Volcano in 1896 and later recorded his impressions in a piece in *Harper's Magazine:*

> The mud-geyser . . . is, I suppose, the most disgusting object in nature . . . On the side of a hill, at the bottom of a deep sloping pit, is a sort of cave, like the lair of a wild beast, which perpetually vomits a compound of mud, putty, nastiness. Over the mouth seems to be a concave rock, which prevents the creature from spouting his filth straight up like a geyser. Against this obstacle, with a thud, every moment the vile fluid is flung, as if the beast were in a rage, and growling

because he could not get out, and then through the orifice the mud is flung in spiteful spits and gushes of nastiness. And the most disgusting part of it is that this awful mixture cannot get out, and the creature has to swallow it again, and is perpetually sick to nausea. It is the most fascinatingly loathsome thing in the world.

BUFFALO FORD

Buffalo Ford (it's officially known as Nez Perce Ford but popularly called Buffalo Ford) is where the Nez Perce Indians crossed the Yellowstone River on their flight from the U.S. Army toward Canada in 1877. Their resistance, which many modern Americans see as heroic, lasted for three months and twenty-two days. They covered more than fifteen hundred miles in their flight and fought at least fifteen engagements. Their bid for freedom ended in the Bear Paw Mountains just thirty miles from the Canadian border.

Buffalo Ford is also one of the most popular fly-fishing spots in the park. The fish caught are native Yellowstone cutthroats, but fish-stocking has a long history in the park. As early as 1889, whitefish and several varieties of trout were stocked in Glen Creek, the Gibbon River, the Firehole River, Twin Lakes, Lava Creek, and the Yellowstone River above the falls. This brought non-native fish into park streams, and incompatible species were thrown together.

Though stocking fish in the park ended in 1958, descendants of stocked fish still populate Yellowstone's rivers.

LEHARDY RAPIDS

LeHardy Rapids got its name from a minor disaster on what was probably the first boat trip on the Yellowstone River by white people. Paul LeHardy was a topographer with the Army Corps

of Engineers reconnaissance expedition led in the park in 1873 by Capt. William A. Jones. At the outlet of the Yellowstone River, LeHardy and another man decided to go by raft instead of horseback for a while. After a pleasant three miles, they came to these rapids and soon realized that it was "now too late for anything except to trust to luck." They ran their raft onto a rock, where the back end got sucked to the shallow bottom. They threw their gear to shore, breaking LeHardy's French shotgun, and hoofed it toward the Canyon.

Regulations now forbid boating on the Yellowstone River in the park in order to preserve it as a refuge for aquatic wildlife. Some brave the lower sections (and huge fines) anyway.

THE FISHING BRIDGE AREA

The commercial facilities in the Fishing Bridge area are now a focus of heated controversy. Some people want the area for a store, service station, museum, campground, recreational-vehicle park, and the like. But grizzly bears want it for eating, sleeping, and raising cubs. What follows is politely known as human-bear conflict. On occasion the results have been not only impolite but bloody.

Environmentalists have crusaded for elimination of most commercial developments at Fishing Bridge. Commercial interests, particularly those from Cody, Wyoming, have fought to retain the developments. Grant Village was built in the late 1970s and the early 1980s in part to allow for the closing of facilities at Fishing Bridge. So far, political pressures have kept most of the facilities open.

The Fishing Bridge Museum has been named a National Historic Landmark as an example of rustic architecture.

FISHING BRIDGE TO EAST ENTRANCE

To get off the loop road here and pick up information about the route to the park's east entrance, see page 250.

THE LAKE HOTEL

Continuing southwest on the park's loop road, visitors soon pass the Lake Hotel, which rose on the shore of Yellowstone Lake a century ago. In those early days it was favored by the elegant carriage-trade folk. They were escorted around the park on prearranged tours in relative luxury. They did not eat, they dined. They sat not on logs but reclined in wingback chairs. And they slept not on the ground but in hotel beds. They rolled through the park in coaches, usually four-horse, eleven-passenger rigs. Their drivers were local men with names like Society Red, Cryin' Jack, Scattering Jesus (who was flighty), White Mountain Smith, and Geyser Bob (a spinner of yarns).

According to the Livingston, Montana, newspaper, Geyser Bob got his name from one of his tales:

"I clum up on Old Faithful one day and got too near the crater and fell in."

"How interesting!" commented the lady [a tourist]. "What happened?"

"Why," said Bob pointing to the Beehive Geyser across the Firehole River, "I came out of the Beehive—over there."

"Well! Well! How long did it take?"

"Oh," said Bob, "if I had come straight through it would have taken about ten minutes, but I stopped on the way for a haircut and a shave!"

No doubt the woman understood that Bob was indulging in the time-honored western sport of stuffing dudes, a descendant of the mountain-man love of yarning. One of the reasons dudes get stuffed, of course, is that they ask such incredible questions. Discussions with park rangers and local guides, with strict promises of anonymity, yield such memorable dude questions as these:

"When do you plant the wildflowers?"

"What time of year do the elk change to moose?"

"What color uniforms do the cattle guards wear?"

One principal amusement at Lake Hotel in the early days was watching bears feed on hotel garbage. On his visit to the park in 1903, President Theodore Roosevelt found the bear situation commendable:

The effect of protection upon bear life in the Yellowstone has been one of the phenomena of natural history. Not only have they grown to realize that they are safe, but, being natural scavengers and foul feeders, they have come to recognize the garbage heaps of the hotels as their special sources of food supply. Throughout the summer months they come to all the hotels in numbers, usually appearing in the late afternoon or evening, and they have become as indifferent to the presence of men as the deer themselves—some of them very much more indifferent. They have now taken their place among the recognized sights of the Park, and the tourists are nearly as much interested in them as in the geysers.

Times sure have changed. It's rare to see a bear today. Even a small black bear will draw a crowd. Feeding the bears hotel garbage led to many problems, both for the bears and park visitors. The park closed the garbage dumps in the early 1970s. Hotels must today comply with strict regulations governing what they do with their garbage, and campers must be careful with their food.

Grizzlies still wander some areas where people often visit, and that can lead to trouble. In grizzly-human encounters, people frequently get hurt, sometimes killed, and the park service often must destroy the bears. Since grizzlies are threatened in Yellowstone, these deaths are controversial.

BRIDGE BAY

If you'd been here at the turn of the century you could have rented a rowboat from a man with an apt name: E. C. Waters. However, the tariff was pretty steep: twelve bucks. One customer who found the charge outrageous complained, "The only satisfaction I had was in telling him that I now knew why Christ walked on the water, that in the face of such charges anybody else would walk that was able to."

Waters was involved with more than small boats. In 1889 he launched the steamboat *Zillah* on Yellowstone Lake. It carried passengers between the Lake Hotel and West Thumb. Waters's business was brimming for twenty years, but then he got too ambitious. In 1905 he built a steamer, with the modest name of *E. C. Waters,* which was capable of hauling five hundred people. Park authorities refused to license it for more than 125 passengers. Waters refused to operate under those terms and moored the idle steamer on Stevenson Island, the large timbered island opposite here. Two decades later the works were removed from the steamer to heat the Lake Hotel and the remainder of the boat was burned.

Today commercial boats operate regularly from Bridge Bay.

GULL POINT DRIVE

This pleasant lakeshore drive runs off toward Gull Point for a couple of miles before rejoining the loop road. Somewhere along this shore of Yellowstone Lake is the source of another tall tale attributed to Jim Bridger. Hot springs empty into the lake here, and hot water rises and stays on the surface. That's why Bridger used to brag about catching fish in the depths of the lake and cooking them in the hot water on the way out.

THE WEST THUMB AREA

Potts Geyser Basin was the source of the first published description of the park's thermal features, a letter by the mountain man Daniel Potts:

The Yellowstone has a large fresh water Lake near its head on the very top of the Mountain which is about one hundred by forty miles in diameter and as clear as a crystal. On the south border of this lake is a number of hot and boiling springs, some of water and others of most beautiful fine clay and resembles that of a mush pot and throws its particles to the immense height of twenty to thirty feet in height. The clay is white and of a pink and water appears fathomless as it appears to be entirely hollow under neath. There is also a number of places where the pure sulphur is sent forth in abundance. One of our men visited one of those whilst taking his recreation there. At an instant the earth began a tremendous trembling and he with difficulty made his escape when an explosion took place resembling that of thunder. During our stay in that quarter I heard it every day.

In October 1876, Thumb Bay nearly brought disaster to the Doane expedition. Lt. Gustavus Doane, who had seen Yellowstone with the Washburn expedition, was ordered to explore the Snake River from its source to its mouth at the Columbia River. He was supposed to make the trip with one noncommissioned officer and five privates, a boat, and sixty days' rations. He was also supposed to make the trip in the autumn or winter, when travel in Yellowstone can be dangerous.

The men packed a disassembled boat into Yellowstone Lake, where they put it together and then towed it along the shore. They swamped the boat at Pumice Point but managed to save the cargo and repair their vessel.

At Thumb Bay, Doane told three of the six men to row across and see what was on the other side. While Doane waited for them to return, a storm came up. Just when he was giving them up for lost, he heard their "boisterous and double-jointed profanity." They made the shore safely, but their "hair and beards were frozen to their caps and overcoats and they were sheeted with glistening ice from head to foot."

From that point the expedition fared worse. The men dragged the boat to Heart Lake and launched again, but the streams were difficult to navigate until the Lewis River entered the Snake. They got low on food and had to live on fish and horse meat, prompting an understated complaint from Doane: "The worn out U.S. Cavalry plug was never intended for food." In the canyon of the Snake below Jackson Hole they wrecked their boat. They hobbled into Fort Hall, cold and weary, some time later and cancelled the expedition.

WEST THUMB TO SOUTH ENTRANCE

To get off the loop road here and pick up information about the road south to Teton National Park and Jackson Hole, see page 251.

WEST THUMB TO THE OLD FAITHFUL AREA

The road between West Thumb and Old Faithful crosses the Continental Divide twice. It was built in 1891 under the supervision of Hiram M. Chittenden, a lieutenant in the U.S. Army Corps of Engineers. Later, Chittenden wrote the first comprehensive history of the park, *The Yellowstone National Park* (1895 and several other editions). It's been a prime resource for every subsequent writer about Yellowstone.

SHOSHONE POINT

Not many people get robbed in Yellowstone anymore, not at gunpoint, anyway. But here at Shoshone Point in 1914 a stagecoach robber pulled off one of the most ambitious robberies in park history.

This was still the era of the carriage trade, when ladies and gentlemen of means took the grand tour of the park in style. Drivers customarily stopped at Shoshone Point to let the nabobs gaze across Shoshone Lake to the distant Tetons.

One day in July, a man in a black kerchief interrupted the contemplative proceedings by holding a rifle on the passengers of a coach and ordering them to put their cash and jewelry on his blanket. One at a time, fifteen coaches drove up, and the kerchiefed man robbed them all. He was not overly strict or greedy, even hinting that a couple of young ladies could hide their pretty baubles in their pretty stockings, which they did. This bit of style, and other quips, earned him a nickname: The Merry Bandit. He was not strict in other ways, either. He didn't notice that three tourists took photographs of him, and a preacher even made a sketch. The bandit collected about a thousand dollars worth of valuables and went on his merry way.

The pictures and other evidence soon led the authorities to a ranch in Idaho, where they picked up the Merry Bandit. His name was Edward Trafton, a poacher, ex-convict, and general rogue. He was sentenced to five years in the federal penitentiary at Leavenworth, Kansas.

CRAIG PASS

Craig Pass, at the top of the Continental Divide, was named for Ida Craig, the first lady to cross it on a new road engineered by Hiram Chittenden. At the top of the pass, Isa Lake drains into both the Atlantic and Pacific watersheds. So does Two Ocean Creek, south of the park. Tales of waters that divided toward both the Atlantic and Pacific got mountain men like the old master Jim Bridger into trouble—Surely such a thing was impossible! said experts of the day. But the trapper Osborne Russell had described it in his journal in the 1830s:

> On the south side about midway of the prairie stands a high snowy peak from which issues a stream of water which, after entering the plain it divides equally, one half running West and the other East, thus bidding adieu to each other; one bound for the Pacific and the other for the Atlantic Ocean. Here a trout of 12 inches may cross the Mountains in safety. Poets have sung of the "meeting of the waters" and the fish climbing cataracts but the "parting of the waters" and the fish crossing mountains I believe remains unsung as yet by all except the solitary Trapper who sits under the shade of a spreading pine whistling blank-verse and beating time to the tune with a whip on his trap sack.

ANOTHER STAGE HOLDUP

Ed Trafton, the Merry Bandit, may have gotten the idea for his 1914 stagecoach robbery from the scoundrel who held up seventeen coaches somewhere in the vicinity of Turtle Rock in August 1908.

Twenty-five vehicles rolled up the road from Old Faithful that summer day. Some were coaches of the companies that offered grand tours through the hotels. Others were wagons

Two Ocean Pass. The water to the right goes to the Atlantic Ocean; the water to the left goes to the Pacific Ocean, allowing trout to cross the Continental Divide. *(Jackson Hole Museum and Teton County Historical Society, Jackson, Wyoming)*

belonging to the Wylie Company, which housed its guests in permanent tent camps. The robber allowed the first eight coaches to pass, which let the military escort get far beyond the scene. Then he stopped the next eight coaches as they came up and made the passengers put their valuables in a bag. Then he waited for the nine Wylie wagons and accosted the passengers in like manner.

Though the alarm was sounded quickly, the robber was never caught. He got away with about two thousand dollars.

THE OLD FAITHFUL AREA, UPPER GEYSER BASIN

Certainly some of the most curious geological phenomena in the world, the geysers and hot springs of the Upper Geyser Basin here along the Firehole River were probably first seen by Anglos in 1833. That summer, a brigade of mountain men led by Manuel Alvarez told Warren Angus Ferris, a clerk with the American Fur Company, about the geothermal wonders. The following May, Ferris left his trapping brigade with two Pend'Oreille Indians, visited the Firehole to see them for himself, and was astounded.

Not everyone responded so enthusiastically to the geysers. Consider the reactions of some tourists whom British master-storyteller Rudyard Kipling observed:

> I have been through the Yellowstone National Park in a buggy, in the company of an adventurous old lady from Chicago and her husband, who disapproved of scenery as being "ungodly." I fancy it scared them. The old lady . . . regarding the horrors of the fire-holes, could only say, "Good Lord!" at thirty-second intervals. Her husband talked about "dreffel waste of steam-power . . ."

Surprisingly, the naturalist John Burroughs, who toured the park with his friend President Theodore Roosevelt in 1903, had similar feelings: "The novelty of the geyser region soon wears off. Steam and hot water are steam and hot water the world over, and the exhibition of them here did not differ, except in volume, from what one sees by his own fireside."

Of course, some people are afraid of geysers, and understandably so. The western illustrator Frederic Remington rode horseback through a thermal area with some army companions and judged the deed reckless because the ground "is very thin and hazardous, and to break through is to be boiled. One instinctively objects to that form of cooking."

Some of the early park visitors looked upon the geysers with a practical eye. They thought they'd make terrific washing machines. A Livingston, Montana, newspaperman, blissfully unaware that his words might later offend Americans of Chinese descent, told this story of a Chinese laundryman:

> It is written in the Archives of Yellowstone Park that a child of the Flowery Kingdom . . .

came to the Upper Geyser Basin to establish a laundry, because there was enough hot water there to run a Presidential Campaign. He pitched his tent over a thermal Spring, wrote his name in weird characters upon a sign board, and when the raiments of the native and pilgrim came in, he chucked the whole invoice into the bubbling spring. Then he threw in a bar of soap, and smiled to see the great forces that upheave mountains and shake continents, and toss the mighty Globe into convulsions most awful, doing plain washing in a Chinese laundry. But the spring was a slumbering geyser. The soap awakened the imprisoned giant; with a roar that made the earth tremble, and a shriek of a steam whistle, a cloud of steam and a column of boiling water shot up into the air a hundred feet, carrying soap, raiment, tent and Chinaman along with the rush, and dropping them at various intervals along the way.

Chinaman Spring, near Old Faithful, got its name from this incident.

Later, Owen Wister, who was made famous by his novel *The Virginian,* reported that doing laundry in geysers had become popular, "but to soap a geyser is very bad for it; disturbs its rhythm, dislocates its circulation, and makes it play when it isn't due to play, has killed one important geyser, I have heard."

That's why the army banned soaping. In 1888 two railroad officials took a tour of the park guided by then Yellowstone Park Association general manager E. C. Waters, who would later initiate commercial boating on Yellowstone Lake. Waters soaped Beehive Geyser for the railroad bigwigs—and they got arrested.

Old Faithful Inn, built in 1904 and called the largest log structure in the world, was designed by Seattle architect Robert C. Reamer, who also designed the gateway arch at the north entrance. Park service historian Aubrey Haines, author of *The Yellowstone Story,* wrote:

The Inn at Old Faithful, inside and out, shortly after its construction. *(Jackson Hole Museum and Teton County Historical Society, Jackson, Wyoming)*

The lobby was the focus of Mr. Reamer's rustic effect. It is a great, balconied cavern, open to the roof, with all supporting beams and braces exposed to view like the skeleton of some enormous mammal seen from within. In one corner is a mighty fireplace with its chimney exposed to the point where it passes through the ridge 85 feet above the floor . . . containing, in all, 500 tons of stone taken from a quarry site five miles to the east. The fireplace chimney is faced with a giant clock hammered out by a blacksmith named Colpitts, who also made the distinctive hardware.

MIDWAY GEYSER BASIN

Geothermal spectacles like those in Midway Geyser Basin led the naturalist John Muir to muse on mud:

> These valleys at the heads of the great rivers may be regarded as laboratories and kitchens, in which, amid a thousand retorts and pots, we may see Nature at work as chemist or cook, cunningly compounding an infinite variety of mineral messes; cooking whole mountains; boiling and steaming flinty rocks to smooth paste and mush, — yellow, brown, red, pink, lavender, gray, and creamy white, — making the most beautiful mud in the world; and distilling the most ethereal essences.

LOWER GEYSER BASIN

The Fountain Hotel in the Lower Geyser Basin was built in 1891 and soon gained a reputation as a great place to watch bears feed on garbage. Black bears sauntered over every evening while guests watched from as little as ten yards away. Some even fed the bears by hand. This practice led to well-known problems in later years.

THE NEZ PERCE WAR

One of the few problems in the park between whites and Indians happened around Nez Perce Creek. It was a minor event in the Nez Perce War of 1877. Some nontreaty Nez Perce (the name is generally pronounced in the West like "fez purse," not "nay pairsay" in the French fashion) had been hunting on their traditional grounds and the government precipitated the war by trying to put them on the reservation by force.

Led by Chief Joseph, six hundred Nez Perce fled eastward, fighting a running series of battles with the U.S. Army. In late August they entered Yellowstone National Park via Targhee Pass chased by six hundred soldiers commanded by Gen. Oliver O. Howard. Before long they came on a prospector and a party of ordinary tourists from Montana.

The Nez Perce took all the whites into captivity, destroyed some tourist wagons, and arbitrarily traded their own poor horses for the tourists'.

Mrs. George Cowan, one of the tourists, had to give up her good mount, and later wrote about the trade:

> It occurs to me at this writing that the above mode of trading is a fair reflection of the lesson taught by whites. For instance, a tribe of Indians are located on a reservation. Gold is discovered thereon by some prospector. A stampede follows. The strong arm of the government alone prevents the avaricious pale face from possessing himself of the land forthwith. Soon negotiations are pending with as little delay as a few yards of red tape will permit. A treaty is signed, the strip ceded to the government and opened to settlers and "Lo, the poor Indian" finds himself on a tract a few degrees more arid, a little less desirable than his former home. The Indian has few rights the average white settler feels bound to respect.

Though she may not have known it, Mrs. Cowan was exactly right. In 1855, the government and the Nez Perce had agreed on a reservation in territory where the modern states Idaho, Washington, and Oregon meet. Five years later a gold rush brought whites onto Indian lands illegally. A treaty soon ceded these lands to the whites, reducing the reservation. But certain Nez Perce leaders, including Joseph, refused to sign the treaty or to restrict themselves to this smaller reservation, thus bringing on the war.

After the forced horse trade with Mrs. Cowan and the others, the Nez Perce turned the tourists loose. One Indian, though, Poker Joe, warned them to ride fast to avoid the wrath of the more unruly Nez Perce. Soon shooting broke out, and two of the whites were wounded. Mrs. Cowan, seeing her husband George shot in the head, fainted, and later assumed he was dead. But Cowan regained consciousness, got shot again in the side as he tried to escape, and dragged himself into the forest. The rest of the party was likewise scattered in the forest, or recaptured.

That night Mrs. Cowan camped with Joseph. She wrote later of him: "The chief sat by the fire, sombre and silent, foreseeing in his gloomy meditations possibly the unhappy ending of his campaign. The 'noble red man' we read of was more nearly impersonated in this Indian than in any I have ever met. Grave and dignified, he looked a chief."

After crossing the Yellowstone River at Nez Perce Ford, which is known to the world unofficially as Buffalo Ford, the Indians released the Montana tourists, who found their way back to the oncoming soldiers and the good news that their comrades were alive. The next day, though, some of the Nez Perce shot up the camp of some other tourists from Montana at the forks of Otter Creek, and those white men had to take to the woods (one was later found dead of a gunshot wound).

The Nez Perce fled toward the eastern border of the park, burned Baronett Bridge, and did some raiding in the Yellowstone valley outside the park (where another white man was killed) and along the Lamar River. Then, after two weeks, the Indians passed out of Yellowstone National Park.

Next, Joseph led his people toward Canada. But Gen. Nelson Miles intercepted them in the Bear Paw Mountains and brought an end to the conflict on Snake Creek, about thirty miles from the Canadian border.

The Nez Perce War had lasted three months and twenty-two days. The flight and pursuit covered over fifteen hundred miles. At least fifteen engagements were fought. White casualties were six officers killed and thirteen wounded, 121 soldiers and citizens killed and 127 wounded. Nez Perce casualties were at least 151 killed, 88 wounded, and 489 captured.

The Nez Perce, for their efforts, won only the admiration of many other Americans.

The next year, 1878, saw more Indian-white skirmishes in the park, a minor siege of troubles known as the Bannock War, and with that, red-white warfare in Yellowstone was finished. By 1883, just six years after the high tragedy of the Nez Perce War, run-ins between Indians and whites had turned to high comedy. W. O. Owen and two companions encountered Indians unexpectedly when they were making, incredibly, the first bicycle tour of the park.

> By severe pedaling the top [of the Continental Divide, probably at Targhee Pass] was reached, when, throwing legs over handles, we began our first coast and flew down the mountain with the speed of the wind. Some distance ahead we observed a large, moving body square in the road, coming our way, but with all our eyes we could not satisfy our minds as to what it might be. At the speed we were going, however, the distance was soon sufficiently shortened to explain the matter, and we ascertained that it was a number of Indians traveling west. Here was a predicament indeed, and how to extricate ourselves was the next problem demanding speedy solution. We had no

means of knowing whether these Americans were peaceable or on the warpath, and, fearing it might be the latter, it was deemed best to make a rush and frighten them before they could realize what was in the wind.

In my heart I believe that no men ever moved with greater velocity on a wheel than did we on this occasion. We dashed into their midst at a speed which I dare not even conjecture, and, with the most unearthly yells that ever reached human ears, squaws, chiefs, horses and innumerable dogs scattered in as many directions as there are points to the mariner's compass. It was a desperate charge, but entirely successful, and, passing the Indians, we reached the foot of the hill in safety.

THE MADISON JUNCTION AREA

Legend has it that the idea of turning Yellowstone into the first national park got its beginning at Madison Junction. While camped within sight of National Park Mountain, the timbered summit to the southwest, members of the Washburn expedition relaxed around an evening fire and talked about all they had seen. The date was September 19, 1870. It was an evening when the spirit of generosity overcame the impulse toward acquisitiveness. According to historian Hiram Chittenden, someone remarked what an

important pleasure resort so wonderful a region must soon become . . . It was suggested that it would be a "profitable speculation" to take up land around the various objects of interest. The conversation had not proceeded far on these lines when one of the party, Cornelius Hedges, interposed and said that private ownership of that region, or any part of it, ought never to be countenanced; but that it ought to be set apart by the government and forever held to the unrestricted use of the people. This higher view of the subject found immediate acceptance

with the other members of the party. It was agreed that the project should be at once set afoot and pushed vigorously to a finish.

If this conversation took place as stated, it was not the first suggestion that the Yellowstone country should be a park reserved for all the people. Earlier ones came from Thomas Meagher, the acting governor of Montana Territory, in 1865, and from David Folsom after he went exploring in the park in 1869.

After that important campfire discussion, one of the Washburn men, Nathaniel Langford, who later became the first superintendent of the park, gave a series of lectures in the East about the Yellowstone country on behalf of the Northern Pacific railroad, which already saw Yellowstone as a potential focus of tourism; Langford later claimed to have put forward the national park idea in these lectures.

In 1871, Dr. Ferdinand Hayden led a government surveying expedition through the park and then became a prime mover in pushing the park legislation through Congress. On March 1, 1872, the act of dedication was signed, setting Yellowstone "apart as a public park and pleasuring ground for the benefit and enjoyment of the people," and providing "for the preservation from injury or spoliation of all timber, mineral deposits, natural curiosities or wonders with said park, and their retention in their natural condition."

The museum at Madison Junction is a National Historic Landmark as an example of rustic architecture.

MADISON JUNCTION TO WEST YELLOWSTONE

To get off the park's loop road here or pick up information about the route to West Yellowstone, see page 252.

MADISON JUNCTION TO NORRIS JUNCTION

The river that runs along this section of the park's loop road takes its name from Col. John Gibbon, who led a detachment of soldiers into Yellowstone, and nearly to their deaths, in 1871. Fortunately, the survey party of Dr. Ferdinand Hayden found the starving soldiers and gave them flour and sugar. A little bread must have seemed like manna to the soldiers, who had been trying to stay alive eating roots, squirrels, and jays.

THE AREA OF NORRIS JUNCTION

The geyser basin, Mount Norris, Norris Pass, and the Norris Museum take their names from Philetus W. Norris, a great character from Yellowstone's lore and the park's second superintendent.

He did serious work for the park, but he wasn't always taken seriously. At least not by newspaper reporters. For instance, this is how one writer described his romantic appearance:

> A broad-brimmed white hat, looped up at the side and decorated with an eagle's feather. Long white hair reached far down upon his brawny shoulders; a white waving beard ornamented his breast. He wore a buckskin hunting shirt, decked with long, flowing fringe. He wore a belt full of cart ridges, and had a revolver hanging at his side. He also carried a hunting knife. He swung a tomahawk in his hand. He rode a gallant steed.

Despite his high-flying style, Norris got things done in an era when the park badly needed an effective superintendent. He accomplished a feat of road-building that seems heroic:

In the summer of 1878 he built a road sixty miles long, from Mammoth to the Firehole River geyser basins, in less than a month. That's two miles a day, without the benefit of a prior survey of the route, and with the construction crews working under the disadvantage of having to guard themselves against the rebellious Indians of the Bannock War.

NORRIS GEYSER BASIN

This is one of the strange places of the earth, Rudyard Kipling wrote on his trip here in 1889:

> We walked chattering to the uplands of Hell. They call it the Norris Geyser Basin on Earth. It was as though the tide of desolation had gone out, but would presently return, across innumerable acres of dazzling white geyser formation. There were no terraces here, but all other horrors. Not ten yards from the road a blast of steam shot up roaring every few seconds, a mud volcano spat filth to Heaven, streams of hot water rumbled under foot, plunged through the dead pines in steaming cataracts and died on a waste of white where green-grey, black-yellow, and pink pools roared, shouted, bubbled, or hissed as their wicked fancies prompted. By the look of the eye the place should have been frozen over. By the feel of the feet it was warm.

In those days, you could stop at the Norris Lunch Station (everything seemed named after the superintendent). The lunch station was run by Lawrence Francis Mathews, an Irishman with a terrific gift of gab. Kipling bellied up at "Larry's" and paid a stiff price for canned beef, biscuits, and beer, but the Irishman's eloquence made it seem "imperial bounty."

NORRIS SOLDIER STATION

Norris Soldier Station is one of the three remaining soldier stations in the park, the others being at Tower Junction and Bechler. During the thirty years that the army administered the park, soldiers lived in these lonely billets, stamping out poaching and visiting each other occasionally during the winter on skis.

FRYING PAN SPRING

The bubbles that come to the surface of the water here reminded some of grease sizzling on a griddle. Thus the name, Frying Pan Spring. Former park service historian Aubrey Haines says in amusement that the park guides used to give out "a cock-and-bull story about how the birds in that locality drank so much hot water they all laid hard-boiled eggs, and anybody who didn't believe it could look in the woods round-about, where the trees were full of nests containing just such eggs."

ROARING MOUNTAIN

Roaring Mountain, the hill on the east side of the road, which still vents steam prodigiously, used to give off an eerie roaring sound as well.

THE NORTH FORK FIRE

About three miles beyond Roaring Mountain, the landscape begins showing intermittent patterns of burn from 1988's largest wildfire, the North Fork Fire (which included the Wolf Lake Fire). The North Fork blaze was caused by human activity outside the southwest border of Yellowstone on July 22. It burned all the way to and beyond Mammoth Hot Springs on the north and Tower Junction to the northeast. It encircled about 560,000 acres, and burned nearly 500,000, more than half of the total acreage burned inside the park during that ferocious fire season.

Because it was not a fire caused by nature, it was fought from the start. But some fires dur-

ing the same season were caused by lightning. Only monitored at first, these fires later proved uncontrollable. The park's policy of letting some fires burn became hugely controversial and according to park spokesmen was widely misunderstood.

Since 1972, along with some other national parks, Yellowstone had followed a policy of permitting natural fire to burn as a part of the park's basic wild processes. According to park researchers and other scientists, fire is an essential natural element in the park. It sweeps the grasslands in the northern part of the park several times in every hundred years, and the lodgepole forests of the central and southern park several times every thousand years.

Yellowstone's managers argue that fire does the park lots of good—it increases plant diversity and provides more food for lots of Yellowstone's animals. It does this by releasing more nutrients in the soil, encouraging the growth of smaller plants, and providing more light to the ground-level plants. Fire also helps to give the park tree stands of varying ages.

Managers argue that fire has always played a role in the park region. It must continue to do that, they say, if the park is to be "an authentic vignette of primitive America."

To let fire do its historic job, the park's policy is to let lightning-caused fires burn when they don't threaten crucial values like human life, property, endangered species, and park boundaries; to suppress all fires caused by man; and to burn some areas deliberately.

Some think that the fires of 1988 proved this policy a failure. The summer was the driest in recorded park history, making the forests tremendously vulnerable to flames. When the administration did not fight some small fires from the outset, they became huge cataclysms, as did many of the fires that were fought from the beginning.

Critics of the natural-fire policy include some members of the media, many businessmen near the park, and even U.S. congressmen. Some of them contend merely that the park managers ought to follow their policy more flexibly and respond more quickly to exceptional circumstances like those of the summer of 1988. Others are dubious about any natural-fire policy at all, and argue for vigorous suppression of all fires or for prescribed burns that do the job of natural fires.

What is certain is that, despite the fire-fighting efforts of more than nine thousand men and women, 850 miles of fire lines, over a hundred fire engines, many bulldozers, dozens of helicopters, and over $100 million, the fires of 1988 became a natural force that humans could not control.

Why? An almost complete lack of moisture parched Yellowstone's trees to kindling that spring and summer. High winds fanned the flames. Even the nights were so dry that the fires kept burning vigorously. Conventional fire-fighting techniques failed. High winds blew embers extraordinary distances ahead of the flames, constantly starting new fires in spite of bulldozed fire lines. The flames jumped not only fire lines and backfires but roads, rivers, and even the Grand Canyon of the Yellowstone. The fires raced along with unusual speed, confronting fire crews with the extreme danger of being trapped or overrun.

Scientists say that fires of this magnitude occur in Yellowstone only once in several centuries.

Park officials have scaled back their initial estimates that the fires scorched over a million acres, about half the park. The major fires were the Fan Fire in the extreme northwest corner of the park; the Hellroaring and Storm Creek fires, which touched the extreme northeast corner of the park; the Clover-Mist Fire in the east-northeast area of the park; the Mink Fire in the extreme southeast corner of the park; the North Fork Fire, spreading all the way from Old Faithful to Tower Junction; and the Snake River Complex in the south-central park.

If park managers are right, the fires will benefit the park's plants and animals. In fact, animals seemed little bothered by the fires — relatively few died. In the immediate aftermath, some animals, especially elk, may have suffered from a lack of forage caused less by the fires than by the drought. Eventually, though, the more open landscape resulting from the fires is expected to create more feed for most mammals, from elk to moose to coyotes to buffalo to bears.

OBSIDIAN CLIFF

Obsidian Cliff stands on the east side of the road. It is a mountain of dark volcanic glass valued by Indians and, later, whites for its sharp cutting edges. Modern visitors who want pieces of obsidian are a park problem, because collecting obsidian, which is a violation of park rules, destroys the site for future visitors.

Obsidian Cliff is the kernel of truth from which one of master trapper Jim Bridger's tall tales came, the story of the glass mountain:

> Coming one day in sight of a magnificent elk, he [Bridger] took careful aim at the unsuspecting animal and fired. To his great amazement, the elk not only was not wounded, but seemed not even to have heard the report of the rifle. Bridger drew considerably nearer and gave the elk the benefit of his most deliberate aim; but with the same result as before. A third and a fourth effort met with a similar fate. Utterly exasperated, he seized his rifle by the barrel, resolved to use it as a club since it had failed as a firearm. Rushing madly toward the elk, he suddenly crashed into an immovable vertical wall which proved to be a mountain of perfectly transparent glass, on the farther side of which,

Sheepeater Indians of the late nineteenth century. *(Jackson Hole Museum and Teton County Historical Society, Jackson, Wyoming)*

still in peaceful security, the elk was quietly grazing. Stranger still, the mountain was not only of pure glass, but was a perfect telescopic lens, and, whereas, the elk seemed but a few hundred yards off, it was in reality twenty-five miles away!

SHEEPEATER CLIFFS

Sheepeater Cliffs rise on the east side of the road. One of the few park features that Superintendent Philetus Norris did not name for himself, the cliffs take their name from a tribe of Indians who lived around Yellowstone even into the nineteenth century. These Sheepeaters were a variety of Shoshone Indians who retained a pre-horse lifestyle, used dogs for hunting and packing, and avoided all other peoples.

The trapper Osborne Russell describes some Sheepeaters he met in the Lamar Valley in the 1830s:

about 30 dogs on which they carried their skins, clothing provisions, etc., on their hunting excursions. They were well armed with bows and arrows pointed with obsidian. The bows were beautifully wrought from Sheep, Buffaloe and Elk horns secured with Deer and Elk sinews and ornamented with porcupine quills and generally about 3 feet long. We obtained a large number of Elk Deer and Sheep skins from them of the finest quality and three large neatly dressed Panther skins in return for awls axes kettles tobacco ammunition etc. They would throw the skins at our feet and say "give us whatever you please for them and we are satisfied. We can get plenty of Skins but we do not often see the Tibuboes" (or People of the Sun).

GARDNER'S HOLE

Swan Lake lies on the west side of the road. The broad valley it decorates is called Gardner's Hole, after a mountain man with the American Fur Company, Johnson Gardner.

A park service sign here identifies to the northwest a conspicuous mountain, Electric Peak. It got this dramatic name in 1872 when one Henry Gannett climbed it with surveying instruments while a thundershower was approaching. Said Gannett:

> About fifty feet below the summit, the electric current began to pass through my body. At first I felt nothing, but heard a crackling noise, similar to a rapid discharge of sparks from a friction machine. Immediately after, I began to feel a tingling or pricking sensation in my head and the end of my fingers, which, as well as the noise, increased rapidly, until, when I reached the top, the noise . . . was deafening, and my hair stood completely on end, while the tingling, pricking sensation was absolutely painful.

THE GOLDEN GATE

At the north end of Gardner's Hole the road passes through the Golden Gate, once called Kingman Pass. Lt. Dan C. Kingman, of the Army Corps of Engineers, was the park's first road

engineer, 1883–86. He devised a plan to build one large loop that would run south from Mammoth to Norris and then circle through the Firehole geyser basins, along the north shore of Yellowstone Lake, to the Grand Canyon of the Yellowstone, and back to Norris—more or less the route of today's Grand Loop Road. His design for a new route from Mammoth to the Golden Gate put the road on a wooden trestle.

Among the many observers struck by the beauty of the Golden Gate was the western artist Frederic Remington, who added a touch of bitterness aimed at the camera, which was then becoming popular:

> It is one of those marvellous vistas of mountain scenery utterly beyond the pen or brush of any man. Paint cannot touch it, and words are wasted. War, storms at sea, and mountain scenery are bigger than any expression little man has ever developed. Mr. Thomas Moran made a famous stagger at this pass in his painting; and great as is the painting, when I contemplated the pass itself I marvelled at the courage of the man who dared the deed. But as the stages of the Park Company run over this road, every tourist sees its grandeur, and bangs away with his Kodak.

THE HOODOOS

This area of weird rock outcroppings may be as haunted as it sounds. Once, the old roadbed gave way here, and a passing stagecoach dropped into a hidden cavern. The passengers suffered less damage than did the team and coach.

BARONETT'S BRIDGE

The first bridge over the Yellowstone, Baronett's Bridge spanned the river downstream of the modern bridge. It was built by Collins Jack Baronett in 1871, before the park existed, to help miners and those who supplied them get into the area from Cooke City, Montana. Called Yellowstone Jack, Baronett was a Scot who had gone to China as a sailor, to California as a goldseeker, to the Arctic as a whaler, and to Australia and Africa, again looking for gold. From the 1860s to the turn of the century Baronett scouted and prospected in the Yellowstone region.

VALLEY OF THE LAMAR RIVER

Frequented by Indians and mountain men before Yellowstone Park was even dreamed of, the Lamar Valley makes an easy route from the tangle of mountains of the Yellowstone Plateau to the Clarks Fork (of the Yellowstone) and so to the buffalo plains beyond.

The trapper Osborne Russell wandered into this valley (which he called Secluded Valley) in the 1830s and, struck by its beauty, spoke for many observers since: "I almost wished I could spend the remainder of my days in a place like this where happiness and contentment seemed to reign in wild romantic splendor."

LAMAR STATION

From 1907 to the 1960s, workers at the Lamar Buffalo Ranch near Lamar Station raised a semidomesticated herd of bison that interbred with the park's wild herd. After the 1960s the buffalo were allowed to thrive, or not, in a natural "vignette of primitive America." This reflected a shift in park management philosophy.

Charles Jones, a.k.a. Buffalo Jones, started the domestic herd at Mammoth Hot Springs between 1902 and 1905. A daring old hand, Jones once caught a mountain lion in a mine shaft and brought it back, alive, tied behind his saddle. Theodore Roosevelt met Jones and wrote that Jones like to rope bears that fed in garbage dumps so he could take the tin cans off their paws. But he could not get along with the other park employees. A teetotaller himself, he challenged the dependability and honesty of men who drank, smoked, or played poker, and ended up by so alienating everyone that they would not speak to him, and he was obliged to resign.

SPECIMEN RIDGE

Specimen Ridge runs nearly parallel to the road on the southeast side. A layer cake of fossil forests, the ridge may be the source of yet another great yarn from the mountain man Jim Bridger. As historian Hiram Chittenden repeats the story,

There exists in the Park country a mountain which was once cursed by a great medicine man of the Crow nation. Everything upon the mountain at the time of this dire event became instantly petrified and has remained so ever since. All forms of life are standing about in stone where they were suddenly caught by the petrifying influences, even as the inhabitants of ancient Pompeii were surprised by the ashes of Vesuvius. Sage brush, grass, prairie fowl, antelope, elk, and bears may there be seen as perfect as in actual life. Dashing torrents and the spray mist from them stand forth in arrested motion as if carved from rock by a sculptor's chisel. Even flowers are blooming in colors of crystal, and birds soar with wings spread in motionless flight, while the air floats with music and perfumes siliceous, and the sun and the moon shine with petrified light!

YOUNT'S CABIN

Harry Yount, known as Rocky Mountain Harry, built a cabin in the 1880s here near the confluence of Soda Butte Creek and the Lamar River. Yount, an old frontiersman, worked briefly as a park gamekeeper. Yount's Peak, the source of the Yellowstone River southeast of the park, is named for him.

SODA BUTTE AND SOLDIER STATION

In the early decades of the park, a soldier station stood opposite Soda Butte, the hard-to-miss travertine mound on the southeast side of the road. The outpost housed soldiers who guarded the park's wild game against poachers.

ENTRANCE STATION

The entrance station here is listed as a National Historic Landmark as an example of rustic architecture.

This beautiful stretch of road curves around the north shore of Yellowstone Lake and climbs out of the park via Sylvan Pass. After a run through Shoshone National Forest, it leads to the resort town of Cody.

PELICAN CREEK

Some trappers camped along Pelican Creek in 1839. Their number included Osborne Russell, one of the few of that rough breed who packed pen and paper as well as shot and powder. Russell's journal tells us that Blackfeet Indians attacked their camp and stole the trappers' "possibles" (as they called their gear) and horses. Russell and company had to walk out for help. No short jaunt—they walked all the way to Fort Hall in what would become Idaho. Just another hazard in the life of the mountain man.

Pelican Creek is now "the best grizzly habitat in the park," according to one park official. It's a likely spot to see bears—and maybe get into trouble with them.

Advancing civilization doesn't make the big silvertip any less dangerous. In the summer of 1984 a Swiss woman was killed by a grizzly north of Pelican Valley. In October of 1986 a Montana man photographing a grizzly was attacked and killed near Otter Creek after approaching the bear too closely. Some bear researchers say that human and bear deaths are unavoidable as long as the two species use the same areas too intensively. Bear deaths can follow human deaths because the park service destroys bears regarded as dangerous.

LAKE BUTTE OVERLOOK

A side road leads to Lake Butte Overlook, which offers a fine panoramic view of Yellowstone Lake and its islands. Park explorer David Folsom found himself deeply moved by the lake in 1869. He wrote about "this inland sea, its crystal waves dancing and sparkling in the sunlight as if laughing with joy for their wild freedom. It is a scene of transcendent beauty which has been viewed by few white men, and we felt glad to have looked upon it before its primeval solitude should be broken by the crowds of pleasure seekers which at no distant day will throng its shores."

SYLVAN PASS: A BEAR INCIDENT

A grizzly bear attacked some men in 1916 while they hauled hay up Sylvan Pass. One teamster was killed. The next day a little dog wandered into their camp, evidently lost. Rather than take the dog in, the foreman left it out in the cold. That night the bear came back. But this time the terrier raised cain and the crew drove the bear off, the dog nipping at his heels. The crew then baited a barrel with garbage and charged the opening with dynamite. When the bear came back, they blew him up—"raised that bear maybe four or five feet" in the air and smashed all his bones. And the little dog got his reward—the foreman kept him as a companion in the park for many years.

This road runs south from West Thumb Junction to the park's boundary, tracing the course of the Lewis River and the path of one of the large wildfires of 1988. Beyond the park boundary, the road runs south to Grand Teton National Park and the town of Jackson.

WEST THUMB

For information about West Thumb or to pick up the major loop road at this point, see page 236.

GRANT VILLAGE

This village was built in the late 1970s and early 1980s in order to replace facilities at Fishing Bridge, Old Faithful, and West Thumb. The park service wanted to centralize camping to reduce human pressure on primary resource areas. Of particular concern were the number of people at Fishing Bridge, near Lake Junction, who often got into trouble with the many grizzly bears. However, closing facilities at Fishing Bridge became a political issue, and the plan is now in bureaucratic limbo. Facilities were kept open at other locations, too, and a lively argument has developed between those who emphasize accessibility and those who emphasize preservation. The park service is caught in the middle.

The Red Fire of 1988 accounts for the burns visible around Grant Village and farther south on this stretch of road. Caused by lightning, the Red Fire was at first allowed to burn unsuppressed. After the park began fighting it, the Red Fire combined with the Shoshone, Falls, and Mink fires to make what was called the Snake River Complex. It threatened Grant Village, the Lewis Lake campground, and on some days closed the road to the south entrance.

For a fuller report on the wildfires of 1988 and a discussion of the park's policies, see page 244.

LEWIS LAKE AND RIVER

Here the road follows the eastern shore of Lewis Lake and then runs beside the Lewis River, with its beautiful meadows and dramatic canyon. The lake and river were named for Meriwether Lewis. He was one of the co-captains of the Lewis and Clark expedition, which explored the West from St. Louis to the Pacific Ocean and back from 1803 to 1806. The expedition never came into the area that is now Yellowstone National Park, but on the return journey William Clark did go down the lower Yellowstone River.

FLAGG RANCH

From Flagg Ranch, the road leads to Grand Teton National Park and Jackson Hole.

This road follows the Madison River to the west entrance of the park and traces the approximate route of a trail mountain men used to enter the Yellowstone territory. However, the road may seem most conspicuous for the evidence of burns left by the North Fork Fire, the largest of 1988's wildfires.

The North Fork Fire started on July 22, touched off by a logger's cigarette outside the park. The park fought the fire immediately, but the flames were not contained until October. In the intervening months, the fire moved across more than half a million acres, actually burning about 385,000. It threatened facilities at Old Faithful, Madison Junction, and Norris; the town of West Yellowstone, Montana; park headquarters at Mammoth and Canyon; and even Tower-Roosevelt Lodge.

The fire uncovered the wreckage of a B-17 bomber that crashed in Jack Straw Basin in the spring of 1943, killing ten airmen. The site had been overgrown and almost forgotten, but fire cleanup crews hauled more than twelve tons of refuse from the crash. The debris included bullets, a wing tip, small bits of clothing and equipment, and parts of practice bombs. The main hulk of the plane, covered by the rescue crews forty-five years ago, was left in place.

Forty-five years after the crash, its cause remains unknown. The plane was returning from California to its base in Lewiston, Montana, when it went down. One soldier parachuted out and survived.

SUGGESTED READING

Readers who have made it to the back of the book may want to read more widely and deeply in Wyoming history. To them we suggest these works, which are not only reliable but readable. Editions mentioned are not necessarily the first but are those that are currently available.

Journals and Books Written by Original Westerners:
Osborne Russell, *Journal of a Trapper* (Lincoln: University of Nebraska Press, 1955); Rose Pender, *A Lady's Experience in the Wild West* (Lincoln: University of Nebraska Press, 1978); Horace Greeley, *An Overland Journey* (New York: Alfred A. Knopf, 1964); Arthur Dickson, *Covered Wagon Days* (Spokane: Arthur H. Clark Company, 1929); Francis Parkman's *The Oregon Trail* is available in many editions.

On the Mountain Men:
Winfred Blevins's *Give Your Heart to the Hawks* (New York: Avon Books, 1975) is a good place to start; Bernard DeVoto's *Across the Wide Missouri* (Boston: Houghton Mifflin Company, 1947) is a grand piece of history writing.

On the Oregon Trail:
John D. Unruh, Jr., *The Plains Across: The Overland Emigrants and the Trans-Mississippi West, 1840–60* (Champaign: University of Illinois Press, 1979).

On Mormons:
Wallace Stegner, *The Gathering of Zion* (New York: McGraw-Hill, 1964); LeRoy R. and Ann Hafen, *Handcarts to Zion: The Story of a Unique Western Migration, 1856–1860* (Spokane: Arthur H. Clark Company, 1960).

On the Indian Wars:
Dorothy Johnson, *The Bloody Bozeman* (Missoula, Mont.: Mountain Press Publishing Company, 1983).

On the Union Pacific Railroad:
Robert G. Athern, *Union Pacific Country* (Skokie, Ill.: Rand McNally & Company, 1971); Dee Brown, *Hear That Lonesome Whistle Blow* (Orlando, Fla.: Holt, Rinehart and Winston, 1977).

On the Early Days of Cattle Ranching:
Jack Gage, *The Johnson County War Is/Isn't a Pack of Lies* (Flintlock Publishing, 1967); Bob Edgar and Jack Turnell, *Brand of a Legend* (Stockade Publishing, 1978).

On Dude Ranching:
Struthers Burt, *Diary of a Dude Wrangler* (New York: Charles Scribner's Sons, 1924).

On the Conflicts between Cattlemen and Sheepmen:
William O'Neal, *Cattlemen vs. Sheepherders* (Austin, Tex.: Eakin Press, 1988).

On Yellowstone National Park:
Winfred Blevins's *Roadside History of Yellowstone Park* (Missoula, Mont.: Mountain Press Publishing Company, 1989) is a brief history; Aubrey Haines's *The Yellowstone Story* (Niwot, Colo.: University Press of Colorado, 1977) is a comprehensive history.

ROUTE INDEX